AMERICA'S NONPROFIT SECTOR

A PRIMER

SECOND EDITION

AMERICA'S NONPROFIT SECTOR

A PRIMER

SECOND EDITION

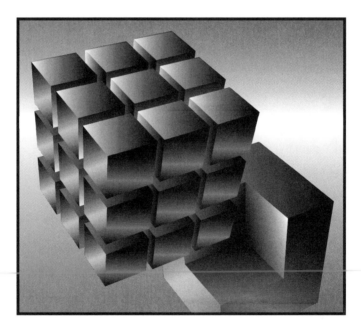

Lester M. Salamon

The Foundation Center

The Foundation Center is grateful to the Charles Stewart Mott Foundation for its generous gift in support of this publication.

Library of Cataloging-in-Publication Data

Salamon, Lester M.
America's nonprofit sector: a primer / Lester M. Salamon. — 2nd ed.
p.   cm.
Includes bibliographical references and index.
ISBN 0-87954-801-0
1. Charities—United States. 2. Nonprofit organizations—United States.
3. Human services—United States. 4. Public welfare—United States.
I. Title.
HV91.S23   1999
361.7'0973—dc21   99-12559
                                                                                          CIP

For
Noah and Matt

Table of Contents

List of
Tables and Figures

PART II:
KEY SUBSECTORS

Chapter Six:

Chapter Seven:

Foreword

By John W. Gardner

The nonprofit sector of American life is a wonder to behold. It includes an incredible range and variety of activities and institutions — from soup kitchens to the Metropolitan Museum of Art, from churches to hospitals, from the Girl Scouts to scientists studying DNA. It is an outlet for our community-serving impulses. It is the arena in which we fulfill our religious needs, serve our compassionate impulses, express our creativity in art and science, engage in citizen political action, and pursue our powerful urges toward education and health care. And much more.

Yet, until little more than 20 years ago, it was so comfortably taken for granted by the American people that no one had done much hard research on the sector.

When Brian O'Connell and I founded Independent Sector in 1980 to serve as an inclusive forum for the sector, it was apparent that we had to encourage the scholars of the nation to fill this unacceptable gap in our knowledge. And none responded more heroically than Lester Salamon. He has become the premier guide to the sector. He asks deeply relevant questions and answers them with hard data and keen analysis.

In this book he tells a story the reader won't find anywhere else. It is a critically important story for the understanding of our society.

John W. Gardner
November 1998

Acknowledgments

The original edition of this book resulted from an expression of frustration on the part of Robert Smucker, then the director of Government Relations for Independent Sector, the Washington-based umbrella group for the nation's not-for-profit organizations, about the lack of an easily accessible guide to the contours and work of America's vast, but under-appreciated, nonprofit sector that could be used to educate policymakers, the press, and leaders of the sector itself.

Since then, the field of nonprofit sector studies has blossomed considerably both in the United States and around the world. Far from reducing the need for a "primer" of this sort, however, this development has intensified the need as increased numbers of students and interested observers have sought to understand what this set of institutions is all about and what role it plays in our national life. It is in response to this growing need, and the desire to provide the growing number of students in this field with the most up-to-date information available, that the present revision was undertaken.

Fortunately, significant improvements have taken place in the basic data sources available to track the nonprofit sector since the original edition of this *Primer* was prepared. At the same time, immense difficulties confront an effort of this sort. Inevitably, data coverage is incomplete, data sources diverge in their estimates of the same parameters, and lapses in data availability make it hard to track changes over the same time periods. All of this makes the task of assembling a primer such as this a bit of a Chinese puzzle.

Fortunately, I have been aided ably in this puzzling by two very dedicated research assistants. Ms. Gretchen van Fossan provided important assistance in assembling the data reported in the first edition of this *Primer*, and Ms. Paige Hull provided similar outstanding assistance in pulling together the data reported in this edition. I am immensely grateful to both of them. In addition, I want to express my special thanks to Murray Weitzman of Independent Sector for sharing with me his early estimates of the scope and size of the independent sector as of 1996 and for responding to my numerous queries about incongruities and ambiguities in the various data sources. Thanks are also due to Frederick Schoff, the director of publications at the Foundation Center, who patiently monitored this project and provided important encouragement along the way. Finally, I am grateful to the Rockefeller Brothers Fund for the support that made the first edition of this *Primer* possible, and to the Charles Stewart Mott Foundation for support that assisted with the production of the first edition and with the preparation and production of the present edition. Needless to say, however, none of these organizations or individuals has any responsibility for any shortcomings this work may still contain or any opinions or interpretations it may reflect. That responsibility is mine alone.

As I hope this book makes clear, nonprofit organizations have long played a critical role in American life. At the same time, this set of institutions has often found itself enveloped in a variety of misperceptions and myths, some of them ideologically inspired. It is my hope that by clarifying the basic scope, structure, operation, and role of this important set of institutions it will be possible to get beyond these myths, to understand the underlying organizations more fully, and therefore to nurture them more effectively. If this *Primer* contributes to these goals it will have served its purpose well.

L. M. S.
Annapolis, Maryland
November 1998

CHAPTER ONE

Introduction

Modern societies, whatever their politics, have found it necessary to make special provisions to protect individuals against the vagaries of economic misfortune, old age, and disability; to secure basic human rights; and to preserve and promote cherished social and cultural values.

Because of growing social and economic complexity, what could be handled at an earlier time, however imperfectly, by a combination of self-reliance, spontaneous neighborliness, and family ties has required more structured responses in modern times. The nature of these responses varies, however, from place to place. In some countries, governments have guaranteed their citizens a minimum income, and a minimum level of health care, housing, access to culture, and other necessities of life. In others, private corporations or private charitable institutions shoulder a far larger share of the responsibility for coping with human needs. And in still others, complex, mixed systems of aid are in force, combining elements of public and private provision, collective and individual responsibility.

In few countries is the system of aid more complicated and confusing, however, than in the United States. Reflecting a deep-seated tradition of individualism and an ingrained hostility to centralized institutions, Americans have resisted the worldwide movement toward predominantly governmental approaches to social welfare provision, adding new governmental protections only with great reluctance, and then structuring them in ways that preserve a substantial private role. While it may no longer be true, as it was when the Frenchman Alexis de Tocqueville visited America in 1835, that, "Wherever at the head of some undertaking you see the government in France, or a man of rank in England,

"America has an intricate 'mixed economy' of welfare that blends public and private action in ways that few people truly understand."

"One of the more important features of the American approach to social welfare provision is the important role it leaves to private, nonprofit organizations."

"The nonprofit sector is perhaps the least well understood component of American society and certainly the one about which the least is known."

in the United States you will be sure to find an association,"[1] the fact remains that nonprofit organizations continue to play a vital role in American life.

The result is an intricate "mixed economy" of welfare that blends public and private action in ways that few people truly understand. In fact, the resulting system is not a system at all, but an ad hoc collection of compromises between the realities of economic necessity and the pressures of political tradition and ideology.

One of the more important features of this American approach to social welfare provision is the important role it leaves to private, nonprofit organizations, to nongovernmental institutions that nevertheless serve essentially public, as opposed to private, economic goals. These organizations do not operate only in the social welfare field, moreover. Rather, they play many other roles as well — serving as vehicles for cultural expression, as mechanisms for political action, as instruments for social cohesion, and more.

Of all the components of American society, however, this is the one that is perhaps the most commonly misunderstood and about which the least is known.

The purpose of this "primer" is to overcome this widespread lack of knowledge about America's nonprofit sector and the role it plays in American life. To do so, however, it is necessary not only to examine the scope, scale, and structure of the nonprofit sector, but also to put this set of organizations into context in relation to government and private businesses operating in the same fields. More specifically, this primer seeks to answer questions such as the following:

- What are nonprofit organizations, what features do they have in common, and why do they exist?
- What different types of nonprofit organizations are there and what is the scale of each major type?
- Where do nonprofit organizations get their funds?
- How extensive is government activity in the fields in which nonprofit organizations are active? Is it true, as many people believe, that government spending vastly outdistances nonprofit spending in these fields?
- What do nonprofit organizations do and how significant a role do they play in the various fields in which they are involved? For example:
  - What share of all hospital beds are in nonprofit hospitals as compared to government hospitals or private, for-profit hospitals?
  - What proportion of all home health facilities are nonprofits as opposed to for-profits?

- What share of all colleges and universities are nonprofits and what proportion of all students enrolled in colleges or universities are enrolled in nonprofit institutions as opposed to public (governmental) ones?
- What have been the recent trends in the relative importance of nonprofit, for-profit, and government providers in these various fields? Are nonprofits generally gaining ground or losing it?

To answer these and related questions, the discussion that follows falls into three major sections containing thirteen chapters in all. The four chapters that comprise Part I provide a broad overview of the nonprofit sector and its role in American life. The first chapter in this section (Chapter 2) defines more precisely what nonprofit organizations have in common and explores the basic rationale for this type of organization. Chapter 3 examines the different types of organizations that make up the American nonprofit sector, and then looks in detail at the public-benefit portion, which is the major focus of the balance of the book. In Chapter 4 attention turns to the governmental and business roles in the fields where nonprofits are active and the relationship between governmental activity and the activity of the nonprofit sector. Chapter 5 puts current realities into historical perspective, reviewing the way government and the nonprofit sector evolved and the recent trends to which they have been exposed.

Against this backdrop, Part II then looks more closely at the scale and role of the major subcomponents of the public-benefit nonprofit sector — health, education, social services, arts and culture, religion, advocacy, and international aid. For each, an attempt is made to identify the role of the nonprofit sector, to compare it to the roles played by government and private, for-profit firms, and to highlight recent trends. Part III then reviews some of the key trends and challenges that nonprofit organizations are facing at the present time and draws out some general conclusions that flow from this work.

Clearly no work of this scale can offer a full evaluation of the nonprofit sector and its contributions to community life. The conscious attempt here, therefore, is primarily to be descriptive, to portray the major components of this complex system and show how they fit together, and to do so in as accessible and nontechnical a fashion as possible.

Even this modest objective poses serious challenges, however, which perhaps explains why it has never been attempted before.[2] No single data source compiles systematic information on all the various facets of the nonprofit sector or of the social welfare system of which it is a significant part. What is more, various data sources covering similar aspects

"American nonprofits not only operate in the social welfare field, but also they serve as vehicles for cultural expression, as mechanisms for political action, as instruments for social cohesion, and more."

of the field often provide widely varying estimates because of subtle differences in definitions and coverage. Thus, for example, an annual estimate of government spending on health compiled by the Social Security Administration yields an estimate that differs considerably from the estimate that the Health Care Financing Administration provides in its annual summary of "national health expenditures." Total spending by hospitals as reported in the "national health expenditures" series is in turn hard to reconcile with the independent estimates provided at five-year intervals in the U.S. Census Bureau's *Census of Service Industries* or the annual surveys conducted by the American Hospital Association. Assembling a full picture of the scope of nonprofit activity and how it compares to the scope of government and business activity in each of the major subfields is therefore a Herculean task, requiring careful sifting of dozens of different data sources and reconciliation of hundreds of definitional and empirical anomalies.

Though complicated, however, such an effort is well worth undertaking, and not just for descriptive reasons. In addition:

- It can better equip both policymakers and the citizenry at large to understand a system that has long seemed to defy comprehension.

- It can clarify the role of the long-overlooked nonprofit sector and bring this sector into focus for the first time.

- It can introduce non-Americans to the important role that nonprofit organizations play in our social and political life.

- It can thus enable all concerned to make more sensible policy choices and comprehend the serious challenges that this set of institutions currently confronts.

These, at any rate, are some of the objectives we seek.

ENDNOTES

1. Alexis de Tocqueville, *Democracy in America*. The Henry Reeve Text, Vol. II (New York: Vintage Books, 1945 [1835]), p. 114.

2. Other accounts provide useful information on the American nonprofit sector, but none of these systematically compares the nonprofit sector to other components of our mixed economy both in general and in particular subfields. See, for example: Waldemar A. Nielsen, *The Endangered Sector* (New York: Columbia University Press, 1979); Michael O'Neill, *The Third America: The Emergence of the Nonprofit Sector in the United States* (San Francisco: Jossey-Bass Publishers, 1989); and Virginia A. Hodgkinson, Murray S. Weitzman, and Stephen M. Noga, *The Nonprofit Almanac, 1992-1993: Dimensions of the Independent Sector* (San Francisco, CA: Jossey-Bass Publishers, Inc., 1992). The 1996 edition of this *Almanac* contains more of these comparative data.

PART ONE

Overview

CHAPTER TWO

What is the Nonprofit Sector and Why Do We Have It?

Nothing, in my opinion, is more deserving of our attention than the intellectual and moral associations of America.
ALEXIS DE TOCQUEVILLE, 1835

Few aspects of American society are as poorly understood or as obscured by mythology as the thousands of day-care centers, clinics, hospitals, higher education institutions, civic action groups, museums, symphonies, and related organizations that comprise America's private, nonprofit sector.

More than a century and a half ago, the Frenchman Alexis de Tocqueville identified this sector as one of the most distinctive and critical features of American life. Yet, despite a steady diet of charitable appeals, most Americans know precious little about the sector or what it does. Indeed, to judge from press accounts and national policy debates, it would seem as if the nonprofit sector largely disappeared from the American scene around the time of the Great Depression of the 1930s, as both public and scholarly attention came to focus instead on government policy and the expansion of the State.

In fact, however, in this, the third century of the American democratic experiment, the private, nonprofit sector remains at least as potent a component of American life as it was when de Tocqueville observed it more than a century and a half ago. This sector contains some of the most prestigious and important institutions in American society — Harvard University, the Metropolitan Museum of Art, the NAACP, to name just a few (see Table 2.1). More than that, it engages the activities and enlists the support of literally millions of citizens, providing a mechanism for self-help, for assistance to those in need, and for the pursuit of a wide array of interests and beliefs. Indeed, almost as many Americans volunteer for nonprofit organizations as take part in our national elections.[1] Finally, this sector has helped give rise to a characteristically, though hardly distinc-

"...almost as many Americans volunteer for nonprofit organizations as take part in our national elections."

TABLE 2.1
Sample Nonprofit Organizations

Harvard University
Princeton University
Montefiore Hospital
American Red Cross
American Cancer Society
Boy Scouts of America
Girl Scouts of America
Rockefeller Foundation
N.Y. Philharmonic Orchestra
Folger Theater
Metropolitan Museum of Art
Planned Parenthood
Catholic Relief Services
C.A.R.E.
Audubon Society
Environmental Defense Fund
National Association for the Advancement
   of Colored People (NAACP)
The Brookings Institution
American Enterprise Institute

TABLE 2.2
Types of Tax-Exempt Organizations under U.S. Law

Tax Code Number	Type of Tax-exempt Organization
501(c)(1)	Corporations organized under an act of Congress
501(c)(2)	Title-holding companies
501(c)(3)	Religious, charitable, educational, etc.
501(c)(4)	Social Welfare
501(c)(5)	Labor, agriculture organization
501(c)(6)	Business leagues
501(c)(7)	Social and recreational clubs
501(c)(8)	Fraternal beneficiary societies
501(c)(9)	Voluntary employees' beneficiary societies
501(c)(10)	Domestic fraternal beneficiary societies
501(c)(11)	Teachers' retirement fund
501(c)(12)	Benevolent life insurance associations
501(c)(13)	Cemetery companies
501(c)(14)	Credit unions
501(c)(15)	Mutual insurance companies
501(c)(16)	Corporations to finance crop operation
501(c)(17)	Supplemental unemployment benefit trusts
501(c)(18)	Employee-funded pension trusts
501(c)(19)	War veterans' organizations
501(c)(20)	Legal services organizations
501(c)(21)	Black lung trusts
501(c)(25)	Holding companies for pensions
501(d)	Religious and apostolic organizations
501(e)	Cooperative hospital service organizations
501(f)	Cooperative service organizations of operating educational organizations
521	Farmers' cooperatives
527	Political organizations

Source: Internal Revenue Service, *1995 Data Book*

tively, American version of the modern welfare state, which features extensive interaction between government and nonprofit groups to help respond to public needs.[2] In fact, without a clear understanding of the nonprofit sector, it is as impossible to comprehend American society and American public policy today as it was in the time of de Tocqueville.

What is the Nonprofit Sector?

But what is this "nonprofit sector"? What do the organizations that are part of this sector have in common? Why do we have such organizations? What purpose do they serve?

A Diverse Sector

Unfortunately, the answers to these questions are somewhat complicated because of the great diversity of this sector. U.S. tax laws contain no fewer than 27 separate sections under which organizations can claim exemption from federal income taxes as nonprofit organizations.[3] Mutual insurance companies, certain cooperatives, labor unions, business associations, as well as charitable and educational institutions are all eligible (see Table 2.2). Of these, the "religious, charitable, and educational" organizations eligible for tax exemption under Section 501(c)(3) are probably the best known — yet included even within this narrow span are a wide assortment of institutions:

- small, one-room soup kitchens for the homeless;
- massive hospital complexes;
- museums, art galleries, and symphony orchestras;
- day-care centers;
- prestigious universities;
- foster care and adoption agencies; and
- advocacy and civic action groups bringing pressure on government and businesses to clean the environment, protect children, promote civil rights, or pursue a thousand other causes.

The Terminological Tangle

Nor does the terminology used to depict the sector provide much help. A great many such terms are used — *nonprofit sector, charitable sector, independent sector, voluntary sector, tax-exempt sector,* and, more recently, *civil society sector.* Each of these terms emphasizes one aspect of the reality represented by these organizations at the expense of overlooking or downplaying other aspects. Each is therefore at least partly misleading. For example:

- *Charitable sector* emphasizes the support these organizations receive from private, charitable donations. But as we shall see, private charitable contributions do not constitute the only, or even the major, source of their revenue.

- *Independent sector* emphasizes the important role these organizations play as a "third force" outside of the realm of government and private business. But as we shall see, these organizations are far from independent. In financial terms they depend heavily on both government and private business.

- *Voluntary sector* emphasizes the significant input that volunteers make to the management and operation of this sector. But as we shall see, most of the activity of the organizations in this sector is not carried out by volunteers at all, but by paid employees.

- *Tax-exempt sector* emphasizes the fact that under U.S. tax law the organizations in this sector are exempt from the national income tax and from most state and local property taxes. But this term begs the question of what characteristics qualify organizations for this treatment in the first place. In addition, it is not very helpful in comparing U.S. experience with that elsewhere because it is so dependent on the peculiarities of U.S. tax law.

- *Civil society sector,* the term that gained particular currency in the 1990s, emphasizes the citizen base of this set of organizations. But in the United States, most nonprofit organizations are not membership associations and many of those who work in these organizations are paid staff members.

- Even *nonprofit sector,* the term we will generally use here, is not without its problems. This term emphasizes the fact that these organizations do not exist primarily to generate profits for their owners. But as we shall see, these organizations sometimes do earn profits, that is, they generate more revenues than they spend in a given year.

> *"Without a clear understanding of the nonprofit sector, it is as impossible to comprehend American society and American public policy today as it was in the time of de Tocqueville."*

A Crucial Distinction:
Philanthropy versus the Nonprofit Sector

The task of comprehending the nonprofit sector is further complicated by a widespread failure to recognize the important distinction between philanthropy, on the one hand, and the private, nonprofit sector, on the other. In many accounts, these two terms are treated interchangeably when in fact one is really just a part of the other.

- The *private nonprofit sector,* as the term will be used here, is a set of organizations that is privately constituted but serves some public purpose, such as the advancement of health, education, scientific progress, social welfare, or the free expression of

> *"The task of comprehending the nonprofit sector is further complicated by a widespread failure to recognize the important distinction between philanthropy, on the one hand, and the private, nonprofit sector, on the other. In many accounts, these two terms are treated interchangeably when in fact one is really just a part of the other."*

TABLE 2.3
Six Defining Characteristics of the Nonprofit Sector

The nonprofit sector is a collection of entities that are
1. organizations;
2. private, as opposed to governmental;
3. non-profit-distributing;
4. self-governing;
5. voluntary; and
6. of public benefit.

ideas. The nonprofit sector thus includes thousands of day-care centers, private hospitals, universities, research institutes, community development organizations, soup kitchens, foster care facilities, social service agencies, employment and training centers, museums, art galleries, symphonies, zoos, business and professional associations, advocacy organizations, and dozens of similar types of institutions.

- *Philanthropy* is the giving of time or valuables (money, securities, property) for public purposes. Philanthropy, or charitable giving, is thus one form of income of private nonprofit organizations. To be sure, some nonprofit organizations have the generation or distribution of charitable contributions as their principal objective. But as we will see, these are not the only types of nonprofit organizations, and private charitable contributions are not the only source of nonprofit income.

Six Defining Characteristics

What, then, do the organizations that comprise the "nonprofit sector" have in common? What are the defining characteristics of this sector?

Broadly speaking, six characteristics seem most crucial (see Table 2.3).[4] In particular, as we will use the term here, the nonprofit sector refers to a collection of entities that are:

- *Organizations,* that is, they are institutionalized to some extent. Purely ad hoc, informal, and temporary gatherings of people are not considered part of the nonprofit sector, even though they may be quite important in people's lives. At the same time, under American law it is not necessary for an organization to be formally incorporated, or even to secure formal recognition by the Internal Revenue Service, in order to function as a nonprofit organization. Typically, however, nonprofit organizations secure legal standing as corporations chartered under state laws. This corporate status makes the organization a legal person able to enter into contracts and largely frees the officers from personal financial responsibility for the organization's commitments.

- *Private,* that is, they are institutionally separate from government. Nonprofit organizations are neither part of the governmental apparatus nor governed by boards dominated by government officials. This does not mean that they may not receive significant government support. What is more, government participation on nonprofit boards is not unheard of, as was the case with Yale

University until the 1870s.[5] But nonprofit organizations are fundamentally private institutions in basic structure.

- *Non-profit-distributing,* that is, they are not dedicated to generating profits for their owners. Nonprofit organizations may accumulate profits in a given year, but the profits must be plowed back into the basic mission of the agency, not distributed to the organizations' founders. This differentiates nonprofit organizations from the other component of the private sector — private businesses.

- *Self-governing,* that is, they are equipped to control their own activities. Nonprofit organizations have their own internal procedures for governance and are not controlled by outside entities.

- *Voluntary,* that is, they are non-compulsory and involve some meaningful degree of voluntary participation, either in the actual conduct of the agency's activities or in the management of its affairs. Typically, this takes the form of a voluntary board of directors, but extensive use of volunteer staff is also common.

- Of public benefit, that is, they serve some public purpose and contribute to the public good.[6]

The Rationale:
Why Do We Have a Nonprofit Sector?

Why does the nonprofit sector exist in the United States, or any other country? Why did such organizations come into existence, and why do we give these organizations special tax and other advantages? Five major considerations seem to be involved.

Historical
In the first place, the nonprofit sector came into existence for reasons that are largely historical. In the United States, as well as in many other countries, society predated the state. In other words, communities formed before governmental structures, or governmental institutions, were in place to help deal with their common concerns. People therefore had to tackle problems on their own and often found it useful to join with others in voluntary organizations to do so. The result was the creation of voluntary fire departments, schools, adoption societies, and many more organizations. Even after governments came into existence, moreover, Americans were often reluctant to use them, fearing the rebirth of monarchy, or bureaucracy. Therefore, citizens still had to take matters into their own hands until they could persuade their fellow citizens that government

help was needed. Once created, these organizations then often continued in existence even after government entered the scene, frequently helping government meet a need.

Market Failure

Beyond this historical reason, the creation of nonprofit organizations has been motivated by certain inherent limitations of the market system that dominates the American economy.[7] Economists refer to these as *market failures*. Essentially, the problem is this: The market is excellent for handling those things we consume individually, such as shoes, cars, clothing, food. For such items, consumer choices in the marketplace send signals to producers about the prices that consumers are willing to pay and the quantities that can be sold at those prices. By contrast, the market does not handle very well those things that can only be consumed collectively, such as clean air, national defense, or safe neighborhoods. These so-called *public goods* involve a serious "free-rider" problem because, once they are produced, everyone can benefit from them even if they have not shared in the cost. Therefore, it is to each individual's advantage to let his or her neighbor bear the cost of these public goods because each individual will be able to enjoy them whether he or she pays for them or not. The inevitable result, however, will be to produce far less of these collective goods than people really want, and thus to leave everyone worse off.

To correct for this, some form of nonmarket mechanism is needed. One such mechanism is government. By imposing taxes on individuals, government can compel everyone to share in the cost of collective goods. Indeed, in classical economic theory the problem of providing collective goods is the major rationale for the existence of government.

But in a democracy government will only supply those collective goods desired by a majority. Where such support is lacking, another mechanism is needed, and one such mechanism is the nonprofit sector. Nonprofit organizations allow groups of individuals to pool their resources to produce collective goods they mutually desire but cannot convince a majority of their countrymen to support. This can happen, for example, when particular subgroups share certain cultural, social, or economic characteristics or interests not shared by all, or most, citizens of a country. Through nonprofit organizations such subgroups can provide the kinds and levels of collective goods they desire. The greater the heterogeneity of the population, therefore, the larger the nonprofit sector is likely to be.

"According to the 'market failure' theory, nonprofit organizations exist to fill the unsatisfied demands for collective goods left by both the market and the state in circumstances where considerable heterogeneity of demands exists; or where information asymmetries make it difficult to rely on the market to control the price or quality of products."

A slightly different kind of market failure occurs where information asymmetries exist, e.g., where the purchasers of services are not the same as the consumers, a situation economists refer to as *contract failure*.[8] This is the case, for example, with nursing homes, where the consumers are often elderly people with limited consumer choice or ability to discriminate among products and the purchasers are their children. In such situations, the purchasers, unable to assess the adequacy of services themselves, seek some substitute for the market mechanism, some provider they can trust. Because nonprofits do not exist principally to earn profits, they often are preferred providers in such situations.

Government Failure

Since the existence of "market failures" — of inherent limitations of the market system — serves, in classical economic theory, as the justification for reliance on government, it is clear that market failures alone cannot explain the existence of a nonprofit sector. Also important are "government failures," inherent limitations of government that help to explain why nonprofit organizations are needed. In the first place, even in a democracy it is often difficult to get government to act to correct "market failures" because government action requires majority support. By forming nonprofit organizations, smaller groupings of people can begin addressing needs that they have not yet convinced others to support. In short, it is not market failure alone that leads to a demand for nonprofit organizations. Rather, it is the failure of *both* the market and the state to supply collective goods desired by a segment of the population, but not by enough to trigger a governmental response.

"'Government operations tend to be everywhere alike. With individuals and voluntary associations, on the contrary, there are varied experiments, and endless diversity of experience."
JOHN STUART MILL, ON LIBERTY

Even when majority support exists, however, there is still often a preference for some nongovernmental mechanism to deliver services and respond to public needs because of the cumbersomeness, unresponsiveness, and bureaucratization that often accompanies government action. This is particularly true in the United States because of a strong cultural resistance to the expansion of government. Even when government financing is viewed as essential, therefore, it is often the case that private, nonprofit organizations are utilized to deliver the services that government finances. The result, as will be detailed later, is a complex pattern of cooperation between government and the nonprofit sector.[9]

Pluralism/Freedom

A fourth reason for the existence of nonprofit organizations has less to do with the efficiency of these organizations or the service functions they perform than with the role they play in promoting a crucial social value — the value of freedom and pluralism. As John Stuart Mill pointed out in his classic treatise, *On Liberty,* "Government operations tend to be everywhere alike. With individuals and voluntary associations, on the contrary, there are varied experiments, and endless diversity of experience."[10] Nonprofit organizations facilitate the exercise of individual initiative for the public good just as the business corporation facilitates the exercise of individual initiative for the private good. This line of argument is similar to what some theorists of the nonprofit sector refer to as the "supply-side" or "stakeholder" theory of the nonprofit sector.[11] The central argument of this theory is that a need for nonprofit organizations is not sufficient to ensure that such organizations are created. At least as important, and perhaps more so, is a supply of people who take the initiative to form such organizations. Such individuals can be motivated by religious or other moral convictions, by ideological concerns, by a desire to win adherents to a religious cause, by dissatisfaction with the existing range of services for those about whom they care, by a sense of justice, by professional interests, by a desire for creative expression, or by any of a host of other considerations. Whatever the motivation, where individuals with such motivations are in plentiful supply, the likelihood is greater that substantial numbers of nonprofit organizations will be formed.

Reflecting this, it should come as no surprise that most of the major reform movements that have animated American life over the past century or more have taken form within the nonprofit sector — the abolitionist movement, the women's suffrage movement, and the more recent movements for civil rights, environmental protection, workplace safety, child welfare, women's rights, and libertarianism. Even if it were the case that government was far more efficient than the nonprofit sector in responding to citizen needs, Americans would thus likely still insist on a vibrant nonprofit sector as a guarantor of their liberties and a mechanism to ensure a degree of pluralism.

"Nonprofit organizations facilitate the exercise of individual initiative for the public good just as the business corporation facilitates the exercise of individual initiative for the private good."

"'In democratic countries the science of association is the mother of science; the progress of all the rest depends upon the progress it has made.'"
ALEXIS DE TOCQUEVILLE, DEMOCRACY IN AMERICA

Solidarity

Finally, the nonprofit sector is a response to the need for some mechanism through which to give expression to sentiments of solidarity. This is particularly important in individualistic societies like the United States, as Alexis de Tocqueville pointed out in his seminal essay over 150 years ago. In fact, it was this facet of the nonprofit sector that Tocqueville had principally in mind when he argued: "In democratic countries the science of association is the mother of science; the progress of all the rest depends upon the progress it has made." The reason, Tocqueville observed, is that "...among democratic nations...all the citizens are independent and feeble; they can do hardly anything by themselves, and none of them can oblige his fellow men to lend him their assistance. They all, therefore, become powerless if they do not learn voluntarily to help one another."

Voluntary associations are critical in democratic societies to create artificially what the equality of conditions makes it extremely difficult to create naturally, namely, a capacity for joint action. It is for this reason that Tocqueville argues that: "If men living in democratic countries had no right and no inclination to associate for political purposes, their independence would be in great jeopardy, but they might long preserve their wealth and their cultivation; whereas if they never acquired the habit of forming associations in ordinary life, civilization itself would be endangered."[12]

The Stakes: Why We Need the Nonprofit Sector

These explanations of the existence of nonprofit organizations help to clarify the contributions that these organizations can make and the stakes that American society consequently has in them. Broadly speaking, these contributions take four major forms:

Service Provision

In the first place, nonprofit organizations perform a service function. This function has been particularly important in a society which, like ours, is reluctant to turn to government to respond to social and economic needs. The nonprofit sector thus functions as a first line of defense, a flexible mechanism through which people concerned about a social or economic problem can begin to respond immediately without having to convince a majority of their fellow citizens that the problem deserves a more general, governmental response. It also provides a vehicle through which specialized demands — for culture and arts or other

TABLE 2.4
The Functions of the Nonprofit Sector

Nonprofit organizations serve four critical functions:
- Service provision
- Value Guardian
- Advocacy/Problem Identification
- Community-building

"The nonprofit sector functions as a first line of defense, a flexible mechanism through which people concerned about a social or economic problem can begin to respond immediately without having to convince a majority of their fellow citizens that the problem deserves a more general, governmental response."

collective goods — can be pursued, and through which public services themselves can be delivered, thus avoiding the enlargement of governmental bureaucracies and keeping the provision of services in private institutions at the community level. In short, nonprofit organizations perform an important service function by:

- addressing unmet needs;
- fostering innovation;
- providing "collective goods" that only a portion of a community wishes to support; and
- adapting general policies to local circumstances and needs.

Value Guardian

Well beyond its service role, however, the nonprofit sector functions as a "value guardian" in American society, as an exemplar and crucial embodiment of a fundamental national value emphasizing *individual initiative in the public good.* Just as private economic enterprises serve as vehicles for promoting individual initiative for the private good, nonprofit organizations provide a mechanism for promoting such initiative in the pursuit of *public* purposes. In the process, they foster pluralism, diversity, and freedom. These values go beyond the more instrumental purposes that nonprofit organizations also serve, such as improving health or providing shelter to the homeless. They are important in and of themselves, as expressions of what has come to be regarded as a central dimension of the American experience — the protection of a sphere of private action through which individuals can take the initiative, express their individuality, and exercise freedom of expression and action.

Advocacy and Problem Identification

In addition to solving problems themselves, nonprofit organizations also play a vital role as mechanisms for mobilizing broader public attention to societal problems and needs. In a complex society such as ours, the right to free expression has little effective meaning unless it is joined to the right of free association, so that individuals can merge their individual voices and thereby make them effective. Nonprofit organizations are among the principal vehicles for doing this. By making it possible to identify significant social and political concerns, to give voice to under-represented people and points of view, and to integrate these perspectives into social and political life, these organizations function as a kind of social safety valve that has helped to preserve

"Nonprofit organizations embody a central dimension of the American experience—the protection of a sphere of private action through which individuals can take the initiative, express their individuality, and exercise freedom of expression and action."

"In a complex society such as ours, the right to free expression has little effective meaning unless it is joined to the right of free association, so that individuals can merge their individual voices and thereby make them effective."

American democracy and maintain a degree of social peace in the midst of massive, and often dramatic, social dislocations.

Social Capital

Finally, nonprofit organizations play a vital role in creating and sustaining what scholars have come to refer to as "social capital," i.e., those bonds of trust and reciprocity that seem to be pivotal for a democratic society and a market economy to function effectively, but that the American ethic of individualism would otherwise make it difficult to sustain.[13] Alexis de Tocqueville understood this point well when he wrote in *Democracy in America* in 1835,

> Feelings and opinions are recruited, the heart is enlarged, and the human mind is developed, only by the reciprocal influence of men upon one another.... these influences are almost null in democratic countries; they must therefore be artificially created and this can only be accomplished by associations.[14]

The perpetuation of a vital nonprofit sector is thus essential to the development and sustenance of a sense of community, which is required to uphold contracts and make it possible for both a market system and a democratic polity to operate.

Conclusion

In short, there is a vitally important set of institutions in American society that, despite many differences, nevertheless share certain common features. It consists of *organizations* that are *private, self-governing, non-profit-distributing, voluntary,* and *of public benefit.* Together they comprise what we will call the nonprofit sector.

The existence of this set of organizations is partly an accident of history. But it has more concrete foundations as well — in the inherent limitations of the market in responding to public needs, in the inherent limitations of government as the sole alternative mechanism to respond to market failures, in the need that a democratic society has for some way to promote cooperation among equal individuals, and in the value Americans attach to pluralism and freedom.

The rationale for the existence of a nonprofit sector is not peculiar to American society, of course. The same arguments apply to other societies as well, particularly those with democratic governmental structures and market-oriented economic systems. But there is no denying that these organizations have come to play a particularly important role in the American setting. While there is reason to question whether American nonprofit organizations always live

"...the existence of a set of institutions that is private, nonprofit, and self-governing has come to be viewed in this country both as a critical component of community life, a convenient and fulfilling way to meet community needs, and a crucial prerequisite of a true 'civil society.'"

up to the expectations that these theories assign to them, it seems clear that the existence of such a set of institutions has come to be viewed in this country as a critical component of community life, a convenient and fulfilling way to meet community needs, and a crucial prerequisite of a true "civil society."

ENDNOTES

1. In 1995, an estimated 93 million Americans reported volunteering for nonprofit organizations. By comparison, 96 million voted in the 1996 Presidential election. Independent Sector, *Giving and Volunteering in the United States* (Washington: Independent Sector, 1996), p.2; U.S. Bureau of the Census, *Statistical Abstract of the United States: 1997.* 117th Edition. (Washington: National Technical Information Service, 1997), p.271.

2. For other examples of countries that have built extensive reliance on the nonprofit sector into their social welfare systems, see the chapters on Germany and the Netherlands in Benjamin Gidron, Ralph Kramer, and Lester M. Salamon, eds., *Government and the Third Sector: Emerging Relationships in Welfare States* (San Francisco: Jossey-Bass, 1992); and Lester M. Salamon and Helmut K. Anheier, *The Emerging Sector* (Manchester, U.K.: Manchester University Press, 1996).

3. Three other types of tax-exempt organizations are also legally recognized but are almost nonexistent. These are §501(c)(22) multi-employer pension plans; §501(c)(23) veterans associations founded prior to 1880; and §501(c)(24) trusts described in section 4049 of ERISA.

4. This definition draws on Maria Brenton, *The Voluntary Sector in British Social Services* (London: Longman, 1985), p. 9. For further discussion of the problem of defining the nonprofit sector, see Lester M. Salamon and Helmut K. Anheier, "In Search of the Nonprofit Sector: The Problem of Definition," *Voluntas*, Vol. 3, No. 2 (1992), pp. 125–151.

5. John S. Whitehead, *The Separation of College and State: Columbia, Dartmouth, Harvard and Yale, 1776–1876* (New Haven, CT: Yale University Press, 1973).

6. The definition of what constitutes a public purpose naturally varies from country to country and over time. In "common law" countries like the United Kingdom and the United States, the definition has evolved through more than three hundred years of legal interpretation of the term "charitable," which was incorporated in the Elizabethan Statute of Charitable Uses in 1601 as the touchstone for exemption from taxation. As summarized in the late nineteenth century, this line of cases established four broad meanings of the concept of public purpose: relief of poverty, advancement of education, advancement of religion, and other purposes beneficial to the community. More recently what is meant by "public purpose" or "public benefit" has been enshrined in formal legislative enactments of the sort embodied in Section 501 (c) of the U.S. Internal Revenue Code defining purposes eligible for tax exemption. On the common law definition of "charitable," see Jeremy Kendall and Martin Knapp,

"The United Kingdom," in Lester M. Salamon and Helmut K. Anheier, *Defining the Nonprofit Sector: A Cross-National Analysis* (Manchester, U.K.: Manchester University Press, 1996), p. 257.

7. This line of argument has been applied to the nonprofit sector most explicitly in Burton Weisbrod, *The Voluntary Nonprofit Sector* (Lexington, MA: Lexington Books, 1978).

8. This line of argument has been developed most explicitly in Henry Hansmann, "The Role of Nonprofit Enterprise," *Yale Law Journal*, Vol. 89 (1990), pp. 835–901.

9. That such cooperation occurs is due, in turn, to certain inherent limitations of the nonprofit sector. Like the market and the state, the voluntary sector suffers from certain inherent failures or limitations. In particular, nonprofit organizations have great difficulty generating needed resources and suffer as well from propensities toward particularism, paternalism, and amateurism. For further detail on these "voluntary failures" and the consequence they have for government–nonprofit cooperation, see: Lester M. Salamon, "Of Market Failure, Voluntary Failure, and Third-Party Government: Toward a Theory of Government–Nonprofit Relations in the Modern Welfare State," *Journal of Voluntary Action Research*, Vol. 16, Nos. 1–2, (1987), pp. 29–49, reprinted in Lester M. Salamon, *Partners in Public Service: Government–Nonprofit Relations in the Modern Welfare State* (Baltimore: Johns Hopkins University Press, 1995), pp. 33–49.

10. John Stuart Mill, *On Liberty*, quoted in Bruce R. Hopkins, *The Law of Tax-Exempt Organizations*, 5th Ed. (New York: John Wiley and Sons, 1987), p. 7.

11. For a discussion of this "supply-side theory," see: Estelle James, "The Nonprofit Sector in Comparative Perspective," in Walter W. Powell, ed., *The Nonprofit Sector: A Research Handbook* (New Haven: Yale University Press, 1987), pp. 397–415; Avner Ben-Ner and Theresa van Hoomissen, "Nonprofit Organizations in the Mixed Economy: A Demand and Supply Analysis," in Avner Ben-Ner and Benedeto Gui, eds., *The Nonprofit Sector in the Mixed Economy* (Ann Arbor: The University of Michigan Press, 1993); Michael Krashinsky, "Stakeholder Theories of the Nonprofit Sector: One Cut at the Economic Literature," *Voluntas*, Vol. 8, No. 2 (1997), pp. 149–161.

12. Alexis de Tocqueville, *Democracy in America*. The Henry Reeve Text, Vol. II (New York: Vintage Books, 1945 [1835]), p. 114–118.

13. See, for example: James S. Coleman, *Foundations of Social Theory* (Cambridge, MA: Harvard University Press, 1990), pp. 300–321; Robert Putnam, *Making Democracy Work: Civic Traditions in Modern Italy* (Princeton: Princeton University Press, 1993), pp. 83–116, 163-185.

14. de Tocqueville, *Democracy in America*. Vol. II, p. 117.

CHAPTER THREE

Scope and Structure: The Anatomy of America's Nonprofit Sector

To say that nonprofit organizations share certain common characteristics and a common rationale is not, of course, to suggest that all nonprofit organizations are identical. To the contrary, the complexity and diversity of this sector is one of the major factors that has diverted attention from it over much of its history. Indeed, nonprofit organizations are so diverse and so specialized that some observers question whether it is appropriate to consider this group of institutions a "sector" at all — a point that could be raised about the "business sector" as well, of course.

Complicating things further is the fact that significant portions of the nonprofit sector are largely informal in character and therefore difficult to capture in empirical terms. This reflects the fact that under American law organizations are not required to incorporate, or even to seek formal recognition by the tax authorities, in order to function as tax-exempt nonprofit organizations. This organizational fluidity is, in fact, one of the prized features of this sector, enabling groups of people to meet together to pursue common purposes without having to seek official approval or even acknowledgment. At the same time, however, it makes it exceedingly difficult to gauge the size of this sector with any real precision.[1]

While recognizing these problems, this chapter seeks to make some sense of the vast array of institutions that comprise the American nonprofit sector, to examine the basic anatomy or architecture of this sector and the scope and scale of some of its constituent parts. In the process, it seeks to strip away some of the confusion and misperception that too often characterize popular understanding of what the nonprofit sector really is and how it functions in American life.

"...this chapter seeks to make some sense of the vast array of institutions that comprise the American nonprofit sector, to examine the basic anatomy or architecture of this sector and the scope and scale of some of its constituent parts."

"If the U.S. nonprofit sector were a separate country, it would exceed the gross domestic products of most of the countries in the world...."

TABLE 3.1
America's Nonprofit Sector:
An Overview

	Amount
Number of Organizations (1995)	1.6 million
Revenues (1996)	$670.3 billion
As share of gross domestic product	8.8%
Employees (1996)	10.9 million
As % of total paid employment	7%
Volunteers (FTE) (1995)	6.3 million
As% of total paid and volunteer employment	11%

Source: See Endnotes 2,3,4,5.

FIGURE 3.1
Anatomy of the Nonprofit Sector*

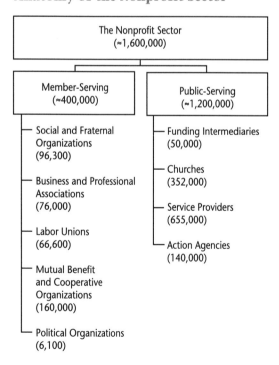

* Estimates of numbers of organizations here include only the more visible and formal parts of the nonprofit sector.

Source: See Endnote 2.

To do so, we first examine the overall scale of this sector and then look in more detail at some of the sector's major components, focusing particularly on what we refer to as "public-benefit service organiza- tions," the portion of this sector that most people have in mind when they refer to the "nonprofit sector." Given the limitations of available data, our focus is inevitably on the more formal and institu- tionalized organizations, although, as we will see, the line between these and the rest of this sector is far from clear.

Overview: Basic Dimensions

As reflected in Table 3.1, the nonprofit sector is not only a quite important, but also a quite sizable, presence in American society:

- As of 1995, this sector included approximately 1.6 million identifiable organizations, or more than 6 percent of all organizations of all types (nonprofit, business, and government) in the country.[2]

- These organizations had revenues as of 1996 of $670 billion, which is equivalent to nearly 9 percent of the U.S. gross domestic product. In fact, if the U.S. nonprofit sector were a separate country, it would exceed the gross domestic products of most of the countries in the world, including Australia, Canada, India, the Netherlands, and Spain.[3]

- These organizations are also an important source of employment. Nearly 11 million people worked as employees of nonprofit organizations in 1996, or approximately 7 percent of the nation's workforce. This was more than three times the number employed in agriculture and larger than the number employed in construction, in trans- portation and communication, and in finance, insurance, and real estate.[4]

- In addition to the paid employment, nonprofit organizations also employed the equivalent of 6.3 million full-time volunteers, boosting their workforce to 17.2 million workers, or about 11 percent of all paid and volunteer employment in the U.S. economy.[5]

A Basic Division: Public-Serving versus Member-Serving Organizations

Included within these figures, however, are two very different categories of organizations.

Member-Serving Organizations

The first are what we may refer to as *primarily member-serving* organizations. These are organizations that, while having some public purpose, primarily exist to provide a benefit to the members of the organization rather than to the public at large. As reflected in Figure 3.1, the member-serving organizations include social clubs, business and professional associations (e.g., chambers of commerce, the American Bankers' Association, local bar associations, labor unions), mutual benefit and cooperative organizations (e.g., farmers cooperatives, benevolent life insurance associations), and political organizations (e.g., political parties and political action committees). Approximately 400,000 such organizations were officially registered with the Internal Revenue Service as of 1995 and a far larger number probably exist more informally. As noted in Figure 3.2, these member-serving organizations account for about 10 percent of all nonprofit employment.

Public-Serving Organizations

The second category of nonprofit organizations are *primarily public-serving* in character. These are organizations that exist primarily to serve the public at large rather than primarily the members of the organization. They may do so in a variety of ways, however — providing health and education services, sponsoring cultural or religious activities, advocating for certain causes, aiding the poor, financing other nonprofits, and many more. Altogether, at least 1.2 million such organizations exist at the present time and they account for 90 percent of the sector's employment.

Treatment in Tax Law

This distinction between primarily member-serving and primarily public-serving nonprofit organizations is far from perfect, of course. Even the member-serving organizations produce some public benefits, and the public-serving organizations often deliver benefits to their members. Yet the distinction is significant enough to find formal reflection in the law.

In particular, public-serving organizations are the only ones entitled to tax-exempt status under Section 501(c)(3) of the federal tax law. What makes this so important is that this gives such organizations a tax advantage not available to other nonprofit organiza-

FIGURE 3.2

Nonprofit Sector Employment by Major Components, 1996

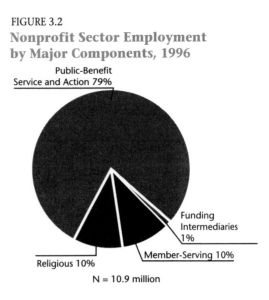

Source: See Endnote 16.

"Included within the American nonprofit sector are two very different categories of organizations: primarily member-serving organizations and primarily public-serving organizations."

tions. In particular, in addition to being exempt from taxes themselves like all nonprofit organizations, 501(c)(3) organizations are also eligible to receive tax-deductible gifts from individuals and corporations; that is, contributions that the individuals and corporations can deduct from their own income in computing their tax liabilities. This gives the individuals and corporations a financial incentive to make contributions to these 501(c)(3) organizations because they can deduct the gifts from their taxable income. The justification for this is that the organizations are serving purposes that are public in character and that government might otherwise have to support through tax revenues.[6]

To be eligible for this status, organizations must operate "exclusively for religious, charitable, scientific, literary, or educational purposes."[7] The meaning of these terms is rooted in English common law, however, and is quite broad, essentially embracing organizations that promote the general welfare in any of a wide variety of ways.[8] Included, therefore, are not only agencies providing aid to the poor, but also most of the educational, cultural, social service, advocacy, self-help, health, environmental, civil rights, child welfare, and related organizations that most people have in mind when they think about the nonprofit sector. The one major exception are public-serving organizations heavily engaged in direct political action (campaigning and lobbying for legislation), for which a special section of the tax code [Section 501(c)(4)] exists.[9]

Focus on Public-Serving Organizations

Because of their essentially public character, the public-serving nonprofit organizations are the ones that most observers have in mind when they speak about the "nonprofit sector" in the United States. These are therefore the organizations that will be the principal focus of this "primer."

What is not widely appreciated, however, is that this public-serving component of the nonprofit sector contains four very different types of organizations, as shown in Figure 3.1. The first are funding intermediaries, that is, organizations that function chiefly to provide funds for other parts of the nonprofit sector. The second are religious congregations, that is, organizations that principally engage in religious worship (e.g., churches, synagogues, mosques). The third are various service-providing organizations, that is, organizations that provide health care, education, counseling, adoption assistance, etc., or that advocate for particular causes. The fourth are the public-benefit political action agencies noted above, which devote a significant portion of their effort to supporting or opposing particular pieces of legislation. Let us look briefly at each of these types, focusing particularly on the first and third.

Funding Intermediaries

Among the public-serving nonprofit organizations in the United States, probably the least well understood, are the *funding intermediaries*. These are organizations whose sole, or principal, function is to channel financial support, especially private charitable support, to other nonprofit organizations.

The Scope of Private Giving

The existence of these funding intermediaries reflects the highly specialized and developed character of the U.S. nonprofit sector, which has led to the emergence of organizations that are dedicated exclusively to fundraising and fund distribution. But it also reflects the importance of private charitable giving in the United States and the scale that such giving has attained. In 1996, for example, Americans contributed an estimated $139 billion to various charitable causes.[10] This represented about 2.2 percent of personal income, considerably higher than for most other countries.[11]

Of this $139 billion, about 85 percent came from individuals, about 9 percent from foundations, and about 6 percent from corporations. The largest share of this support (an estimated $66 billion, or almost half) went to religious organizations, mostly for sacramental religious activities. Another $12.7 billion went to public or governmental institutions, particularly higher education institutions. This left an estimated $45.5 billion for all the rest of the private, nonprofit service organizations (see Table 3.2).[12]

TABLE 3.2
Private Charitable Giving in the U.S., 1996, by Type of Recipient, and Purpose

Type of Recipient	Amount ($ billions)	Percent
Religious congregations	$66.3	48%
Government agencies	12.7	9
Foundations	8.3	6
Nonprofit Service Providers	45.5	33
Education	15.0	11
Health	11.2	8
Social/legal services	9.5	7
Arts, culture	4.2	3
Civic	5.6	4
Other Nonprofit	6.1	4
Total	$138.9	100%

Source: See Endnote 10.

FIGURE 3.3
Nonprofit Funding Intermediaries

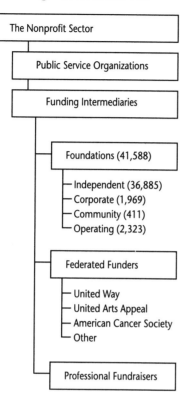

Source: Foundation data from Renz et al. *Foundation Giving* (1998), p.5

Although, as we shall see, private charitable giving is by no means the only, or even the largest, source of support for American nonprofit service organizations, it is nevertheless quite important because of the role it plays in helping to ensure the sector's independence and autonomous character.

The role of the funding intermediaries is to help generate this private funding, to manage it once it is accumulated, and to make it available for use by the other organizations in the sector. Broadly speaking, as shown in Figure 3.3, three distinct types of such funding intermediaries exist: (a) foundations, (b) federated funders, and (c) professional fundraisers. Let us look briefly at each.

Foundations

Private foundations (e.g., the Ford Foundation, the Rockefeller Foundation, the W.K. Kellogg Foundation) are among the most visible components of the nonprofit sector — so much so that there is a tendency to overstate their role and confuse them with the public-serving nonprofit sector as a whole. This latter problem is particularly acute among overseas observers because the term *foundation* is used quite differently in many other countries. In particular, there is often little distinction between foundations and other parts of the nonprofit sector elsewhere, whereas in the United States the term foundation is typically reserved for organizations with the more specialized function of making grants to other nonprofit organizations, typically out of the earnings from an endowment.[13]

Altogether, as noted in Table 3.3, there were over 41,000 foundations in the United States as of 1996, with total assets of $267.6 billion.[14] These foundations take four different forms, however.

Independent Grantmaking Foundations. The most important type of foundation by far are the so-called independent grantmaking foundations. These are nonprofit organizations set up to administer an endowment typically left for charitable purposes by a

TABLE 3.3
U.S. Grantmaking Foundations, 1996 ($ billions)*

Type	Number	Assets	Grants
Independent	36,885	$226.6	$10.7
Corporate	1,969	9.5	1.8
Community	411	15.9	1.0
Operating	2,323	15.7	0.3
Total	41,588	$267.6	$13.8

Source: *Foundation Giving* 1998, p.5.
*Figures may not add due to rounding.

single individual, and to distribute all or some of the earnings from that endowment to nonprofit organizations pursuing public purposes. Of the more than 41,000 foundations in existence as of 1996, almost 37,000, or nearly 90 percent, were independent foundations, as shown in Table 3.3. These independent foundations controlled 85 percent of all foundation assets and accounted for 77 percent of all foundation grants.

Corporate Foundations. Somewhat different from the independent foundations are the corporate or company-sponsored foundations. Unlike the independent foundations, which receive their endowments from wealthy individuals, corporate foundations receive their funds from business corporations that want to avoid the fluctuations that come from financing corporate charitable activities from current income alone. By creating corporate foundations, corporations are able to maintain more professional and stable giving programs because the foundations can receive excess funds during years of corporate prosperity to build up endowments for use when corporate profits are lower. Altogether, there were nearly 2,000 corporate foundations in 1996 and they controlled 4 percent of all foundation assets and accounted for 13 percent of all foundation grants. This excludes, of course, the amounts that corporations give to charitable purposes directly, rather than through separate foundations.

Community Foundations. A third form of foundation is the community foundation. Where both independent and corporate foundations receive their funds from a single source, community foundations receive them from a number of sources in a given community. The basic concept of a community foundation is that wealthy individuals in a community, rather than tying their bequests to particular organizations that may go out of business or become less relevant over time, can pool them through a community foundation and put a board of local citizens in charge of deciding what the best use of the resources might be at a given point in time. Altogether, 411 community foundations were in existence in 1996, and they accounted for nearly 6 percent of all foundation assets and over 7 percent of all foundation grants — up from 5 percent in 1989.

TABLE 3.4
Ten Largest U.S. Foundations, 1996

Name	Assets ($ billions)
Ford Foundation	$8.2
W.K. Kellogg Foundation	7.6
David and Lucille Packard Foundation	7.4
J. Paul Getty Trust	7.2
Lilly Endowment Inc.	6.8
Robert Wood Johnson Foundation	5.6
The Pew Charitable Trusts	4.0
MacArthur Foundation	3.4
Robert W. Woodruff Foundation	3.0
The Rockefeller Foundation	2.7
Total	$55.9

Source: *Foundation Giving* (1998), p. 73

FIGURE 3.4
Distribution of Foundations and Foundation Assets, by Size Class, 1996

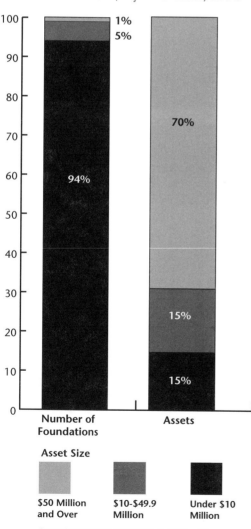

Asset Size

$50 Million and Over

$10-$49.9 Million

Under $10 Million

Source: Computed from *Foundation Giving* (1998), p. 16.

Operating Foundations. Finally, although most American foundations specialize in grantmaking, there were 2,323 foundations in 1996 that functioned both as grantmakers and operators of actual charitable programs, a pattern that is much more common overseas. These so-called operating foundations accounted for 6 percent of foundation assets and 2 percent of all foundation grants.

The Relative Position of Foundations.
Because of the scale and recent growth of the American foundation universe — the number of foundations has nearly doubled over the past decade and a half and the real value of their assets has increased two and a half times — there is often a tendency to exaggerate the role that foundations play and the contribution that they make. It is therefore important to bear a number of crucial facts in mind in assessing their position in the American nonprofit sector.

- In the first place, although the number of American foundations is quite large, most foundations are quite small. In fact, as shown in Figure 3.4, the top 1 percent of all foundations — 645 institutions in all — controlled 70 percent of all foundation assets as of 1996. By contrast, those with less than $10 million in assets represented 94 percent of all foundations but accounted for only 15 percent of all the assets. In other words, it is only a relative handful of foundations that account for the vast majority of foundation resources. (See Table 3.4 for a list of the top ten foundations in terms of assets.)

- In the second place, although the overall scale of foundation assets seems quite large, it pales in comparison to the assets of other institutions in American society. Thus, as Figure 3.5 shows, compared to the $268 billion in foundation assets, U.S. money market funds had assets of $891 billion (3 times as much), U.S. life insurance companies had assets of $2,239 billion (8 times as much), U.S. mutual funds had assets of $2,349 billion (8 times as much), U.S. pension funds had assets of $3,031 billion (11 times as much), U.S. commercial banks had assets of $3,349 billion (12 times as much),[15] and U.S. nonfinancial corporations had financial assets of $5,327 billion (20 times as much). In other words, while private foundations control significant assets, they hardly represent a major force in the American economy.

- Finally, private foundation grants, while important, hardly represent the dominant share even of the private philanthropic support that American nonprofit organizations receive. As shown in Figure 3.6, foundations (including corporate foundations) accounted for only about 10 percent of the $138.9 billion in private philanthropic contributions that Americans made in 1996. Even when we focus exclusively on the giving that flows to nonprofit service organizations of the sort that foundations support, and exclude giving to religious congregations, the foundation share of the total is still less than 20 percent. Since private charitable contributions represent only slightly over 10 percent of the total income of these nonprofit organizations, moreover, this means that the foundation share of total nonprofit income is only about 2 percent.[16]

In short, the United States has an extraordinary number of private, charitable foundations. These foundations control significant assets and make important contributions to the American nonprofit sector. Nevertheless, it would be wrong to exaggerate the role that these organizations play. They are by no means the dominant source of charitable donations and represent an even smaller share of the overall income of American nonprofits.

Federated Funders

Beyond the foundations, a second broad group of "funding intermediaries" in the American nonprofit sector are so-called federated funders. These are organizations that collect private donations on behalf of a number of service organizations. Examples here would be the United Jewish Appeal, the Lutheran social services network, the American Cancer Society, the American Heart Association, federated arts appeals, and the like.

Perhaps the best known of these federated funding organizations is the United Way. United Way is a network of some 1,900 local "community chests" that raise funds from individuals and corporations on behalf of a number of local social service agencies. What is distinctive about the United Way system, however, is its use of a particular mode of fundraising, namely, "workplace solicitation." This essentially involves a direct charitable appeal to workers in their workplace coupled with a system allowing employers to deduct the pledged contributions made by their employees automatically from the

FIGURE 3.5

Financial Assets, Foundations and Other U.S. Institutions, 1995 ($ billions)

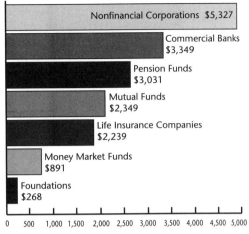

Source: *Statistical Abstract of the United States*, 1997, Table 74, p. 510.

"Though an important source of independence for American nonprofit organizations, private foundations nevertheless account for less than 10 percent of all private charitable giving, and less than 2 percent of all nonprofit income."

FIGURE 3.6

Sources of Private Giving, 1996
(including religion)

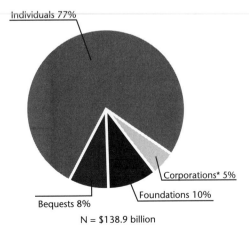

N = $138.9 billion

*Corporate foundations included with foundations

Source: See Endnote 16.

employees' paychecks each pay period. In order to ensure employer support, United Way has typically involved the corporate community actively in the organization of each year's United Way "campaign," and has historically restricted the distribution of the proceeds of the campaign to a set of approved United Way "member agencies." This latter feature has come under increasing attack in recent years, however, with the result that many local United Ways have established "donor option" plans, which permit donors to designate which agencies will receive their contributions.

Because of its obvious efficiencies, United Way's workplace campaigns have been quite effective, so much so that many other federated fundraising organizations have sought to break the monopoly that United Way has long had on the workplace as a solicitation site.[17] In 1997, for example, local United Ways throughout the United Sates collected a total of $3.25 billion in contributions.[18] While this is quite significant, it represented just over 2 percent of all private charitable donations to American nonprofit organizations, or a fourth as much as is provided by foundations. In the human service field in which it focuses, United Way provides closer to 25 percent of all the charitable support, but it is still important to remember that charitable support is just one of the sources of nonprofit income, and by no means the largest source.

While United Way is the best known of the federated funding organizations, it is by no means the only one. Also prominent are the numerous united health appeals organizations, such as the American Cancer Society, the American Heart Association, the American Diabetes Association, and others. These organizations sponsor public appeals through mail, by telephone, or via house-to-house solicitations to generate funds for use in health research and related purposes. The American Heart Association, for example, raised $345.2 million in 1995/6 from a combination of direct public appeals, special events, and bequests which it then used to support medical research, public health education campaigns, and medical education.[19]

Recent years have witnessed an expansion of the role of federated fundraising, even as individual nonprofit organizations have increased their direct appeals as well. Federated fundraising minimizes costs, especially for direct mail and related types of campaigning, but it also creates serious challenges in figuring out how to distribute the proceeds of federated campaigns and how to create donor identification with the causes and agencies being supported.

Professional Fundraisers

A final group of financial intermediaries of great importance to the nonprofit sector are professional fundraisers, the individuals and firms professionally involved in raising private contributions on behalf of private, nonprofit organizations. Larger nonprofit organizations typically employ one or more professional fundraisers on their regular staffs, and the typical large university or cultural institution may have a "development office" that employs 50 or more fundraisers. These professional fundraisers have their own professional association, the National Society of Fund-Raising Executives (NSFRE), as well as extensive networks of workshops and training courses. As of 1997, NSFRE had over 17,000 members throughout the United States.[20] In addition, a significant number of for-profit fundraising firms exist. For example, the American Association of Fund-Raising Counsel, Inc. represents approximately 25 of these firms. Such firms work on retainers from nonprofit organizations to manage fundraising campaigns.

Summary

In short, the American nonprofit sector contains a significant number of major institutions whose principal function is to serve as financial intermediaries, generating philanthropic contributions from the public, managing philanthropic asset pools, and transferring the resulting proceeds of both activities to other nonprofit organizations for their use. The existence of these organizations is at once a reflection of the maturity and specialization of the American nonprofit sector and of the premium that is placed on private, charitable support for it. But it can also be a source of confusion for those unacquainted with this class of organization.

Religious Congregations

In addition to the funding intermediaries, a second broad class of public-serving nonprofit organizations are the numerous sacramental religious organizations. Included here are the close to 350,000 religious congregations — churches, mosques, synagogues, and other places of worship — as well as an assortment of conventions of churches, religious orders, apostolic groups, and religious auxiliaries.[21]

The placement of these religious organizations in the primarily "public-serving" category is, of course, open to question. Although they often engage in a variety of service functions, religious congregations really exist primarily to serve the needs of their members rather than the public more generally. They are grouped in the public-serving category here because of the favored position they occupy in American law: They are the only organizations that are automatically entitled to tax exemption under Section 501(c)(3) of the tax code, and thus to the receipt of tax-deductible donations, without even having to file an application for formal recognition from the Internal Revenue Service. They are also exempt from the reporting requirements that the law places on all other types of 501(c)(3) organizations.

This favored position reflects the strong separation of church and state built into the American constitution.[22] Because the power to tax is the power to destroy, it is felt that to require religious congregations to secure approval from government to be incorporated or exempted from taxation would be to give government too much potential control over them. A self-declared religious congregation is therefore automatically treated as a 501(c)(3) organization exempt from taxes and eligible to receive tax-deductible gifts.

What constitutes a religious congregation or church for this purpose is open to dispute, however. Federal authorities have historically been loath to define the term very precisely in view of the First Amendment's prohibitions on any laws regarding the establishment of religion or the free exercise thereof. But the appearance of various self-styled religious organizations that turn out to be fronts for nonexempt activities has led the courts and the Internal Revenue Service to be somewhat more precise. Thus, churches and religious organizations are expected, among other things, to have some recognized creed or form of worship, to be sacerdotal in character, to have regular religious services, and to operate, like other 501(c)(3) organizations, for other than private gain.[23]

Service Providers

We come now to what in many respects is the heart of the public-serving nonprofit sector: the broad assortment of organizations that are neither funding intermediaries nor sacramental religious congregations, but rather service-providing organizations, broadly conceived. Included are providers of health services, education, day-care, adoption services, counseling, community organization, employment and training assistance, shelter, food, arts, culture, music, theater, and hundreds of others. Also included, however, are organizations engaged in research, advocacy, information-sharing, civic action, and overseas relief and development. As shown in Figures

"A self-declared religious congregation is automatically considered to be exempt from taxes and eligible to receive tax-deductible gifts."

3.1 and 3.2, these organizations account for 40 percent of the known nonprofit organizations but 80 percent of total nonprofit employment.

To make sense of this welter of organizations, it is useful to group them into five basic categories:[24]

- health care, including hospitals, clinics, nursing and personal care facilities, home health care centers, and specialty facilities (e.g., kidney dialysis units);
- education, including elementary and secondary education, higher education, libraries, vocational schools, noncommercial research institutes, and related educational services;
- social and legal services, including individual and family social services, job training and vocational rehabilitation services, residential care, day-care, and legal aid services;
- civic, including advocacy organizations, civil rights organizations, neighborhood-based organizations; and
- arts and culture, including bands, orchestras, theater groups, museums, art galleries, and botanical and zoological gardens.

Service versus Action Organizations

Legally, two broad classes of these service organizations exist. The principal distinction between these two classes is the extent to which they engage in active legislative "lobbying," i.e., actively promoting the passage or defeat of specific pieces of legislation.[25] The first class includes organizations that are primarily service providers and that can engage in "lobbying" activities only as a subsidiary activity. Such organizations are recognized as tax-exempt under Section 501(c)(3) of the tax code as "charitable" organizations. The second class is composed of organizations that are primarily engaged in lobbying and other legislative activity. Such organizations must register under Section 501(c)(4) of the tax code as "social welfare organizations." As such, they are not eligible to receive tax-deductible gifts from corporations or the general public.

Because of this restriction, many 501(c)(3) organizations, restricted from engaging "substantially" in lobbying activities themselves, organize (c)(4) "political action" affiliates to handle their lobbying activities for them without jeopardizing the tax-deductible status for the rest of the organization's operations. For purposes of our discussion here, however, we will treat both the primarily service organizations and the primarily "action" organizations as service providers.

"Service-providing organizations, including those engaged in research, advocacy, and information-sharing, comprise 40 percent of all nonprofit organizations but account for 80 percent of all nonprofit employment."

"Service-providing nonprofit organizations operate in five broad fields: health care, education and research, social and legal services, civic, and arts and culture."

FIGURE 3.7

Composition of the U.S. Public-Benefit Service Sector, Organizations and Expenditures, 1996

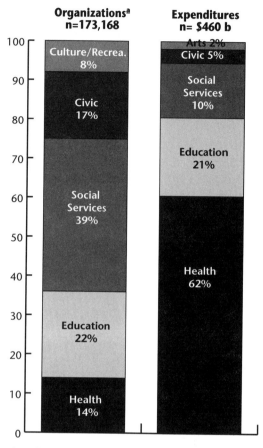

Source: See Endnotes 24 and 25
[a]As of 1992. Includes organizations with one paid employee.

"Even the public-benefit service component of America's nonprofit sector alone is a major economic force, with expenditures of $460 billion, or 6 percent of the nation's gross domestic product."

Numbers of Organizations

Solid data on the scope of this nonprofit service sector, or of its constituent parts, are difficult to piece together and sensitive to differences in record-keeping (e.g., some organizations treat their branches as separate organizations and others as integral parts of a single parent organization; many organizations carry out a multitude of activities and cannot easily be classified in one category). Based on the available data, however, it appears that there were approximately 760,000 active nonprofit, public-benefit service organizations as of 1996, the latest date for which data are available.[26] As noted earlier, most of these are quite small, and many may be inactive.[27] At any rate, detailed information is available only on those with at least one paid employee or that file the required Form 990 with the Internal Revenue Service. As of 1992, there were approximately 170,000 such organizations.[28]

As shown in Figure 3.7, these organizations are not distributed evenly among the various service fields. Rather:

- *The social service agencies* are the most numerous. Close to 40 percent of all nonprofit service organizations fall into this category. Included here are child day-care centers, individual or family counseling agencies, relief agencies, job training and vocational rehabilitation facilities, residential care institutions, and the like.

- The next largest group of nonprofit service organizations are *educational and research institutions,* including private elementary and secondary schools as well as private universities and colleges, libraries, and research institutes. Close to 38,000 such nonprofit educational institutions exist and they comprise 22 percent of the sector's institutions.

- The third most numerous type of nonprofit agencies are the *civic organizations*, which include neighborhood associations, advocacy organizations, community improvement agencies, civil rights organizations and the like. Seventeen percent of nonprofit service organizations take this form.

- *Health organizations,* including hospitals, nursing homes, and clinics, comprise 14 percent of the organizations.

- The smallest component of the nonprofit service sector in terms of numbers of organizations is the arts and recreation component, which includes symphonies, art galleries, theaters, zoos, botanical gardens, and other cultural and recreational institutions. Together, these cultural and recreational organizations represent 8 percent of the known nonprofit organizations.

Expenditures: A Major Economic Force

Because of the growth of government spending in recent decades and the prominence given to government policies, it is widely believed that this nonprofit service sector has shrunk into insignificance. Yet nothing could be further from the truth. To the contrary, in addition to their social value, nonprofit organizations are also a major economic force. In particular, these nonprofit public-benefit service organizations had expenditures in 1996 of approximately $460 billion, or over 6 percent of the country's gross domestic product and more than 30 percent of total expenditures on services.[29] In many local areas, in fact, the expenditures of the nonprofit sector easily outdistance those of local government. For example, a recent study of the nonprofit sector in Baltimore, Maryland, revealed that nonprofit expenditures in this metropolitan area exceeded the total expenditures of the city government and the five surrounding county governments.[30]

The distribution of expenditures differs widely, however, from the distribution of organizations. In particular, as Figure 3.7 also shows:

- *Health dominance.* The health subsector, composed in part of huge hospital complexes, accounts for the lion's share of the sector's total resources even though it comprises a relatively small proportion of the organizations. In particular, with 14 percent of the organizations the health subsector accounts for 62 percent of all nonprofit service-organization expenditures.

- *Significant education presence.* The education subsector accounted for another 21 percent of the expenditures. Health and education organizations alone thus make over 80 percent of the sector's expenditures.

- *Balance of the sector.* By contrast, the social service, civic, and arts and recreation organizations, which represent altogether two out of every three (65 percent) of the organizations, accounted for only 17 percent of the expenditures.

Quite clearly, this is a sector with a great deal of diversity in the size of its component organizations.

"Important as private giving is to the vitality and independence of the nonprofit sector, it is hardly the largest source of revenue for nonprofit public-benefit service organizations. Rather, the most important source of revenue is fees and charges, followed by government."

FIGURE 3.8
Sources of Nonprofit Public-Benefit Organization Income, 1996

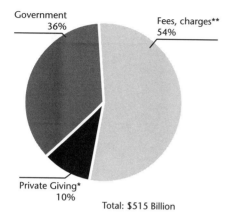

Government
36%

Fees, charges**
54%

Private Giving*
10%

Total: $515 Billion

Source: See Endnote 31.
*Includes estimated indirect giving through churches.
**Includes investment income.

"Not only are fees, charges, and other commercial income the major source of support for America's nonprofit public-benefit service organizations overall, but also they are the major source of support in four of the five different fields."

Where Do Nonprofit Service Agencies Get Their Funds?

Compared to their $460 billion in operating expenditures, America's nonprofit, public-benefit service organizations had revenues in 1996 of approximately $515 billion.[31] Included in the revenue figure are sums that were spent for nonoperating expenses such as capital equipment and buildings, as well as fund balances.

Where did these resources come from? What are the major sources of nonprofit revenues?

Unfortunately, there is a great deal of misunderstanding about the answer to this question. One common belief has been that large charitable foundations provide most of the income of America's nonprofit sector. Another is that charitable contributions as a whole, including individual and corporate gifts as well as foundation grants, account for the bulk of nonprofit service-organization income.

As we saw earlier in this chapter, however, private foundations account for only 10 percent of the private charitable contributions that are given in the United States. And total charitable contributions amounted to only $45.5 billion in income to nonprofit service organizations in 1996, $54 billion if estimated indirect contributions through churches are included.[32] Compared to total revenues of $515 billion this means that private giving from all sources constituted only 9 percent of nonprofit income, 10 percent if estimated contributions through churches are included. Clearly, important as private charitable support may be to the independence of the nonprofit sector, it hardly comprises the major source of income.

What, then, are the major sources of income? The answer to this question may be found in Figure 3.8. As this figure shows:

- *Fees, service charges, and other commercial income.* The major source of support of America's nonprofit public-benefit service organizations are fees, service charges, and other commercial income. Included here are college tuition payments, charges for hospital care not covered by government health insurance, other direct payments for services, and income from investments and sales of products. This source alone accounts for 54 percent of all nonprofit service-organization revenues.

- *Government.* The second most important source of income of America's nonprofit public-benefit service organizations is government. Government grants, contracts, and reimbursements account for 36 percent of nonprofit service-organization income. This reflects a widespread pattern of partnership between government and the nonprofit sector in carrying out public purposes, from the delivery of health care to the provision of education.[33]

- *Private giving.* The 10 percent of total income that nonprofits receive from private giving makes this only the third largest source of nonprofit service-organization income.

"Even with volunteer time included, private giving represents only 20 percent of all nonprofit support."

Variations by Subsector

Not only are fees, charges, and other commercial income the major source of support for America's nonprofit public-benefit service organizations overall, but also this source is the major source of support for four of the five different types of organizations. At the same time, some variations are also apparent. In particular, as shown in Figure 3.9:

- *Clear fee dominance in health and education.* The health and education portions of the nonprofit sector, which are by far the largest, receive the overwhelming preponderance of their income from fees and charges. This source accounts for 54 percent and 65 percent, respectively, of the income of these two types of nonprofit organizations. In the case of health, however, government is also a significant source of support, providing 41 percent of total revenue, whereas in the education field private giving plays a somewhat larger role.

FIGURE 3.9
Sources of Nonprofit Organization Revenue, by Type of Agency, 1996

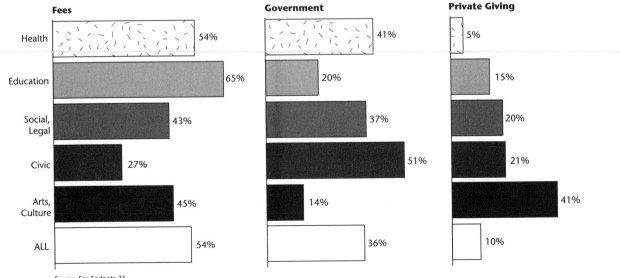

	Fees	Government	Private Giving
Health	54%	41%	5%
Education	65%	20%	15%
Social, Legal	43%	37%	20%
Civic	27%	51%	21%
Arts, Culture	45%	14%	41%
ALL	54%	36%	10%

Source: See Endnote 31.

FIGURE 3.10

Sources of Nonprofit Public-Benefit Service Organization Income, Including Volunteers, 1996

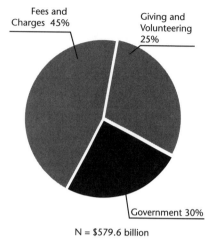

N = $579.6 billion

Source: See Endnote 32.

- *Heavy reliance on fees in social services and arts and recreation.* Fees also turn out to be the major source of income in the fields of arts and recreation (45 percent) and social services (43 percent). In the former, however, private giving is a close second, whereas in the latter, government support plays this role.

- *Government support in community development and civic organizations.* In only one field — community development and civic — are fees and service charges not the major source of nonprofit income; here government support performs this role, with fees and private giving in second and third place, respectively.

In short, in none of the major fields of nonprofit activity is private giving the major source of income. Needless to say, this does not mean that particular agencies may not get the preponderance of their income from private giving. But for the sector as a whole, and for the major classes of organizations, such giving now lags behind fees and government support as a source of nonprofit income.

Volunteer Time

In addition to the cash income they receive, nonprofit service organizations also have access to the services of numerous volunteers. Recent estimates indicate that 95 million Americans volunteered an average of 4.2 hours per week to various charitable and other organizations in 1995, and public-serving nonprofit service organizations are the beneficiaries of a significant portion of this.[34] In fact, the volunteer labor available to these organizations translates into the equivalent of almost five million full-time employees. If these organizations had to hire such employees, the cost would be over $100 billion.[35] Therefore, it is possible to consider this volunteer time as contributing another $100 billion to the revenues of the public-benefit service sector, of which half goes to social services and civic organizations, and nearly the other half to health, education, and arts organizations. Thus, including the assigned value of volunteers brings the total revenue of these organizations to $618 billion in 1996 and boosts the share represented by private contributions of time and money to 25 percent. In some fields, moreover, the inclusion of volunteers changes the picture even more dramatically. In social services, for example, the share of total support coming from philanthropy jumps from 20 percent to 56 percent once the value of volunteer time is factored in. For civic organizations it climbs to 48 percent, and for arts and recreation organizations to 78 percent.

Comparison to Other Countries

The scale of the nonprofit sector is larger in the United States than in most other countries. At the same time, however, measured as a share of total employment, the American nonprofit sector is hardly the largest in the world. Rather as figure 3.11 shows, at least four countries are known to exceed it in relative size — the Netherlands (12.4 percent), Ireland (11.5 percent), Belgium (10.5 percent), and Israel (9.2 percent) compared to the 6.9 percent in the U.S.[36]

Clearly, while America may have a particularly highly developed nonprofit sector, similar organizations are very much present in other parts of the world as well. Indeed, a veritable "global associational revolution" appears to be under way, a significant upsurge of organized, private, voluntary activity in virtually every corner of the globe.[37]

FIGURE 3.11

Nonprofit Sector Employment as a Percent of Total Nonagricultural Employment, U.S. vs. Selected Countries

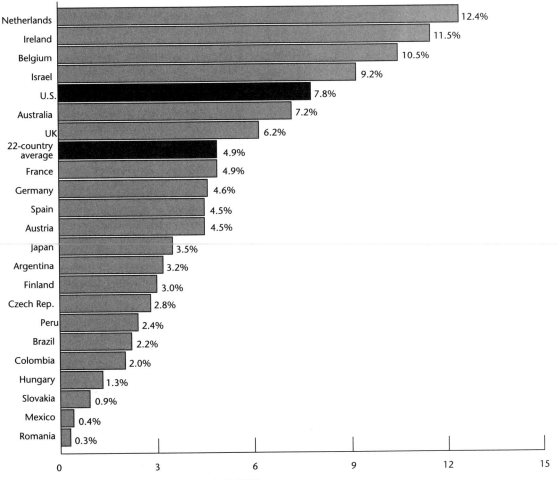

Source: Salamon and Anheier, *The Emerging Sector Revisited* (1998).

Summary

Four principal conclusions flow from this overview of the American nonprofit sector:

(1) *The nonprofit sector is composed of many different types of organizations.* Some of these are essentially member-serving organizations, and others are primarily public-serving. Among the public-serving organizations, a great deal of specialization also exists. Some organizations are essentially funding intermediaries, others are places of sacramental religious worship, and others provide the human and other services for which the sector is best known.

(2) *The nonprofit sector is much larger than is commonly believed.* America's nonprofit, public-benefit service organizations had operating expenditures in 1996 that were the equivalent of 6 percent of the gross national product. In many locales, the expenditures of the nonprofit sector outdistance those of all local governments.

(3) *Private giving comprises a much smaller share of the income of the nonprofit sector than is commonly recognized.* Important as private giving is to the vitality and independence of the nonprofit sector, it is hardly the largest source of nonprofit service-organization revenue. Rather, most of the income of this sector comes from fees and service charges, with government a close second.

(4) *While the American nonprofit sector is larger than its counterparts elsewhere in absolute terms, it is not in relative terms.* Nonprofit organizations have long been present in other countries as well, and their role and scope appear to be on the rise almost everywhere.

ENDNOTES

1. One recent estimate puts the number of informal grass-roots organizations in the United States as of the early 1990s at 7.5 million, or about 30 per 1,000 inhabitants, though this is based on rather rough projections. By comparison, the number of organizations formally registered as tax-exempt entities under any of the 26 relevant provisions of the Internal Revenue Code was approximately 1.164 million as of 1995. See: David Horton Smith, "The Rest of the Nonprofit Sector: Grassroots Associations as the Dark Matter Ignored in Prevailing 'Flat Earth' Maps of the Sector," *Nonprofit and Voluntary Sector Quarterly*, Vol. 26, No. 2 (June 1997), p. 118. Internal Revenue Service data from: U.S. Internal Revenue Service, *1995 Data Book* (Washington: U.S. Treasury Department), p. 25.

2. The estimate of 1.6 million identifiable nonprofit organizations noted here was derived by adding to the 1,164,789 organizations listed as registered tax-exempt organizations on the Internal Revenue Service's Exempt Organization

Master File two categories of organizations known to be underrepresented in the IRS records: the approximately 300,000 out of 375,000 religious congregations that exercise their right not to register with the Internal Revenue Service or to file the information return required of all other registered organizations; and the approximately 25 percent of all other charitable nonprofit organizations that are not recorded in IRS records but that prior research has documented to exist in communities throughout the country.

The IRS data were derived from *IRS Data Book: 1995,* p. 25. Data on the number of churches was compiled from several sources: *Yearbook of American & Canadian Churches,* Kenneth B. Bedell, ed. (New York: National Council of Churches, 1996), pp. 250–256 for Christian churches; television interview of Adburahman Alamoudi, Executive Director of American Muslim Council, National Public Radio, September 15, 1997, for Islamic mosques; Council of Jewish Federations for Jewish synagogues. The number of churches listed voluntarily with the IRS was derived from Mr. Ron Williams, IRS Personal Interview, October 27, 1997. The estimate of the number of 501(c)(3) organization other than churches not listed with the Internal Revenue was based on survey work conducted by the present author in cooperation with a team of colleagues in sixteen American cities of various sizes in the early 1980s. See: Lester M. Salamon, *Partners in Public Service: Government–Nonprofit Relations in the Modern Welfare State* (Baltimore: Johns Hopkins University Press, 1995), p. 59, n.1.

The list of 1.164 million organizations provided by the Internal Revenue Service itself very likely includes numerous defunct, inactive, or informal organizations. For example, only 572,600 of these organizations, or less than half, filed the information forms that prevailing laws require of all nonprofit organizations with expenditures in excess of $25,000 (Internal Revenue Service, *Statistics of Income Bulletin,* Publication 1136, February 1997, Table 21). Whether the non-filers were simply organizations that fell below the IRS reporting requirement of $25,000 in income, or whether they are organizations that have ceased to exist but are still carried on the IRS lists, is difficult to determine. Among the public-benefit service organizations of greatest interest to us here, moreover, this over-estimating problem may be even more severe. Of the 493,983 501(c)(3) charitable organizations other than churches and foundations included in the IRS listings, only approximately 165,000, or about one-third, filed one of the required information forms with IRS in 1995, according to data presented in Virginia A. Hodgkinson, Murray S. Weitzman et al., *Nonprofit Almanac: Dimensions of the Independent Sector 1996/97* (San Francisco: Jossey-Bass Publishers, 1996), p. 218. This suggests that a significant portion of the "registered" organizations either no longer exist or have revenues that fall below the IRS' $25,000 reporting threshold. They are consequently very likely grassroots organizations without paid staff.

3. Revenue data derived from Independent Sector, *America's Nonprofit Sector in Brief* (Washington, D.C.: Independent Sector, Spring 1998) and U.S. Census Bureau, *1996 Census Annual Survey* (June 1998). Data on gross domestic products of foreign countries from U.S. Census Bureau, *Statistical Abstract of the United States: 1997,* p.838.

4. Employment data derived from estimates prepared by Independent Sector, *America's Nonprofit Sector in Brief* (Washington, D.C., 1998) and from data in U.S. Department of Labor, Bureau of Labor Statistics, *Employment and Earnings,* 1996, (Washington, D.C., 1998).

5. Volunteer data derived from *Giving and Volunteering in the United States, 1996 edition* (analyzed by Virginia A. Hodgkinson and Murray S. Weitzman), (Washington, D.C.: Independent Sector, 1996), p. 1–30. The nonprofit share of total volunteers was estimated from computer tapes made available by Independent Sector.

6. The justification for tax exemption in the case of religious organizations is naturally different from this, resting on the First Amendment's bar against any law that might prohibit the "free exercise" of religion. Taxation of churches has been judged to involve the kind of excessive entanglement of government with religion that the First Amendment has been interpreted to prohibit. Bruce Hopkins, *The Law of Tax-Exempt Organizations,* 6th edition. (New York: John Wiley and Sons, 1992), pp. 202–3.

7. The formal language of the law is somewhat more complex than this. Section 501(c)(3) status is available for: "Corporations, and any community chest, fund or foundation, organized and operated exclusively for religious, charitable, scientific, testing for public safety, literary, or educational purposes, or to foster national or international amateur sports competition (but only if no part of its activities involve the provision of athletic facilities or equipment), or for the prevention of cruelty to children or animals."

8. The English Statute of Charitable Uses of 1601, which is the basis of the legal definition of the term charitable, specifically included the following activities within the term charitable: "...relief of aged, impotent, and poor people;...maintenance of sick and maimed soldiers and mariners; schools for learning, free schools, and scholars in universities; repair of bridges, ports, havens, causeways, churches, seabanks, and highways;...education and preferment of orphans;...relief, stock or maintenance of houses of correction;...marriages of poor maids; supportation, aid, and help of young tradesmen, handicraftsmen and persons decayed; relief or redemption of prisoners or captives; aid or ease of any poor inhabitants concerning payments of fifteens, setting out of soldiers and other taxes." For further detail, see: Hopkins, *The Law of Tax-Exempt Organizations* (1992), pp. 69–108.

9. The reason for this is that Section 501(c)(3) of the Internal Revenue Code law puts certain restrictions on the extent to which organizations can engage in "lobbying" activities, that is, activities intended to affect the passage or defeat of particular pieces of legislation. Organizations that intend to devote a substantial part of their activities to influ-

encing legislation must seek tax-exempt status under Section 501(c)(4) of the Internal Revenue Code, which is reserved for "civic leagues or organizations not organized for profit but operated exclusively for the promotion of social welfare...." Like "charitable" organizations exempted under section 501(c)(3), the "welfare organizations" granted exemption under section 501(c)(4) must be primarily public-serving and not member-serving in orientation, but they are allowed to be more action-oriented in political terms. In return, however, they cannot receive tax-deductible gifts. We have therefore depicted these organizations in Figure 3.1 in a special category. For more detail on the similarities and differences between 501(c)(3) and 501(c)(4) organizations, see Hopkins, *The Law of Tax-Exempt Organizations* (1992), pp. 564–568 and Chapter 10 below.

10. This estimate is a composite of estimates of bequest, foundation, corporate, and individual giving. The estimates of bequest, foundation, and corporate giving were derived from: *Giving USA 1997*. Ann E. Kaplan, editor. (New York: AAFRC Trust for Philanthropy, 1997), p. 16. The estimate of individual giving is based on an adjustment prepared by Mr. Murray Weitzman of Independent Sector of a projection of 1996 individual giving originally reported in: *Impact of Tax Restructuring on Tax-Exempt Organizations*. A report by Price Waterhouse LLP and Caplin & Drysdale, Chartered (Washington, D.C.: Council on Foundations and Independent Sector, 1997), p. 33. This estimate of $108.1 billion differs markedly from the $119.9 billion estimate of individual giving provided in *Giving USA 1997*. The major reason for this disparity arises from different methods of estimating the charitable contributions of persons who do not itemize deductions on their tax returns and for whom solid data on giving are consequently not available. Such individuals now constitute over 70 percent of all taxpayers, creating serious problems in estimating the overall scale of private charitable giving in the United States. For a variety of reasons, the estimates developed by Price Waterhouse, which are based on an econometric analysis of an Internal Revenue Service public use sample of individual income tax filers, seem more reasonable than those reported in *Giving USA*.

11. Comparable data for the United Kingdom, for example, reveal that private giving represents at most only about 1.4 percent of gross domestic product. Charities Aid Foundation, *Charity Trends*. 13th edition. (London: Charities Aid Foundation, 1990), p. 10.

12. See note 7 above for the derivation of the individual, bequest, foundation, and corporate giving totals. The allocation of giving among recipient types is based largely on data provided by Murray Weitzman of Independent Sector. The estimate of charitable contributions received by foundations comes from: *Giving USA 1997*, p. 201. The estimate of giving to government agencies (e.g., higher education institutions) is derived by subtracting the estimates of giving to other independent sector organizations from total estimated giving.

13. While foundations in their present form have existed since the turn of the century, they were given legal definition only in 1969, with the passage of the Tax Reform Act. This Act differentiated foundations from other nonprofit institutions that have endowments and imposed extra restrictions on the foundations. The key defining feature of a foundation as opposed to other nonprofit institutions is that they typically receive their support from a single individual and utilize their resources chiefly to make grants or other "qualifying distributions" to other nonprofit organizations. To be treated as other than a foundation, nonprofit organizations must therefore meet a "public support test," demonstrating that they receive their support from multiple sources. "Community foundations," which, as noted below, receive their support from multiple sources also, fall into a special category in the law.

14. Loren Renz, Crystal Mandler, and Rikard Treiber, *Foundation Giving,* 1998 Edition. (New York: The Foundation Center, 1998), p. 5. All data on foundations here come from this source. (Cited hereafter as *Foundation Giving,* 1998).

15. U.S. Bureau of the Census, *Statistical Abstract of the United States,* 1997, 117th edition (Washington, DC: U.S. Government Printing Office, 1997), p. 510.

16. See note 7 for the source of the estimates of the various sources of giving. The estimates of foundation and corporate giving here differ from those mentioned in note 7 and the accompanying text in that the foundation figure includes giving by corporate foundations and the corporate giving figure is correspondingly reduced. This was done to make the estimates consistent with Foundation Center usage, which is the basis for all other foundation data here. Data on corporate foundation giving for 1996 were derived from *Foundation Giving 1998,* p. 5. Giving to religion was estimated by deducting from overall private giving to religious congregations an estimate developed by Independent Sector of the gifts these congregations made to other nonprofit organizations. It was assumed that all of the giving to religious congregations originates with individuals. I am grateful to Murray Weitzman of Independent Sector for sharing these estimates with me.

17. During the Carter Administration, several alternative funds, such as the Black United Fund and the United Health Appeal, secured permission to solicit contributions in the federal workplace. This was later revoked by the Reagan Administration, provoking a legal battle that has ended with a broadening of the access to the federal workplace and a greater willingness of the United Way to accept the donor option approach. For this and other features of United Way, see: Eleanor Brilliant, *The United Way: Dilemmas of Organized Charity* (New York: Columbia University Press, 1991).

18. United Way Press Release, August 18, 1997.

19. American Heart Association, World Wide Web Site, January 20, 1998.

20. World Wide Web site, www.nsfre.org, January 5, 1998.

21. Included here are an estimated 345,170 Christian churches, 1,500 Islamic mosques, and 1,859 Jewish synagogues. Data on churches from: *Yearbook of American and Canadian Churches,* 1996. Edited by Kenneth B. Bedell, (New York: National Council of the Churches of Christ in the United States, 1996), pp. 250–256. Data on mosques from American Muslim Council. Data on synagogues from Council of Jewish Federations. For a discussion of the definitions of these various types of religious organizations, see: Hopkins, *The Law of Tax-Exempt Organizations* (1992), pp. 270–272. The 350,000 religious congregations included here do not include the religiously affiliated service organizations offering day-care, family counseling, and other services, such as the agencies that are part of the Catholic Charities network or the Lutheran Social Services network. These agencies are included among the service agencies discussed later. For additional detail on religious organizations, see Chapter 11 below.

22 The First Amendment to the U.S. Constitution declares, "Congress shall make no law respecting an establishment of religion, or prohibiting the free exercise thereof."

23. Organizations that are church-related but that would be eligible for tax-exempt 501(c)(3) status for other than religious reasons (e.g., church-affiliated educational organizations, hospitals, orphanages, old-age homes) are required to be recognized under these other provisions and are not treated as churches. Typically such organizations must therefore secure separate tax-exempt status and are not covered by the exemption accorded the church *qua* church. Reflecting this, we do not treat them here as religious congregations, but rather as service organizations. On the treatment of churches and church-related charitable organizations, see: Hopkins, *The Law of Tax-Exempt Organizations* (1992), pp. 775–77.

24. This classification follows *U.S. Census of Service Industry* usage and is embraced here for convenience sake. The chapters in Part II of this volume separate out legal aid from other social services and group it with political action and international aid.

25. Lobbying is thus different from "advocacy." Advocacy includes the generation of information about public problems, the education of policymakers and the general public about such problems, and responses to inquiries from policymakers. Where advocacy crosses the line to become "lobbying" is when it is focused on a particular piece of legislation or administrative action. Organizations exempt under Section 501(c)(3) of the Internal Revenue Code are not limited in the extent of advocacy they can carry out, but they are limited in the extent of "lobbying" in which they can engage. Such lobbying cannot be a "substantial" part of the organization's activity, which has been interpreted to mean that it cannot absorb more than 20 percent of the organization's expenditures. For further detail, see: Hopkins, *The Law of Tax-Exempt Organizations* (1992), pp. 300–326, and Chapter 10 below.

26. This estimate was developed by subtracting from the 765,677 organizations registered as 501(c)(3) or 501(c)(4) organizations on the Internal Revenue Service's Master File of Exempt Organizations the estimated 78,866 churches that choose to register with the Internal Revenue Service even though they are not required to, and the approximately 51,330 funding intermediaries, and then adding the 25 percent of organizations that prior research has identified to exist locally but not to be included in the IRS listings. For further detail, see note 2 above. IRS data are from U.S. Internal Revenue Service, *Annual Report of the Director* (1997).

27. Reflecting this, only about a third of these organizations file the Form 990 that the Internal Revenue Code requires for all tax-exempt organizations with at least $25,000 in expenditures.

28. Included here are 129,956 organizations identified by the U.S. Census Bureau in its 1992 Census of Service Industries in the categories that meet our definition of public-benefit service organizations, plus 28,924 schools, colleges, and universities identified in the *Digest of Education Statistics,* and 14,288 civic organizations identified from the IRS records. Supplementation of the census data is necessary because the census did not cover schools and colleges in 1992. Deleted from the census data are certain member-serving organizations that do not meet our definition. In addition, the census tally of civic organizations groups these organizations with social and fraternal organizations that fall into the member-serving category in our grouping. Accordingly, we drew on IRS data to estimate the number of such civic organizations. For further information, see: U.S. Census bureau, *1992 Census of Service Industries* (Washington: U.S. Government Printing Office, 1996); and U.S. Department of Education, National Center for Education Statistics, *Digest of Education Statistics,* 1997, Table 5.

   An alternative estimate of the number of nonprofit public-benefit service organizations is available from data assembled by the Internal Revenue Service from the information forms (Form 990) that nonprofit organizations are required to file with the IRS. Only organizations with expenditures of $25,000 or more are required to file these forms, however. As of 1993, there were 152,186 such organizations that met our definition of a public-benefit service organization. Included here are all 164,247 501(c)(3) organizations that filed Form 990 in1993 except for 5,345 philanthropic intermediaries and 6,716 religious-support organizations. (*Nonprofit Almanac 1996/97,* pp.247–250). For a variety of reasons, the Census data appear more reliable and complete than the IRS Form 990 data. What is more, the classification of organizations in the IRS data differs from that used by the Census Bureau and other economic data agencies, making it difficult to line up the number of agencies with the extent of expenditures using the IRS data.

29. Nonprofit expenditure data provided by Murray Weitzman, Independent Sector, Washington, D.C., 1998. These data were adjusted to fit the definitions used here

using data drawn from U.S. Bureau of the Census, Current Business Reports BS196, *Service Annual Survey: 1996* (Washington, D.C.: U.S. Government Printing Office, 1998). (Cited hereafter as Census Bureau, *Service Annual Survey: 1996*). In particular, social and fraternal organizations were deleted and Social Services Not Elsewhere Classified treated as part of civic. Excludes religious organizations and foundations. Data on gross domestic product and personal consumption expenditures on services from *Economic Report of the President* (February 1997), p. 300.

30. Lester M. Salamon, David Altschuler, and Jaana Myllyluoma, *More Than Just Charity: The Baltimore Nonprofit Sector in a Time of Change* (Baltimore: The Johns Hopkins Institute for Policy Studies, 1990), p. 9.

31. Computed from estimates provided by Murray Weitzman, Independent Sector, December 1997, adjusted to reflect the definitions used here as detailed in Endnote 29. Social service organization revenue sources computed from special tabulations of Form 990 data supplied by the National Center for Charitable Statistics.

32. This assumes that approximately 12 percent of all religious contributions find their way to non-sacramental service organizations. Based on data provided by Murray Weitzman, Independent Sector, December 1997.

33. For more detail on this government–nonprofit financial link, see Chapter 5 and Lester M. Salamon, *Partners in Public Service: Government-Nonprofit Relations in the Modern Welfare State* (Baltimore: Johns Hopkins University Press, 1995.)

34. *Giving and Volunteering in the United States. 1996 Edition.* Virginia Ann Hodgkinson and Murray S. Weitzman. (Washington, D.C.: Independent Sector), p.1–30.

35. The estimate of 4.7 million full-time equivalent workers and $103 billion in imputed value from volunteer inputs is based on applying to the 1995 estimates of total full-time equivalent volunteer workers of 9,233 million and total imputed value of volunteer work of $201.5 billion the estimated share of total volunteer time that is devoted to public-benefit service organizations. This latter was derived from data tapes generated from a 1996 survey conducted by the Gallup organization for Independent Sector. According to our own calculations, religious activities absorbed 24.4 percent of all volunteer time, for-profit organizations and governments 21.5 percent, professional organizations 3.0 percent, and other charitable nonprofit organizations 51.1 percent. Aggregate figures on the amount of volunteer time were derived from Independent Sector, *Giving and Volunteering in the United States, 1996 Edition*, (Washington, D.C.: Independent Sector, 1996). Full-time equivalent conversion was based on a full-time work-year of 1,700 hours. Volunteer time was valued at the average hourly wage for nonagricultural workers.

36. Lester M. Salamon and Helmut K. Anheier, *The Emerging Sector Revisited: A Summary* (Baltimore: MD: Johns Hopkins Institute for Policy Studies, 1998), p.8.

37. Lester M. Salamon, "The Rise of the Nonprofit Sector," *Foreign Affairs*, Vol. 73, No. 4 (July/August 1994), pp. 109–122.

CHAPTER FOUR

The Nonprofit Sector in Context: The Government and Business Presence

Important as the nonprofit sector is to American society and the American social welfare system, it hardly operates in a vacuum. Nor does it have a monopoly on providing for public needs. To the contrary, one of the signal developments of the past half century of American life has been the expansion of governmental social welfare activity, so much so that some observers have feared that government may have displaced the nonprofit sector altogether.

As we have seen, this fear has been largely unwarranted. The presumed conflict between an activist government and a vibrant nonprofit sector has not really materialized in the American setting. Although tensions clearly exist, a widespread partnership has developed between the two sectors, and with for-profit businesses as well, creating a "mixed economy" of welfare in which public and private, nonprofit and for-profit action are mixed in often complex and confusing ways.[1] Thus:

- Nonprofit organizations help to identify problems and mobilize pressure on government to respond.

- Government establishes programs and raises resources and then turns to both nonprofit and for-profit organizations to deliver the services.

- Private households purchase welfare services on their own from both nonprofit and for-profit providers.

- For-profit businesses form alliances with nonprofit organizations and local governments to improve schools, upgrade neighborhoods, and promote the arts.

The purpose of this chapter is to outline the basic scope and structure of governmental involvement in this "mixed economy," focusing particularly on the

"The presumed conflict between an activist government and a vibrant nonprofit sector has not really materialized in the American setting. Although tensions clearly exist, a widespread partnership has developed instead...."

"In 1994, federal, state, and local governments in the United States spent $1.4 trillion–21 percent of the U.S. gross domestic product and nearly 60 percent of all government spending–on 'social welfare services.'"

social welfare sphere; and to assess how valid the claim is that government has surpassed the nonprofit sector in the provision of social welfare services. In addition, it seeks to document the role that private for-profit businesses have come to play in the traditional fields of nonprofit activity.

To do so, the discussion falls into three major sections. The first provides an overview of government social welfare spending, the distribution of this spending between federal and state and local governments, and the relationship between the levels of such spending in the United States and that in other countries. Against this backdrop, we then zero in on those areas where nonprofit organizations are involved and compare the level of government involvement in these areas with the levels of nonprofit activity in the same fields. Finally, we examine the role that for-profit providers are now playing in these same fields.

What emerges from this analysis are five basic conclusions:

- First, government social welfare spending is quite extensive in the United States.
- Second, despite the expansion of federal government activity, state and local governments still play a significant role in many fields.
- Third, government social welfare spending in the United States, however significant, is still well below comparable levels in most of the other advanced industrial societies.
- Fourth, far from being overshadowed by government, the nonprofit sector in the United States is almost as large as government in the fields where both are actively involved.
- Fifth, for-profit businesses have secured a firm foothold in many fields where nonprofits once predominated.

The remainder of this chapter examines the bases for these conclusions.

The Government Role: Basic Parameters

Overview

In 1994, the latest year for which data are available, federal, state, and local governments in the United States spent a total of $1.4 trillion on "social welfare services." Included here are old-age pensions, unemployment insurance, veterans benefits, education, health care, welfare aid for the poor, nutrition assistance, day-care, social services, housing, and related services.[2] This represented approximately 21 percent of the total U.S. gross domestic product and nearly three-fifths (58 percent) of all government spending — federal, state, and local.[3] As noted in Figure 4.1:

- The largest portion (37 percent) of this social welfare spending went for social security, veterans' benefits (excluding health and education), and other social insurance and pension benefits. Included here is the federal social security program, which provides pension benefits to retired workers; unemployment insurance, which provides cash payments to unemployed persons in covered occupations for a limited period following loss of a job; disability payments to persons injured while working; and pension payments to injured war veterans.[4] These benefits are typically conditioned only on past work or military experience and are not income-related.

- More than a quarter (28 percent) of government social welfare spending goes for health benefits. This included payments for Medicare, the federal health program providing health insurance for the elderly; for Medicaid, a joint federal-state program providing reimbursement to hospitals and nursing homes for health services to the poor; and for veterans' health care.

- About one-fourth (24 percent) of government social welfare spending goes for education, of which the lion's share (18 percent) is for elementary and secondary education and 6 percent for higher education.

- This leaves just over 10 percent to be split among all the rest of the activities, including the basic needs-based "welfare" program, housing aid, and an assortment of child nutrition, vocational rehabilitation, institutional care, and related social services. Included here is the Aid to Families with Dependent Children (now Temporary Assistance to Needy Families) Program, the basic cash assistance program for low-income female-headed families with children; Food Stamps, which provides food assistance to the needy; public housing; and a variety of employment assistance and social service programs.

Quite clearly, the basic, universal, non-needs-tested assistance programs for the elderly and for education dominate the government role in the social welfare field, and the assistance targeted particularly on the poor is far more limited. In particular, of the $1.4 trillion in government social welfare spending, less than 20 percent is targeted on the needy. By contrast, the overwhelming majority flows to the broad middle class.

"Less than 20 percent of the $1.4 trillion in government social welfare spending is targeted on the needy. The rest takes the form of pension, health, and education benefits for the broad middle class."

FIGURE 4.1

Government Spending on Social Welfare in the U.S., 1994

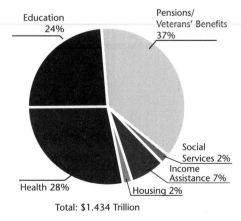

Education 24%

Pensions/ Veterans' Benefits 37%

Social Services 2%

Income Assistance 7%

Housing 2%

Health 28%

Total: $1.434 Trillion

Source: See Endnotes 2 and 4.

51

FIGURE 4.2

Federal vs. State/Local Spending on Social Welfare, 1994

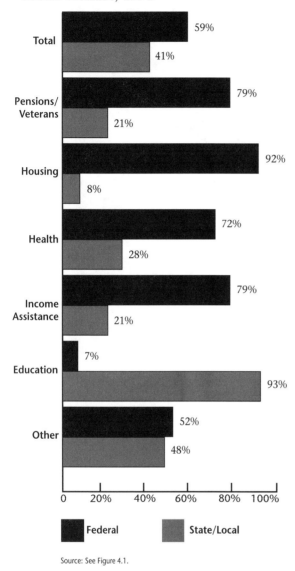

Source: See Figure 4.1.

"...state and local governments retain a substantial role in financing, as well as delivering, government social welfare services in the United States, ...and this was true well before the 'devolution' innovations of the mid-1990s."

Federal versus State and Local Roles

Much of the impetus for the growth of government social welfare spending over the past four or five decades has come from the national level, giving rise to the common assumption that state and local involvement, once dominant, has now effectively disappeared. In fact, however, state and local governments retain a substantial role in financing, as well as delivering, government social welfare services in the United States. In particular:

- Of the $1.4 trillion in government social welfare spending in 1994, only 59 percent came from the federal government. The remaining 41 percent came from state and local governments.

- As shown in Figure 4.2, federal spending dominates in the areas of pensions (Social Security and veterans' payments) and housing aid.

- State and local governments have the decidedly dominant role in education, especially elementary and secondary education. Overall, 93 percent of public education spending originates at the state and local level.

- In addition, state and local governments account for nearly half of the support for a broad range of other social service activities, including day-care, child placement and adoption services, foster care, and legal assistance.

- Even in the health care and need-based income-assistance areas, the states provide between 20 and 30 percent of all support. This reflects state and local financing of much of public health and the "matching" requirements built into the federal Medicaid and welfare programs.

- Beyond their financing role, moreover, state and local governments frequently play a major role in the implementation of even the federally financed activity. Thus, the federal Medicaid and TANF (welfare) programs are essentially administered by state and local governments. State and local governments also operate the federal Social Service Block Grant and Community Development Block Grant programs as well as other federally financed social service activities.

In short, the expansion of federal social welfare activity has by no means displaced the state and local governments, and this was true well before the "devolution" innovations of the mid-1990s. To the contrary, federal aid has helped to expand the role of state and local governments, and these governments retain a vital role both in the financing and delivery of social welfare services.

Comparison to Other Countries

While the government role in social welfare provision is quite extensive in the United States, it still lags behind that in most other developed countries of the world. Compared to the 21 percent of gross domestic product that government social welfare spending represents in the United States, most of the developed nations of Europe devote 30 percent or more of their gross domestic product to government-funded social welfare activities (Figure 4.3).[5] This reflects the different conceptions about public versus individual responsibility for social welfare between the United States and Europe. What is treated as a public responsibility in Europe is often considered a private responsibility, to be financed out of private earnings, in the United States. Significantly, moreover, although the United States boasts a higher rate of private charitable giving than do almost all of these other countries, the difference does not come close to evening out the disparities in government social welfare spending. As we have seen, private giving constitutes at most about 2 percent of gross domestic product in the United States. Even if no charitable activity occurred at all in these other countries, therefore, the inclusion of charitable contributions would narrow the disparity in the share of gross domestic product devoted to social welfare purposes between the United States and these other advanced industrial countries by only 2 percent, leaving a gap of anywhere from 6 percent to 20 percent of gross domestic product — a quite substantial difference.[6]

Government versus the Nonprofit Sector

At first glance, the $1.4 trillion in government social welfare spending appears to overshadow by a substantial margin the $460 billion in nonprofit expenditures, not to mention the $54 billion in private charitable support to nonprofit service providers.[7] This is even more the case given that the government spending data are for 1994 and the nonprofit expenditure data for 1996.

For purposes of comparing the scale of government activity to the scale of nonprofit activity, however, it is not appropriate to include all of what is here referred to as "social welfare expenditures." The nonprofit sector is not, for example, involved in providing pensions or veterans' benefits, and its involvement in elementary and secondary education is quite limited, as will be detailed more fully below. With these two major components excluded, we are left with $650 billion in government spending on welfare services of the sort that nonprofit organizations also provide.

FIGURE 4.3

Government Social Welfare Spending as a Share of G.D.P., U.S. vs. W. Europe, 1994/95

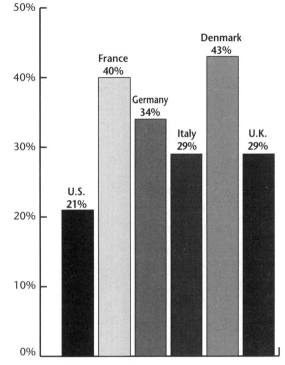

Source: U.S. from Bixby, (1997:40); all other from OECD, National Accounts, (Paris, 1997), Table 5.

"Compared to the 21 percent of gross domestic product that government social welfare spending represents in the United States, most of the developed nations of Europe devote 30 percent or more of their gross domestic product to government-funded social welfare services, and the 2 percent of U.S. personal income that goes to private charitable giving hardly makes up the difference."

FIGURE 4.4

Spending on Selected Social Welfare Functions*: Government vs. Private Nonprofit Organizations, 1994/96

Billions of $

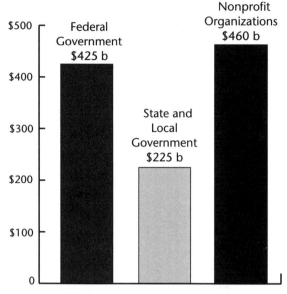

*Excludes old-age pensions, veterans pensions, and public elementary and secondary education. Government data cover 1994; nonprofit data cover 1996.

Of this $650 billion, $225 billion represents state and local government spending and $425 billion represents federal spending. What this means is that for every four dollars of government spending in the fields where government and the nonprofit sector are both involved, nonprofit organizations spend almost three dollars. Put somewhat differently, nonprofit expenditures in these fields outdistance those of either the federal government, or state and local governments, taken separately (see Figure 4.4).

To be sure, a significant share of the revenue that supports nonprofit expenditures comes from government support, but the key point is that the scale of nonprofit activity, even measured solely in monetary terms, is almost as large as government activity as a whole, more than twice as large as state and local government activity alone, and 12 percent larger than the federal role alone! These disparities would widen further, moreover, if we were to include the $100 billion worth of volunteer labor that the nonprofit sector also brings into the field.

The For-Profit Role

In addition to government and nonprofit organizations, for-profit businesses are also increasingly active in many of the fields where nonprofit organizations operate. This reflects in part the presence of governmental funding to underwrite the costs of human services for the poor, and in part the growing demand for such services among middle-class clients who can pay market prices. Thus, as of the mid-1990s:

- For-profit businesses accounted for 14 percent of all general hospitals, 44 percent of all specialty hospitals, 67 percent of all clinics and nursing homes, and 78 percent of all home health facilities (see Figure 4.5).[8]

- For-profit penetration is less pronounced in other fields, but it is still evident. Thus, as Figure 4.5 shows, as of the early 1990s, for-profit firms already represented 20 percent of all family service agencies, almost 70 percent of all day-care centers, 45 percent of all live theaters, 13 percent of all museums and art galleries, 81 percent of all vocational education centers, and even 5 percent of all four-year colleges.

"...for-profit businesses are also increasingly active in many of the fields where nonprofit organizations operate."

Summary

In short:

(1) Government is thus a major presence in the social welfare field in the United States. In fact, over half of all government spending in the United States goes for social welfare purposes, broadly conceived.

(2) Although the growth of federal government spending has been critical in creating this government presence, state and local governments have played an important part as well and retain a significant presence. In fact, fully 40 percent of all government social welfare spending originates at the state and local government level, and state and local governments help to implement many of the federally financed programs as well.

(3) Although sizable, the level of government social welfare spending in the United States, when measured as a share of gross national product, lags significantly behind that in most other advanced industrial societies. In part this reflects the greater reliance Americans place on private charity and the nonprofit sector. But in even greater part it probably reflects the greater reliance Americans place on private purchase of social welfare services.

(4) Reflecting the importance of private purchase of social welfare services, for-profit firms have established a significant presence in the human service field, equalling or exceeding the nonprofit sector in many areas.

(5) Finally, despite the significant presence of both government and the for-profit sector, the nonprofit sector has maintained a very significant role. In fact, the level of nonprofit expenditures on welfare services outdistances the levels of either federal government or state and local government expenditures on these same services. Far from withering away with the growth of government, the nonprofit sector seems to have blossomed as well, though it now faces increasing competition from for-profit firms.

In short, a complex "mixed economy" of welfare exists in the United States, with nonprofit, for-profit, and governmental institutions all deeply involved, sometimes on their own, but increasingly in collaboration with each other. This reality flies in the face of some of our political rhetoric, which tends to portray these sectors as inherently in conflict. But it seems to be the reality that actually exists. As we will see in the next chapter, moreover, it is also a reality that has developed over a considerable period of time.

ENDNOTES

1. For a statement of the theoretical rationale for this arrangement, see: Lester M. Salamon, "Of Market Failure, Government Failure, and Third-Party Government: Toward a Theory of Government–Nonprofit Relations in the Modern Welfare State," *Journal of Voluntary Action Research*, Vol. 16, Nos. 1 & 2 (January-June 1987), pp. 29–49.

FIGURE 4.5

For-Profit vs. Nonprofit Role in Selected Human Service Fields, 1992/96

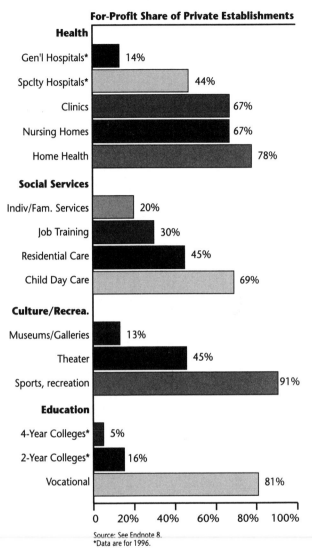

For-Profit Share of Private Establishments

Health
- Gen'l Hospitals* — 14%
- Spclty Hospitals* — 44%
- Clinics — 67%
- Nursing Homes — 67%
- Home Health — 78%

Social Services
- Indiv/Fam. Services — 20%
- Job Training — 30%
- Residential Care — 45%
- Child Day Care — 69%

Culture/Recrea.
- Museums/Galleries — 13%
- Theater — 45%
- Sports, recreation — 91%

Education
- 4-Year Colleges* — 5%
- 2-Year Colleges* — 16%
- Vocational — 81%

Source: See Endnote 8.
*Data are for 1996.

"Far from withering away with the growth of government, the nonprofit sector seems to have blossomed as well, though it now faces increasing competition from for-profit firms."

2. "Social welfare services" are defined by the U.S. Social Security Administration as "the cash benefits, services, and administrative costs of public programs that directly benefit individuals and families." See: Ann Kallman Bixby, "Public Social Welfare Expenditures, Fiscal Year 1994," *Social Security Bulletin,* Vol. 60, No. 3 (1997), p. 40. Unless otherwise noted, the data on government social welfare spending in this chapter are drawn from this source and from unpublished Social Security Administration data made available to the author.

3. Data on gross domestic product from U.S., *Economic Report of the President 1997.* (Washington: U.S. Government Printing Office, 1997), p. 300.

4. The data reported here have been grouped somewhat differently from the way they are presented in the *Social Security Bulletin* data series cited in note 2 above. In particular, "pensions" here includes all of "social insurance" except Medicaid plus all of "veterans' programs" except for "veterans' health and medical programs" and "veterans' education programs." "Income assistance" here includes "public aid" except for "vendor medical payments" (largely Medicaid) and "social services." Health includes "Health and medical programs" from the *Bulletin* listing plus Medicare and "vendor medical payments." "Education" here includes what is listed in the bulletin under "education" plus what is listed under "veterans' education." "Social services" here includes what is listed in the *Bulletin* under "other social welfare" plus what is listed as "social services" under "public aid." These adjustments are needed to make the categories correspond more fully to the substantive program areas.

5. Based on data in Organization for Economic Cooperation and Development (OECD), *National Accounts,* Vol. II (Paris: OECD, 1997), Table 5.

6. Although it is difficult to draw firm conclusions about the consequences of these divergent spending patterns, some crucial social indicators suggest that at least some Americans pay a price for the country's generally lower rates of social welfare spending. Thus, of the countries listed in Figure 4.3, the U.S. has the highest rate of infant mortality, perhaps the best summary indicator of social well-being, and the lowest life expectancy rate. *Statistical Abstract of the United States 1997*, pp. 832–33.

7. This figure differs from the one in Table 3.2 above because it includes giving that reaches service providers indirectly through churches.

8. Hospital data from American Hospital Association, *Hospital Statistics 1996*, special analyses. Education data from U.S. Department of Education, *Digest of Education Statistics* (1997). Remaining data from U.S. Census Bureau, *Census of Service Industries 1992,* Subject Series, pp. 5-9, 5-10; Geographic Area Series, pp. US–9, US-10. All data are from 1992 unless otherwise noted. For further detail see subsequent chapters.

CHAPTER FIVE

How Did We Get Here? Historical Developments and Recent Trends

That the nonprofit sector retains a significant role in the American social welfare system is due in no small measure to how that system has evolved. This evolution has also been responsible, in more recent years, for a variety of strains that nonprofit organizations have experienced. To understand the current position of the nonprofit sector in America's "mixed economy," therefore, it is necessary to understand how that "mixed economy" has developed and what it has undergone in recent years.

To do so, this chapter is divided into two major sections. The first examines the two major eras of reform that gave rise to the mixed system of social welfare provision we have just described — one in the 1930s, which first established a significant governmental role, and the other in the 1960s, which expanded government's cooperation with private, nonprofit groups. The second section then examines the strains to which the government–nonprofit partnership that blossomed in the 1960s and 1970s was exposed during the 1980s, and the consequences these have had for the nation's nonprofit groups.

Historical Background[1]

The New Deal System
The basic foundation of America's current social welfare system was set during the New Deal era of the 1930s, much later than in most other industrialized countries. Prior to this, considerable popular sentiment in the United States opposed extensive government involvement, certainly extensive *federal* government involvement, in social welfare; and the task of responding to the poverty and distress created by the massive urbanization and industrialization of

> *"That the nonprofit sector retains a significant role in the American social welfare system is due in no small measure to how that system has evolved."*

"...the United States emerged from the Second World War with a social welfare system that, despite the New Deal innovations, remained characterized by ...patchy coverage, limited funding, and state and local dominance...."

the late nineteenth and early twentieth centuries was left largely to local governments and private, charitable groups.

The Great Depression of the 1930s made clear, however, that such a private and localized system of aid, however well intentioned, was not capable of providing on its own the protections that an urban-industrial society required. In response to the widespread distress of the depression era, President Franklin D. Roosevelt was therefore able to push through a system of federal protections.

At the heart of the resulting New Deal system of social welfare aid were three principal programs:

- **Old-age pensions** (the Social Security Program), financed largely by worker contributions to a Social Security Trust Fund;

- **Unemployment insurance**, providing temporary income coverage for persons who lose their jobs, financed partly by worker contributions and partly by employer contributions; and

- **Needs-tested cash assistance** (Old Age Assistance, Aid to Families with Dependent Children, Aid to the Blind) for specific categories of people considered unable to work and thus ineligible for help from the regular insurance programs (e.g., widows with young children).

These innovations represented major steps toward providing individuals some protection against the impersonal threats of an increasingly urban-industrial society. At the same time, however, because of the political opposition they faced, they were far from complete. Thus, neither Social Security nor Unemployment Insurance provided universal coverage. Eligibility was work-conditioned and even then extended only to certain types of workplaces (e.g., small businesses and farms were excluded). Cash assistance was available for those not covered by the social insurance programs, but it, too, was limited to narrow categories of people (widows with children, the aged, the blind), and, though part of the cost was covered by the national government, responsibility for determining benefit levels and eligibility was vested in state governments, which were often quite restrictive.

As a consequence, the United States emerged from the Second World War with a social welfare system that, despite the New Deal innovations, retained many features of the pre-New Deal era. In particular, well into the 1960s the system remained characterized by:

- **Patchy coverage.** Key segments of the population remained uncovered, or inadequately protected. For example, expansion of Social Security coverage turned out to be much slower than hoped, so that farm workers, employees of small businesses, and others remained outside its protections. In addition, no assistance was available for health care costs. And cash "welfare" assistance, controlled by local officials, was held down so as not to interfere with wage rates on low-pay agricultural and household jobs, and was denied altogether to poor, intact families.

- **Limited funding.** Reflecting these limitations, spending on social welfare protections remained quite limited. As of 1950, for example, less than 9 percent of the U.S. gross national product was devoted to government social welfare spending.[2] Although some growth was evident in the 1950s, it was fairly limited, as shown in Figure 5.1.

- **State and local government dominance.** Despite the federal entrance in the 1930s, state and local governments continued to dominate the field. Well into the 1960s, state and local spending on social welfare outdistanced federal spending, as Figure 5.1 also shows.

"Well into the 1960s, state and local spending on social welfare outdistanced federal spending, reflecting the dominance of education spending in the social welfare field...."

FIGURE 5.1

Historical Trends in Government Social Welfare Spending, Total vs. Federal and State, 1950-1994: Current and Constant 1994 Dollars*

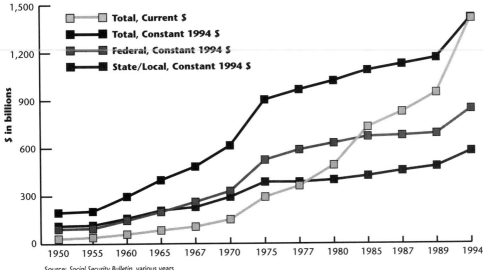

Source: *Social Security Bulletin*, various years
* Adjusted using services component of personal consumption expenditures.

- **Educational salience.** The major reason for the state and local prominence was that education continued to dominate the field, and education has traditionally been a state and local government function in the United States. As Figure 5.2 shows, up through the mid-1950s, education constituted the largest component of social welfare spending, accounting for 40 percent of the total. It was edged out slightly by pension benefits after that, but remained a very close second until the early 1970s.

The "Great Society" System

These central features of the American social welfare system underwent a significant transformation in the 15 years between 1965 and 1980. Prompted by a wave of urban riots and evidence of continued, and deepening, poverty, a major effort was made during the "Great Society" era of the mid-1960s to complete the reforms of the 1930s and add to them in ways that would help the disadvantaged move into productive roles in society. This was followed in the early 1970s by a shift in the payment system in the basic Social Security program that turned out to have a profound impact on that program and on social welfare spending more generally. More particularly, the changes of this period included:

- expansion of employment and training, social service, and housing aid for the disadvantaged.
- creation in 1965 of a new national health insurance plan for the elderly (Medicare).

FIGURE 5.2

Historical Trends in Government Social Welfare Spending, by Field, 1950-1994, in Constant 1994 Dollars*

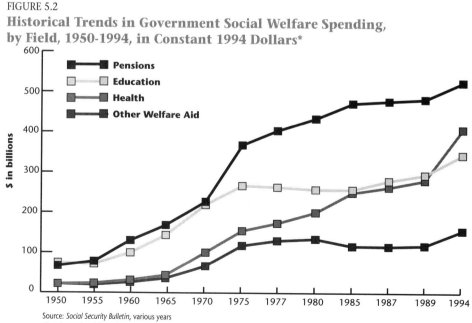

Source: *Social Security Bulletin,* various years

•Based on price deflator for services component of personal consumption expenditures.

- creation in 1965 of a joint, federal-state program to finance health care for the poor (Medicaid).

- creation of a network of "Community Action Agencies" and preschool education programs in low-income neighborhoods.

- establishment in 1972 of an automatic cost-of-living adjustment in the basic Social Security program to adjust benefit levels automatically to inflation.

Coupled with shifts in the basic demographic contours of the population (in particular, an expansion of the elderly population), these changes significantly reshaped the basic social welfare system, although in ways that are not fully understood. In particular, the system came to have the following distinguishing features:

- **Rapid growth in spending.** Between 1965 and 1980, government spending on social welfare accelerated significantly in the United States, as shown in Figure 5.1. Such spending grew by 637 percent in current dollars, and 259 percent in inflation-adjusted dollars, during this 15-year period, or by more than 15 percent a year in real dollar terms. In the process, it expanded from 11.5 percent of gross national product in 1965 to 19.5 percent in 1976 before falling slightly to 18.5 percent as of 1980. During the first part of this period, 1965–1975, the principal source of growth was actual program expansion triggered by the creation of a host of new federal programs. Between 1975 and 1980, the principal source of growth was inflation, which boosted pension and health payments considerably.

> *"Relatively little of the growth in government social welfare spending between 1965 and 1980 resulted from expanded welfare aid for the poor....Rather, Social Security and Medicare were the main causes."*

- **Federal preeminence.** Around 1967, federal government spending on social welfare finally surpassed state and local government spending for the first time. What is more, it widened its lead subsequently, reaching over 60 percent of the total by 1980, as Figure 5.1 shows. Because the total was expanding as well, of course, this does not mean that the federal government displaced state and local governments, as we have already seen. But a significant shift in the relative positions did occur.

- **Relatively limited growth in aid to the poor.** Significantly, what accounted both for the overall growth in social welfare spending and the emergence of the federal government as the dominant player between 1965 and 1980 was not expanded welfare aid for the poor. Although such aid did grow, its rate of growth barely kept pace with the growth of other components of social welfare, as shown in Figure 5.2. By 1980, therefore, it still accounted for only 13 percent of all social welfare spending, compared to 12 percent 30 years earlier. This reflected the fact that: most Great Society "War on Poverty" programs were pilot efforts and few were fully funded; the basic structure of welfare aid remained patchy and "categorical"— that is, available only to narrow categories of people, such as families headed by women with dependent children; and only a few programs, such as Food Stamps, reached a broad cross section of the poor.

"When public aid expanded in the 1960s, it did so in ways that promoted, rather than displaced, the nonprofit sector."

- **Predominance of pensions and health.** What mostly accounted for the great surge of spending that occurred in the 1965–1980 period, rather, were the great middle-class programs, Social Security and health care (mostly Medicare). Total government spending on these two fields went from 48 percent of the total in 1950 to 62 percent in 1980, and this at a time when the overall total was growing massively. The reasons for this were several: the size of the elderly population expanded considerably during this period; medical costs, covered by the newly created Medicare program, accelerated thanks to technological changes and related factors; and changes introduced in the Social Security program in 1972 provided automatic cost-of-living increases at a time when inflation was quite high.

Implications for Nonprofits: The Emergence of a Government–Nonprofit Partnership

The pattern of development of the American social welfare system detailed here had important implications for the evolution of the nation's private, nonprofit sector.

For one thing, the continued, patchy character of the public social welfare system established in the 1930s meant that private agencies continued to perform a significant role even after it had become clear during the Great Depression that primary reliance on private action was not sufficient.

Even more important, however, when public aid expanded in the 1960s, it often did so in ways that promoted, rather than displaced, the nonprofit sector. This was so because of the peculiar way government — particularly the federal government — operates in the United States. Because of ingrained American attitudes of hostility to centralized government, it is rare for the federal government to deliver services directly. Rather, it tends to operate through other entities — state governments, city governments, banks, other private businesses, and, increasingly in the 1960s, private nonprofit organizations. The result is an elaborate system of "third-party government," in which the national government generates the funds but then turns the actual delivery of services over to other public and private organizations.[3]

The private, nonprofit sector was a major beneficiary of this mode of government operation. Reflecting this, long-standing interrelationships between government and nonprofit organizations, many stretching back to colonial times, expanded greatly.[4] For example:

- **Medicare**, the massive new federal health insurance program for the elderly created in 1965, essentially reimburses hospitals for care they provide to the elderly but leaves to the recipient the choice of which hospital to use. Because the preponderance of hospital beds are in private, nonprofit hospitals, these institutions have received the preponderance of the benefits.

- Private, nonprofit universities benefited from expanded federal support for **research,** as well as from new programs of scholarship aid and loan guarantees.

- **New social service and community development programs** provided grants-in-aid to state and local governments, which in turn often contracted with local nonprofit organizations to provide such services as "meals on wheels" to the elderly, day-care, residential care, adoption assistance, and the like.

As of 1980, therefore, approximately 25 percent of all government spending in the fields where nonprofit organizations were active flowed to such organizations. The federal government alone provided $40 billion in support to the private nonprofit sector that year, as shown in Table 5.1.[5] State and local governments, in turn, provided additional amounts from their own resources. By comparison, total private charitable giving to these organizations that same year totalled $26.8 billion. No wonder the influential Commission on Private Philanthropy and Public Needs (the Filer Commission) concluded in the mid-1970s that government had become "a major 'philanthropist,' the major philanthropist in a number of the principal, traditional areas of philanthropy."[6] In fact, contrary to some beliefs, far from displacing the nonprofit sector, the expansion of government activity actually stimulated nonprofit growth in the United States, equipping nonprofit organizations to carry out far more functions than they had been able to conduct in the past.

TABLE 5.1

Federal Government Support to Nonprofit Organizations, 1980 ($ billions)

Field	Amount	%
Health	$24.9	61%
Social Services	6.5	16
Education, research	5.6	14
Community development	2.3	6
Foreign aid	0.8	2
Arts, culture	0.3	1
Total	$40.4	100%

Source: Salamon and Abramson (1982), p. 43.

The 1980s and 1990s: The Era of Retrenchment and Beyond

The 1980s: Selective Retrenchment

After a decade and a half of rapid growth, government social welfare spending entered a period of retrenchment in the latter 1970s and the 1980s. The initial impetus for this was a desire on the part of the Carter administration in the latter 1970s to avoid growth in the federal deficit. But this gave way in the early 1980s to a much more basic assault by the Reagan administration on at least a portion of the Great Society program structure. Between 1977 and 1982, therefore, the inflation-adjusted value of federal spending dropped 31 percent in the social services field, where many of the Great Society programs were concentrated (see Table 5.2). In addition, federal spending on education was reduced by 35 percent; and even spending on income assistance for the poor, which is driven by "entitlement" formulas, declined by 8 percent. Although it was hoped that state and local governments would offset these reductions, in fact the value of state and local government spending declined also in these fields. Outside of health and pensions, therefore, federal social welfare spending declined by 17 percent in inflation-adjusted terms, and state and local spending declined by 7 percent, for an overall decline of 10 percent between 1977 and 1982.

Although Congress resisted at least a portion of the further cuts proposed in the balance of the decade, the significant tax cut it enacted in 1981 seriously deepened the federal deficit and placed a limit on further growth. The result was a considerable slowing in the growth of government social welfare spending.

"...a basic assault took place on at least a portion of the Great Society program structure in the early 1980s."

TABLE 5.2

Changes in Government Social Welfare Spending, Fiscal Year 1982 vs. Fiscal Year 1977, in Constant Dollars*

Area	% Change, 1977-82		
	Federal	State/Local	Total
Pensions	13%	29%	16%
Health	27	23	26
Education	-35	-6	-10
Housing	16	44	19
Income assistance	-8	-18	-10
Social services	-31	-14	-25
Total	9%	4%	7%
Total w/o pensions & health	-17%	-7%	-10%

* Based on implicit price deflators for services component of personal consumption expenditures.
Source: Compiled from data in *Social Security Bulletin*, Vol. 51, No. 4 (April 1988), pp. 23-26 and Vol. 46, No. 8 (August 1983), pp. 10-12. Implicit price deflators from *Economic Report of the President* (February 1998).

Thus, as reflected in Figure 5.3, compared to the 145 percent growth rate it recorded in the twelve years between 1965 and 1977, real government social welfare spending grew by a much slower 21 percent between 1977 and 1989, or by less than 2 percent per year.

Even this growth was selective, however. The retrenchment of the 1980s hit some programs more than others and missed some altogether, as Figure 5.3 also reveals. In particular:

- **Cuts concentrated in programs for the poor.** Programs targeted on the poor and low-income populations were the ones that experienced most of the cuts during this period. Thus, as of 1989, spending on income assistance programs was still 15 percent below its 1977 value in inflation-adjusted terms, and spending on other social services was down by 28 percent. This was largely due, moreover, to federal spending decisions: federal funding of income assistance as of 1989 was 16 percent below its 1977 value, and federal funding of social services down a massive 40 percent.

- **Limited education gains.** Education spending also suffered from the cutbacks of the 1980s. Such spending barely kept pace with inflation during most of this period, growing by only about 1 percent per year until the very end of the decade. In fact, after adjusting for inflation, the federal contribution to education spending by 1989 was 36 percent below what it had been for 1977, and it was only growth at the state and local level that produced a net gain.

- **Continued growth in health spending.** While federal social service, income assistance, and education spending declined, however, federal *health* spending continued its steep rise throughout this period of so-called retrenchment. Fueled by escalating health costs and the aging of the population, such spending grew by 61 percent between 1977 and 1989 even after adjusting for inflation.

- **Significant growth in pension expenditures.** Despite a steady decline in veterans' payments, pension expenditures also experienced continued growth during this period, rising by some 19 percent after adjusting for inflation. This was due to the automatic cost-of-living increases built into the Social Security program coupled with the continued growth of the elderly population.

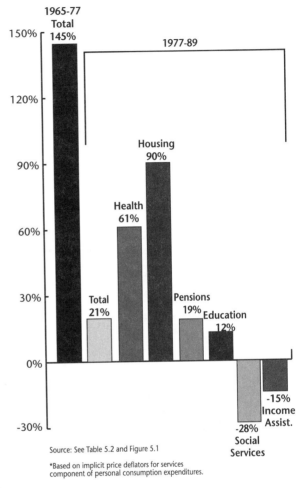

FIGURE 5.3

Changes in Government Social Welfare Spending, 1977-1989 vs. 1965-1977, in Constant Dollars*

Source: See Table 5.2 and Figure 5.1

*Based on implicit price deflators for services component of personal consumption expenditures.

"The retrenchment of the 1980s...shifted the center of gravity of the social welfare system more towards the middle class and away from the poor, and more towards health and away from other human services."

FIGURE 5.4

Selective Retrenchment, 1977-1989: Shares of Spending, 1977, vs. Shares of Spending Growth, 1977-1989

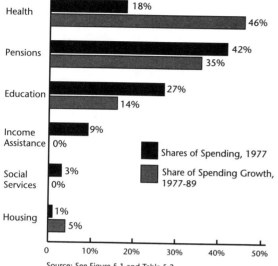

Source: See Figure 5.1 and Table 5.2

- **Housing program expansion.** Alone among the programs at least moderately targeted on the poor, housing assistance experienced significant growth during this period. This reflects in part the low base from which it started and in part the commitments that had been entered into long before the Reagan administration came to power.

Put somewhat differently, of the $225 billion in real growth in government social welfare spending between 1977 and 1989, about 46 percent went for health, and another 35 percent went for old-age and veterans' pensions and unemployment insurance, as shown in Figure 5.4. These two components thus accounted for over 80 percent of all the growth, even though they represented only 60 percent of the spending when the period began. By contrast, income assistance and other social service programs experienced not only no growth, but actual declines. The overall effect was thus to shift the center of gravity of the social welfare system more towards the middle class and away from the poor, and more towards health and away from other human services.

The 1990s: Partial Recovery

Developments in the late 1980s and early 1990s moderated these trends, but hardly reversed them. Fearing that it might have gone too far in its restrictions on eligibility in some of the needs-tested income assistance programs, Congress moved in the mid-1980s to broaden it, and to extend coverage in the Medicaid program as well. With the election of Bill Clinton to the presidency in 1992, moreover, modest growth resumed in spending on programs providing support for needy children and families, and on efforts to make the poor more self-sufficient, although this was held in check, and partially reversed, by a conservative Republican majority in the Congress elected in 1994 on a pledge to cut back further on government social welfare involvement.

Reflecting these developments, overall government spending on social welfare increased markedly in the early 1990s (see Figure 5.5):

- As before, growth continued strong in government health spending, despite efforts to control health costs. Such spending increased by 39 percent after adjusting for inflation. Contributing importantly to this growth was the expansion of Medicaid eligibility in the latter 1980s and the opening of Medicare to payments for home health care;

- Significant growth was also registered in income assistance spending for the first time in a decade;
- Even social service spending resumed, growing by 19 percent during this five-year period.

Although some recovery occurred, it was quite partial. Thus, federal spending on social services and education as of 1994 remained more than 30 percent below what it had been in 1977; and even with state and local spending growth, in the social services field overall spending, not just federal spending, remained 15 percent below its 1977 level as of 1994.

Implications for the Nonprofit Sector

In justifying the budget reductions of the early 1980s, the Reagan administration suggested that cutbacks in government social welfare spending would create more opportunities for private, nonprofit organizations. To those who pointed out that such organizations relied extensively on government support to enable them to carry out their existing functions, the administration expressed the hope that private giving would fill any resulting gap.

FIGURE 5.5

Changes in Government Social Welfare Spending, 1989-1994, After Adjusting for Inflation*

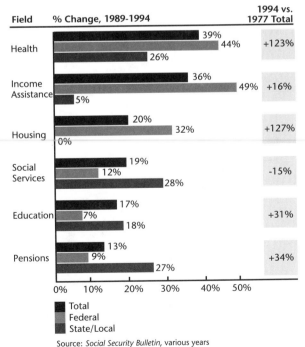

Field	% Change, 1989-1994	1994 vs. 1977 Total
Health	Total 39%, Federal 44%, State/Local 26%	+123%
Income Assistance	Total 36%, Federal 49%, State/Local 5%	+16%
Housing	Total 20%, Federal 32%, State/Local 0%	+127%
Social Services	Total 19%, Federal 12%, State/Local 28%	-15%
Education	Total 17%, Federal 7%, State/Local 18%	+31%
Pensions	Total 13%, Federal 9%, State/Local 27%	+34%

Legend:
- Total
- Federal
- State/Local

Source: *Social Security Bulletin*, various years

*Based on implicit price deflators for services component of personal consumption expenditures.

To what extent have these hopes and expectations come to fruition? How has the nonprofit sector fared during the retrenchment of the 1980s and the partial recovery of the 1990s? The answer is somewhat mixed.[7]

Overall growth. In the first place, as shown in Figure 5.6, the nonprofit sector did experience significant growth during the 1977–1996 period. In fact, the sector outpaced the growth of the economy as a whole, expanding its revenues by 96 percent after adjusting for inflation, compared to a 62 percent growth in the overall gross domestic product.[8] If the nonprofit sector experienced strains as a consequence of the budgetary stringency of the 1980s, therefore, it found ways to overcome them.

Uneven growth. In the second place, however, this growth was very uneven. For one thing, it seems to have been much more substantial during the early part of the period than during the latter part. Thus, between 1977 and 1992, the nonprofit sector outpaced the growth of the economy by almost 2:1 (83 percent vs. 46 percent). During the most recent period (1992–96), however, the sector's growth barely kept pace with that of the economy as a whole (7 percent vs. 11 percent). The major reason for this appears to be a slowing in the rate of growth of the massive health component of the nonprofit sector,

FIGURE 5.6

Changes in Nonprofit Revenues, by Subsector, 1977-1996, in Constant Dollars

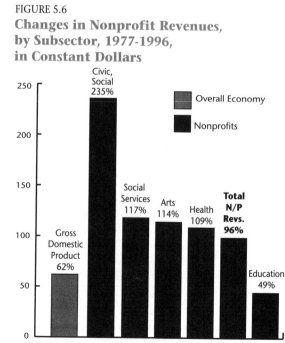

Source: See Endnote 8.
*Based on implicit price deflator for services component of personal consumption expenditures.

which has been subjected in recent years to a variety of cost control measures, ranging from "prospective payment" under the Medicare program to the adoption of "managed care" arrangements by major corporations. After growing by more than 8 percent a year between 1977 and 1992, therefore, the revenues of nonprofit health organizations grew by a much more modest 1 percent a year between 1992 and 1996.

In addition to being uneven over time, the growth rate of the nonprofit sector has also been uneven among components of the sector. As shown in Figure 5.6, *civic* organizations registered the largest percentage gain, boosting their revenues by more than 200 percent between 1977 and 1996. As a result, this component increased its share of overall sector revenues from 13 percent in 1977 to 15 percent in 1996. *Social service organizations* were the second most rapidly growing component of the sector, increasing their revenues by 117 percent, followed closely by arts and recreation.

Ultimately, however, the major source of sector growth was the health field. Even though they experienced some slowing in recent years, nonprofit health providers — chiefly hospitals — boosted their income by close to 110 percent between 1977 and 1996. Given the scale of this component of the sector, this translated into a substantial share of the total growth. In fact, with 56 percent of the sector's income when the period began, health organizations absorbed 64 percent of the sector's total growth, thus strengthening their already commanding presence (See Figure 5.7). By contrast, *education organizations* lost ground in relative terms, accounting for only 15 percent of the growth even though they started with 30 percent of the revenue.

Growth Fueled Mainly by Increased Fee Income. That nonprofit organizations were able to survive the important shifts in government policy during the 1980s and experience substantial growth is due in important part to the continued inflation in health care costs as well as to social and demographic changes that boosted the demand for the services that nonprofit organizations provide. Thus, for example, the lengthening of life expectancy and growth in the labor force participation rates of women have increased the need for nursing home care and child day-care.[9] In addition, many nonprofit organizations were apparently able to adapt to changes in government funding policies by repackaging traditional social services as behavioral health services and secure government support through the rapidly expanding health programs.

FIGURE 5.7
Shares of Nonprofit Growth, 1977-1996, by Type of Agency

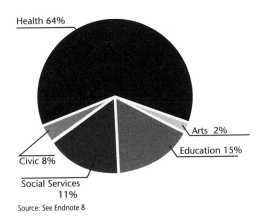

Health 64%

Arts 2%

Education 15%

Civic 8%

Social Services 11%

Source: See Endnote 8

"The principal source of increased revenue fueling the significant growth that the nonprofit sector experienced between 1977 and 1996 was commercial income (service fees, investment income, and income from sales of products)."

FIGURE 5.8
Sources of Nonprofit Growth, 1977-1996

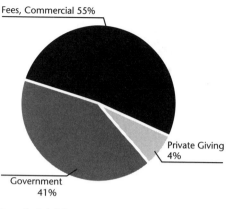

Fees, Commercial 55%

Private Giving 4%

Government 41%

Source: See Endnote 8

"Private giving accounted for only 4 percent of real nonprofit revenue growth between 1977 and 1996. As a consequence, it actually lost ground as a source of nonprofit revenue, falling from 17 percent of the total in 1977 to only 10 percent in 1996."

Reflecting these developments, the principal source of increased revenue fueling the significant growth that the nonprofit sector experienced between 1977 and 1996 was *commercial income* (service fees, investment income, and income from sales of products). As Figure 5.8 shows, this source alone accounted for well over half of the sector's revenue growth between 1977 and 1996. Such commercial income was important not only to health, education, and arts organizations, where it has historically been a major source, but also to civic and social service organizations. In the case of the latter, as Figure 5.9 reports, fee income replaced government as the most important source of support. Since these are the organizations that have historically been most available to the poor, this *marketization* of the social service field has especially important potential implications for the operation of the nonprofit sector.[10]

In addition to commercial income, government support also experienced considerable growth. Indeed, despite the retrenchment of the 1980s, nonprofit receipts from government actually grew faster than those from any other single source (by 131 percent between 1977 and 1996). As a consequence, although starting the period with 30 percent of total nonprofit income, government generated 41 percent of nonprofit income growth. This was largely due to the rapid escalation of government health expenditures noted above. Health providers thus boosted their income from government by more than 150 percent during this period. Indeed, health organizations captured over 75 percent of the growth in support that government provided to the sector during this period.

While fee income and government support grew substantially, *private charitable giving* registered far more tepid growth. Indeed, it was the unavailability of sufficient private charitable support that induced many nonprofits to turn more aggressively to fee income. Thus, although nonprofit income from private giving increased by 19 percent in real dollar terms over the 1977–96 period, this was well behind the overall growth of the economy, and even further behind the growth of the nonprofit sector. Indeed, private giving accounted for only 4 percent of the growth in nonprofit revenue during this period. Far from filling in for government cutbacks, therefore, private giving slipped further as a share of total nonprofit income — from 17 percent as of 1977 down to 10 percent as of 1996.

Growing competition from for-profit providers.
Finally, as they sought to take greater advantage of the growing commercial markets for their services, nonprofit organizations encountered increased competition from for-profit providers that have increasingly entered these fields. Indeed, government policy during the 1980s explicitly encouraged for-profit involvement in an effort to increase competition and, hopefully, promote greater efficiency. Coupled with the advantages private businesses enjoy by virtue of their easier access to capital and their ability to focus on the "bottom line" rather than the mission-related activities, such as charity care, that motivate many nonprofit providers, the result has been a striking growth of for-profit involvement in many traditional fields of nonprofit activity.

Between 1977 and 1992, for example, for-profit firms captured 80 percent of the growth in day-care centers and 70 percent of the growth in day-care employment even though they started the period with only 57 percent of the former and 46 percent of the latter (See Table 5.3). In the field of home health and clinic care, the disparity was even more striking: starting with 44 percent of the facilities and 29 percent of the employees in 1977, for-profit firms captured close to 90 percent of the growth of facilities and over 60 percent of the growth of employment over the subsequent 15 years. These and similar pressures in other fields have inevitably put a significant squeeze on many nonprofit providers.

"As nonprofit organizations have moved more aggressively into the commercial market for services, they have encountered growing competition from for-profit businesses attracted to these markets as well."

FIGURE 5.9
Sources of Nonprofit Revenue Growth, 1977-1996, by Field

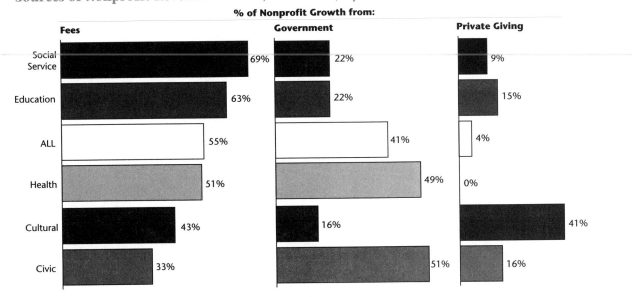

% of Nonprofit Growth from:

	Fees	Government	Private Giving
Social Service	69%	22%	9%
Education	63%	22%	15%
ALL	55%	41%	4%
Health	51%	49%	0%
Cultural	43%	16%	41%
Civic	33%	51%	16%

Summary

The American social welfare system is thus a complex "mixed economy" of federal, state, and local government, private for-profit, and private nonprofit activity. Although sizable governmental expenditures are made for social welfare, much of this goes for old-age pensions, veterans' payments, and public schools. Expenditures for the poor and the disadvantaged, by contrast, represent only a fraction of the total, albeit still a sizable amount.

Alongside the governmental system, moreover, stands a private nonprofit one that rivals it in size. Private philanthropy plays an important part in supporting this nonprofit system, but income from government and fees play an even larger part.

Recent changes in government spending have placed considerable strains on both of these systems. The nonprofit sector has been affected significantly by these changes, although the impact has been disguised somewhat by the aggregate totals and muted by a number of steps nonprofit organizations have taken in response. Thus, while the sector as a whole has grown, most of the growth has been concentrated in a few areas, principally health and, to a lesser extent, social services. These segments have grown, first, because they have cultivated fee income, and second, in the case of health, because the government support flowing to them has been much less affected by the budget stringency of the past few years. In the process, however, the nonprofit sector may be having to shift its focus more heavily away from those in greatest need.

What these observations make clear, among other things, however, is that the American nonprofit sector cannot be understood at the aggregate level alone. To make sense of what is going on, it is therefore necessary to move from the sector overview provided in this section to a more in-depth look at the separate components into which the sector is divided. It is to this task that we therefore now turn, beginning with the largest component, health.

TABLE 5.3
For-Profit Expansion in Social Services and Home Health, 1977-1992

	For Profit Share of			
	Establishments		Employees	
	Number 1977	Growth 1977-92	Number 1977	Growth 1977-92
Day Care	57%	80%	46%	70%
Other Social Services	23	38	15	19
Outpatient Health	44	89	29%	62%

Source: *U.S. Census of Service Industries,* 1977 and 1992.

ENDNOTES

1. The discussion in this section draws on material in Lester M. Salamon, *Welfare: The Elusive Consensus — Where We Are, How We Got Here, and What's Ahead* (New York: Praeger Publishers, 1977).

2. Bixby, *Social Security Bulletin* (1990), p. 22.

3. For further elaboration of this point, see: Lester M. Salamon, "Rethinking Public Management: Third-Party Government and the Changing Forms of Government Action," *Public Policy* (1981), Vol. 29, pp. 255–275; and Lester M. Salamon, *Beyond Privatization: The Tools of Government Action* (Washington: The Urban Institute Press, 1989); Ralph Kramer, *Voluntary Agencies in the Welfare State* (Berkeley, CA: University of California Press, 1981). For a discussion of a similar phenomenon in the United Kingdom, see: Jennifer Wolch, *The Shadow State* (New York: The Foundation Center, 1990).

4. On the early history of government–nonprofit relations in the United States, see: Waldemar Nielsen, *The Endangered Sector* (New York: Columbia University Press, 1979), pp. 25–48; Amos Warner, *American Charities* (New York: Thomas Y. Crowell and Co., 1896); Lester M. Salamon, "The United States," in Lester M. Salamon and Helmut K. Anheier, *Defining the Nonprofit Sector: A Comparative Analysis* (Manchester, U.K.: Manchester University Press, 1997), pp. 280–291.

5. Lester M. Salamon and Alan J. Abramson, *The Nonprofit Sector and the New Federal Budget* (Washington: The Urban Institute Press, 1986), p. 62.

6. Commission on Private Philanthropy and Public Needs. *Giving in America: Toward a Stronger Voluntary Sector* (Washington: Commission on Private Philanthropy and Public Needs, 1975), p. 89.

7. For more detail on the Reagan program and its implications for the nonprofit sector, see: Lester M. Salamon and Alan J. Abramson, "The Nonprofit Sector," in *The Reagan Revolution*, John L. Palmer and Isabel Sawhill, eds. (Washington: The Urban Institute Press, 1982), pp. 219–243; and Lester M. Salamon, "Nonprofit Organizations: The Lost Opportunity," in *The Reagan Record*, John L. Palmer and Isabel Sawhill, eds. (Cambridge, MA: Ballinger Publishing Co., 1984), pp. 261–286. On the more recent developments, see: Lester M. Salamon, *Holding the Center: America's Nonprofit Sector at a Crossroads* (New York: Nathan Cummings Foundation, 1996).

8. Author's estimates based on data in Virginia Hodgkinson et al., *Nonprofit Almanac: Dimensions of the Independent Sector* (San Francisco: Jossey-Bass, 1996), pp. 190–191; unpublished data supplied by Independent Sector; and U.S. Bureau of the Census, *Service Annual Survey: 1996*. Social and fraternal deleted from civic, social, and fraternal; and social services n.e.c. grouped with civic. Inflation adjustment based on implicit price deflator for services component of personal consumption expenditures as reported in *Economic Report of the President* (February 1998), p. 290.

9. For further detail on these changes, see Chapter 12 below.

10. For further detail on this phenomenon, see: Lester M. Salamon, "The Marketization of Welfare: Changing Nonprofit and For-Profit Roles in the American Welfare State," *Social Service Review,* Vol. 67, No. 1 (March 1993), pp. 17–39.

PART TWO

Key Subsectors

CHAPTER SIX

Health Care

Of all the components of the nonprofit service sector, the largest by far is health care. As Chapter Three indicated, nonprofit health providers absorbed close to 60 percent of all nonprofit revenues in 1996 and over 25 percent of all private charitable contributions. This reflects the tremendous scale of the health care field. But it also reflects the substantial role that nonprofit organizations play in this field.

The purpose of this chapter is to explore this nonprofit role in the health field and to put it into context in relation to the roles of government and for-profit providers. To do so, we begin by looking more closely at the overall scale, character, and sources of health care expenditures in the United States. We then zero in on the four subfields where nonprofit organizations are particularly prominent: 1) hospital care, 2) nursing home care, 3) in-home or outpatient clinic care, and 4) health insurance. In each of these subfields, we seek to determine what role nonprofit organizations play, how this compares with the roles of government and for-profit organizations, and what the major trends have been in recent years.

Perhaps the central conclusion that emerges from this analysis is that nonprofit organizations play a vital part in the delivery of health services in the United States. At the same time, their position has been under serious challenge in recent years.

"Nonprofit organizations play a vital part in the delivery of health services in the United States. At the same time, their position has been under serious challenge in recent years."

FIGURE 6.1

Growth of U.S. Health Care Spending, 1965-1996

(In billions of 1996 dollars)*

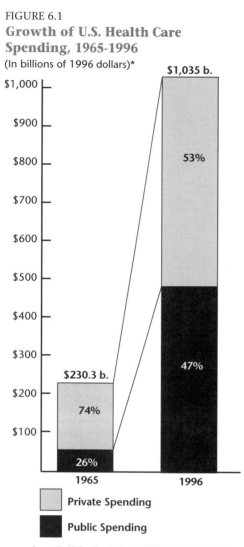

Source: *Health Care Financing Review*, 1997 and Health Care Financing Administration, March 1998, Advance Data.

*Based on implicit price deflator for services component of personal consumption expenditures.

"Although government spending on health has grown faster than private spending over the past three decades, private spending still accounts for more than half of the total. Very little of this private revenue comes from private philanthropy, however.

Overview: National Health Spending

Basic Contours

Health has emerged in recent years as one of the largest and fastest growing components of national spending. As Chapter Four made clear, close to 30 percent of government social welfare spending goes for health care. But an even larger amount of private spending goes into this field as well. As of 1996, in fact, health care accounted for 13.6 percent of the U.S. gross domestic product — a total of $1.035 trillion in spending.

Recent Growth

Health expenditures are not only large, but they have also been growing rapidly. As Figure 6.1 shows, total health spending grew nearly fivefold between 1965 and 1996, after adjusting for inflation, roughly twice as fast as the nation's overall gross national product. As a result, health expenditures went from about 6 percent of gross national product in 1965 to nearly 14 percent by 1996.[1]

Although health expenditures have grown rapidly over this 30-year period, the pace of growth seems to have slowed somewhat in the 1990s, largely as a result of the so-called "managed care revolution," the widespread replacement of fee-for-service insurance by managed care insurance plans that impose more severe limits on the amounts that health care providers can charge for various services. After expanding at an average rate of 10–13 percent per year (before adjusting for inflation) during the 1970s and 1980s, therefore, health spending growth dropped to 4–5 percent per year in the mid-1990s.

Sources of Growth

A principal source of the growth in health spending between 1965 and 1996, as Figure 6.1 shows, was the increase that occurred in *government* health spending. Such spending grew eightfold between 1965 and 1996, after adjusting for inflation, compared to a threefold increase in private health spending. This reflects primarily the creation of the federal Medicare and Medicaid programs in 1965. As a result, government spending on health increased from 26 percent of the total in 1965 to 47 percent of a much larger total in 1996.

Even so, the private-sector contribution to the growth was larger in absolute terms, so that private sources remained dominant by the end of the period. At the same time the growth rate of non-private health spending dropped especially extensively in the 1990s, from more than 10 percent a year in the 1970s and 1980s to under 3 percent in the mid-1990s.[2]

The Role of Philanthropy

Although the nonprofit sector plays a major role in the health field, as will be documented more fully below, very little of the revenue in this field comes from private philanthropy. In particular, of the $1.035 trillion in health care spending in 1996, only $16.3 billion, or less than 2 percent, came from private philanthropic giving.[3] Such giving is somewhat more important in financing certain sub-fields, such as medical research and construction, but even here it is far from the dominant source.[4]

The Role of Nonprofit Providers

While private philanthropy may constitute a relatively limited part of overall health finance, however, the private, nonprofit sector nevertheless plays a very significant role in health care *delivery*. To understand this role, however, it is necessary to divide the health sector into its component parts and look more closely at the four components where nonprofit organizations are most important: hospital care, clinic care, nursing home care, and insurance.

Hospital Care

Overview

Scale. Hospital care represents the largest single component of health care in the United States, and also the one where nonprofit organizations are most prominent. As Figure 6.2 shows, just over one-third of all health spending goes for hospital care — a total of $358.5 billion in 1996. By comparison, private practitioners (dentists and physicians) received 24 percent of total health expenditures, while nursing homes received 8 percent.

Sources of funding. Unlike health care as a whole, government is the dominant source of funding for hospitals, as shown in Figure 6.3. More than 60 percent of all hospital revenue comes from government, up from 55 percent just a decade before. Of this total, the federal government contributes by far the lion's share — 51 percent of total hospital income — with state and local governments providing 11 percent. The remaining funding, about 38 percent in 1996, comes from private sources, including 34 percent from private fees and insurance payments and 4 percent from private philanthropy and miscellaneous sales.

FIGURE 6.2

Where Health Spending Goes, 1996

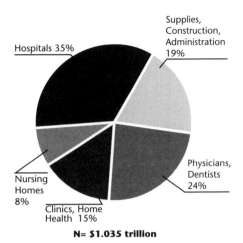

Hospitals 35%

Supplies, Construction, Administration 19%

Physicians, Dentists 24%

Clinics, Home Health 15%

Nursing Homes 8%

N= $1.035 trillion

Source: Health Care Financing Administration, Unpublished Data (March 1998), Table 11.

"Hospital care represents the largest single component of health care in the United States, and also the one where nonprofit organizations are most prominent."

79

Number and types of hospitals. This sizable hospital spending supports a relatively small number of quite large institutions. As of 1996, there were 6,363 hospitals in the United States registered with the American Hospital Association. Of these, the overwhelming majority (83 percent) are general hospitals, the type with which most people are familiar (see Figure 6.4). The remainder include some 710 psychiatric hospitals and another 385 other specialized hospitals.[5]

Nonprofit vs. Government and For-Profit Roles in the Hospital Industry

Nonprofit hospitals. While government provides most of the hospital spending, nonprofit institutions deliver most of the hospital services. As reflected in Figure 6.5, just about half (50 percent) of all hospitals in the country are organized as nonprofits. These nonprofit hospitals account for 56 percent of the country's hospital beds and 70 percent of all hospital expenditures.

FIGURE 6.3

Sources of Health Care Spending, 1996

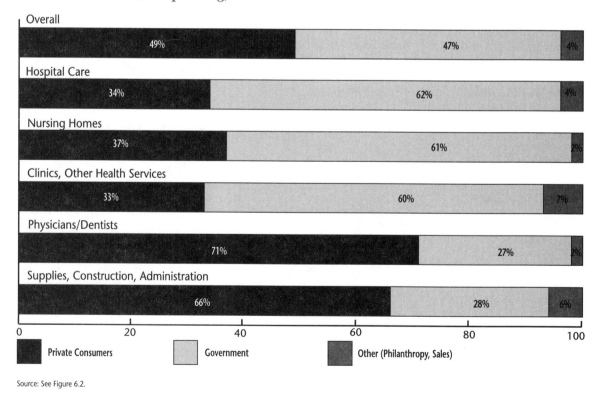

Source: See Figure 6.2.

Nonprofits are especially prominent among the country's general hospitals, which form the heart of the nation's hospital industry. Despite a flurry of for-profit hospital formation in the 1980s, 55 percent of these institutions remain private, nonprofit organizations and they account for 64 percent of the general hospital beds and 72 percent of the general hospital expenditures. By contrast, only 25 percent of the specialty hospitals are nonprofit organizations and they account for only 15 percent of the specialty hospital beds.

Government hospitals. About a third (31 percent) of all hospitals are operated by governmental authorities, chiefly at the state and local levels (see Figure 6.5). Most of these are general hospitals, many of them in central city areas. However, government is also quite prominent in the specialty hospital field. Thus, 31 percent of the specialty hospitals are operated by governmental authorities, and these government institutions account for 53 percent of all specialty hospital expenditures and 62 percent of all specialty hospital beds.

For-profit hospitals. For-profit corporations play a considerably smaller role in the hospital field, with 19 percent of all institutions and 14 percent of all hospital beds (see Figure 6.5). However, for-profit corporations have carved out a particular niche for themselves in the specialty hospital field. Forty-four percent of all specialty hospitals are for-profit institutions. Although these institutions tend to be smaller than the typical public hospital, they are nevertheless a significant component of the industry.

Hospital Trends

Overall decline. Despite the substantial growth in hospital expenditures, the hospital sector has been under considerable strain in recent years as efforts have been made to constrain the growth of both public and private health costs. Reflecting this, between 1980 and 1996, the total number of hospitals declined by 9 percent in the United States and the number of hospital beds declined by about 22 percent — a net reduction of over 600 hospitals and over 300,000 hospital beds (see Figure 6.6).

FIGURE 6.4
Types of Hospitals, 1996

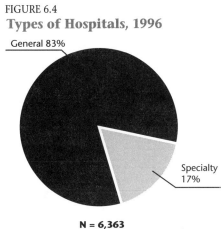

N = 6,363

Source: American Hospital Association, Special Tabulations, 1998.

FIGURE 6.5
Nonprofit Share of Hospital Industry, 1996

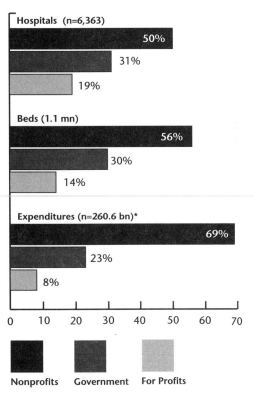

*Covers only expenditures of hospitals responding to AHA survey.

Source: See Figure 6.4.

FIGURE 6.6
Hospital Trends, by Ownership, 1980-1996

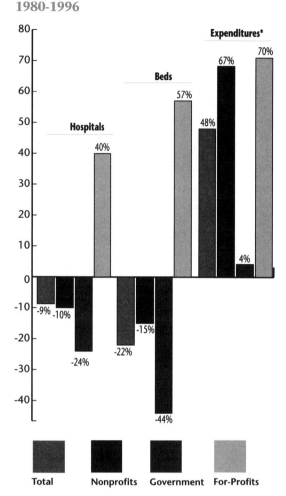

*Constant 1996 dollars

Source: See Figure 6.3.

Variation among types. Not all segments of the hospital industry were affected equally by these pressures, however. In particular, the declines were most marked among general hospitals while the number of specialty hospitals grew by 28 percent. Because of the different roles they play in these different fields, moreover, government, nonprofit, and for-profit hospitals fared differently. In particular, government and nonprofit hospitals experienced most of the decline while for-profit institutions actually grew. Let us look more closely at these divergent patterns and the changes that lie behind them.

Sharp decline of government hospitals. The recent contraction in the hospital industry was especially marked among government institutions. Between 1980 and 1996, the number of government-owned and -operated hospitals declined by one-fourth, and the number of beds in government-owned hospitals declined by over 40 percent.

Two major developments lie behind these results:

- First, increased fiscal pressure on publicly run, inner-city hospitals squeezed by rising health costs, reduced Medicaid reimbursement, and limited fee income. As a result of these pressures, 544 of the 2,167 publicly owned, general hospitals were forced to close their doors between 1980 and 1996, reducing the beds available in these institutions by more than 90,000.

- Second, in the 1970s a movement away from the institutionalization of mentally ill and other long-term ill persons in large, publicly run facilities. The number of government-run specialty hospitals declined by nearly 20 percent between 1980 and 1996 as a result of this "deinstitutionalization" policy, and the number of beds in such facilities declined by over 60 percent.

Significant decline of nonprofit hospitals. Though somewhat less marked, the past 15 years have also seen a marked decline in the number of nonprofit hospitals. At least 375 nonprofit general hospitals, or about 12 percent of the total, ceased operations, merged, or were taken over by for-profit institutions during this period. At the same time, there was a net gain of 19 nonprofit specialty hospitals. In all, therefore, the number of beds in nonprofit institutions declined by more than 100,000.

This dislocation in the nonprofit hospital sector reflects many of the same changes that afflicted the government sector, including increased pressures on hospital reimbursement rates and a resulting push to release patients earlier from costly general hospitals and move them into home health and other less costly alternatives. Also at work, however, have been the more recent shifts to managed care, which have put a special premium on expensive information technologies that nonprofit hospitals have found it difficult to finance. Nonprofit hospitals have thus found themselves squeezed between two sets of forces: first, the overall pressures to reduce the number of general hospital beds; and second, the specific pressures on nonprofit hospitals to convert to for-profit status, or accept for-profit take-overs, to facilitate their access to credit.

Expansion of for-profit providers. While both government and nonprofit hospitals have declined in number and scope over the past 15 years, for-profit hospitals have grown substantially. The number of for-profit hospitals increased by 40 percent during this period and the number of beds they controlled increased by 57 percent. In the process, for-profits boosted their share of the institutions from 13 percent to 19 percent, and their share of the beds from 7 percent to 14 percent.

For-profits have been particularly aggressive in the field of specialty care, the most dynamic component of the hospital industry during this era. For-profit providers moved actively into this field, carving out a new niche of short-term specialty care while long-term specialty institutions (e.g., psychiatric institutions), most of them publicly run, were closing. Thus, while the number of specialty hospitals overall increased by just over 238, the number of for-profit specialty hospitals increased by 296, or 157 percent, more than offsetting the decline in specialty government hospitals. Moreover, for-profit businesses experienced some of the only growth in the general hospital field, adding 31,000 beds while government and nonprofit institutions lost 195,000. In short, the shift toward managed care and the general pressures on hospital bottom lines are not only reducing the overall number of hospitals and hospital beds; they are also producing a shift in the basic structure of the hospital industry toward greater for-profit presence and a reduced presence for both government and nonprofit providers.

"The shift toward managed care and the general pressures on hospital bottom lines are not only reducing the overall number of hospitals and hospital beds; they are also producing a shift in the basic structure of the hospital industry toward greater for-profit presence and a reduced presence for both government and nonprofit providers."

FIGURE 6.7
Nonprofit Share of Private Clinics and Other Health Services, 1992/96

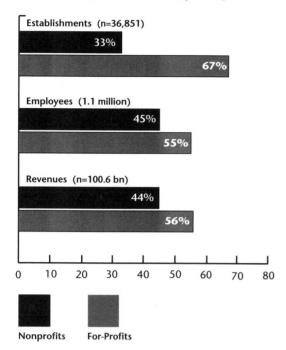

Establishments (n=36,851)
33%
67%

Employees (1.1 million)
45%
55%

Revenues (n=100.6 bn)
44%
56%

0 10 20 30 40 50 60 70 80

Nonprofits   For-Profits

Source: Author's calculations based upon *U.S. Census of Service Industries,*
1992, Tables 1A and 1B, and U.S. Census Bureau *Service Annual Survey:* 1996 (1998).
Revenue data for 1996; all other 1992.

"Nonprofit organizations play a major role in the provision of outpatient and home health care, although they have recently faced immense competition from for-profit providers."

Clinics and Home Health Care

Overview
The second largest component of the health field in which nonprofit organizations have a substantial role is outpatient care other than in doctors' offices. Included here is a wide assortment of activities including clinic care, home health care, kidney dialysis centers, drug and alcohol treatment centers, public health services, school health, and a variety of miscellaneous health services. As reflected in Figure 6.2, this component of the health care field accounted for 15 percent of all health expenditures in 1996, or about $150 billion.

Of this total, nearly one-fourth goes for *government public health activities,* which include local public health screening and the federal government's Public Health Service and the Center for Disease Control. An even larger share (nearly 40 percent) goes for a variety of *outpatient clinics* (e.g., kidney dialysis centers, drug treatment centers, rehabilitation centers). These institutions bear a strong resemblance to the short-term specialty facilities that are gaining ground within the hospital industry, except that they are tailored to "outpatient" care. Another 20 percent of this portion of health care spending goes for the relatively new field of *home health care* (i.e., skilled nursing or medical care provided in the home). Finally, the remaining 18 percent goes for *other personal health services,* such as drug abuse treatment and school health.

Like hospital care, clinic and home health care spending is mostly financed by government. As Figure 6.3 shows, government provides 60 percent of all the spending in this field. This is partly due to the fact that this field includes the direct public health activities and school health services. But it also reflects the broadening of Medicare coverage, beginning in the late 1980s, to include home health services. This triggered a considerable surge in the home health care industry.

Nonprofit Role
Nonprofit organizations play a major role in the provision of outpatient and home health care, although they have recently faced considerable competition from for-profit providers. In particular, as Figure 6.7 shows, nonprofit organizations represent

a third of the roughly 37,000 private health clinics identified by the U.S. Census Bureau in its latest *Census of Service Industries.*[6] What is more, the nonprofit facilities seem to be larger on average than the for-profit ones, so that they account for 45 percent of the employees and, as of 1996, 44 percent of the revenues.

Recent Trends

The outpatient care field has been an extremely dynamic one in recent years, and nonprofit providers have hardly been immune from the resulting shifts. Two major changes in particular have been evident: first, a particularly rapid growth in expenditures; and second, an increased presence of for-profit providers. In all likelihood, moreover, these two trends are hardly independent of each other.

Growth in spending. Despite the rapid pace of growth in overall health spending over the past several decades, the pace of growth in outpatient care and home health spending still exceeded it by a substantial margin. Indeed, as Figure 6.8 shows,

"Two major changes have been evident in the outpatient care field in recent years: first, a particularly rapid growth in expenditures; and second, an increased presence of for-profit providers."

FIGURE 6.8
Recent Trends in Clinic and Home Health Care
% Growth

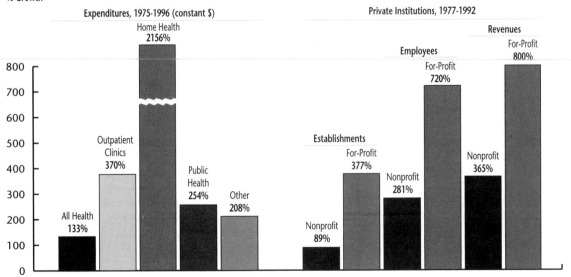

Source: Expenditures, see Figure 6.2. Private institutions, see *U.S. Census of Service Industries,* 1977 and 1992.

between 1975 and 1996 spending on outpatient care grew three times faster than overall health spending, and spending on home health grew 15 times faster. Even public health spending exceeded the growth rate of overall health expenditures.

Several factors seem to account for this phenomenon:

- In the first place, deinstitutionalization of long-term hospital patients during the 1970s and early 1980s increased the need for home health care and specialty, outpatient clinics to care for the deinstitutitionalized patients.

- Secondly, the pressures being put on hospital revenues by shifts in Medicare and private health insurance away from cost-based reimbursement of hospitals have given hospitals strong financial incentives to release patients earlier. This has, in turn, produced a corresponding increase in the demand for less expensive outpatient care. The growth of the outpatient care industry has consequently been the other side of the coin of declining hospital utilization noted above.

- Finally, these changes have been facilitated by the broadening of Medicare coverage to embrace reimbursement for home health care services in the late 1980s. As a consequence, government funding of home health jumped from under 40 percent in 1990 to nearly 60 percent of a much larger total by 1996.[7]

Increased competition from for-profit providers. Interestingly, nonprofit providers have benefitted far less from these changes than have for-profit ones. Indeed, the past decade and a half has witnessed an explosion of for-profit involvement in the outpatient clinic and home health field. Thus, as Figure 6.8 shows, between 1977 and 1992 the number of for-profit outpatient clinics and related health service establishments jumped from around 5,000 to close to 25,000, a 400 percent increase. During the same period, the number of people employed by for-profit facilities swelled from just around 70,000 to more than 600,000, while revenues increased a comparable 800 percent. While nonprofit providers also benefited from the growth in this field, they did so far less extensively. As a consequence, they lost their once-dominant position in this industry, dropping from 55 percent of the establishments and 64 percent of the employees in 1977 to 33 percent of the establishments and 45 percent of the employees by 1992. By 1996, in fact, nonprofit providers of home health and allied health services accounted for only 29 percent of the revenues in this field, well below the 63 percent

"...between 1975 and 1996 spending on outpatient care grew three times faster than overall health spending, and spending on home health grew 15 times faster."

share they enjoyed in 1977.[8] Clearly, as institution-alized medical care has moved out of large, general-purpose hospitals and long-term care institutions into outpatient care facilities and specialty hospitals, for-profit institutions have moved aggressively into these fields, aided by their superior access to capital compared to nonprofit firms and by the prospect of substantial revenues produced by shifts in medical insurance. In the process, however, nonprofit providers have found themselves facing increasingly stiff competition and declining market share.

Nursing Home Care

Overview
Nursing home care is the third major component of the health field where nonprofit organizations are active. As noted in Figure 6.2, nursing homes absorbed about 8 percent of all health spending in 1996, a total of some $80 billion. Of this, over 60 percent now comes from government and about 40 percent from private sources, all but 2 percent of this in the form of fees (see Figure 6.3). Most of the government revenue comes from the Medicaid program, but Medicare has recently increased its funding of nursing home care as well.[9]

Nonprofit versus Government and For-Profit Roles
Unlike the hospital and outpatient clinic portions of the health field, for-profit dominance has long been a distinguishing feature of the nursing home industry. Yet here as well nonprofits play a significant role. Thus, as shown in Figure 6.9, nonprofit institutions represent 27 percent of the estimated 22,179 nursing homes.[10] By contrast, two-thirds of these institutions are for- profit firms, while the balance (about 6 percent) are public institutions.

Reflecting their somewhat larger size, nonprofit organizations accounted for 28 percent of the employees in the nursing home field, and 31 percent of the private nursing home revenues as of 1996.[11]

"... for-profit dominance has long been a distinguishing feature of the nursing home industry. Yet here as well nonprofits play a significant role."

FIGURE 6.9

Nonprofit Share of Nursing Home Industry, 1992/96*

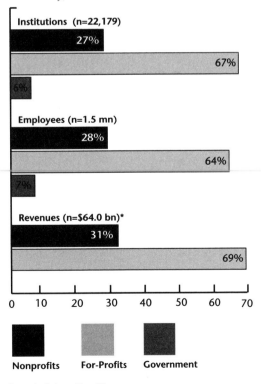

Source: See Endnotes 10 and 11.
•Revenue data apply to 1996; all other data for 1992.

FIGURE 6.10
Recent Trends in the Nursing Home Field, 1977-1996

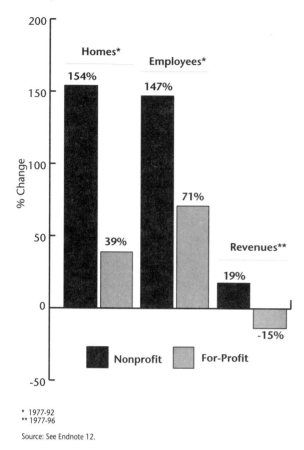

* 1977-92
** 1977-96

Source: See Endnote 12.

"While for-profit firms have long dominated the nursing home industry, recent years have witnessed a resurgence of nonprofit involvement in this field, one of the few fields where this is the case...This may suggest the critical safety valve function that nonprofit institutions perform when profitability and social need diverge."

Trends

While for-profit firms have long dominated the nursing home industry, recent years have witnessed a resurgence of nonprofit involvement in this field, one of the few fields where this is the case. Thus, as shown in Figure 6.10, the number of nonprofit nursing homes increased by 154 percent between 1977 and 1992, compared to a much smaller 40 percent growth in the number of for-profit homes. Similarly, the number of employees at nonprofit firms increased at twice the rate as that of for-profit firms. Finally, and perhaps most dramatically, nonprofits experienced a 20 percent rise in revenue, after adjusting for inflation, over the period 1977–1996 while for-profit homes actually lost ground in inflation-adjusted terms.[12]

That nonprofits are outdistancing for-profits in this field is partly a result of the larger base against which the for-profit growth is measured. Thus, for example, while close to 3,600 nonprofit nursing homes were added during the 1977–1992 period, 4,175 for-profit homes were added as well. The nonprofit growth was measured against a base of 2,300 whereas the for-profit growth was measured against a base of almost 11,000.

Equally important, however, may be the economic circumstances facing the nursing home industry during much of this period. In the immediate aftermath of the enactment of Medicaid, which made government support available for nursing home care for the first time, the nursing home industry experienced immense growth, with expenditures increasing by more than 100 percent in inflation-adjusted terms and the number of beds growing by 75 percent. While all segments of the nursing home industry participated in this growth, for-profit homes expanded most rapidly, adding homes and beds at rates that easily exceeded those of the nonprofit providers.

In more recent years, however, the nursing home industry has confronted a series of challenges. For one thing, the industry may have over-built, leading to reduced utilization rates. In addition, efforts began in the early 1980s to constrain the growth of Medicaid spending, which put a squeeze on nursing home revenues. Finally, nursing homes have recently confronted competition from home health agencies and other outpatient care facilities.[13]

In the face of these more difficult economic circumstances, the growth of for-profit nursing homes has slowed considerably. Nonprofit homes, by contrast, responding to social and religious needs rather than purely economic incentives, have expanded apace. What this suggests is the critical safety valve function that nonprofit institutions perform, especially in circumstances where profitability and social need diverge.

Health Insurance

In addition to contributing significantly to the delivery of health services, nonprofit organizations have also historically played a crucial role in health *finance*. Most importantly, nonprofit organizations were the early vehicle used for the creation and spread of pre-paid health insurance, which revolutionized the financing of hospital care by spreading the risks among entire communities, thereby bringing such care within the financial reach of middle-and working-class families. Begun in the 1930s, the resulting Blue Cross and Blue Shield insurance programs spread rapidly across the country in the 1940s and 1950s.[14]

More recently as well, the nonprofit form has been used to pursue new health financing experiments. Thus the health maintenance organization (HMO) phenomenon, which has revolutionized health care finance in recent years, got its start through a nonprofit organization, Kaiser Permanente. And several large foundations, such as Robert Wood Johnson and the Commonwealth Fund, have made major investments in reshaping thinking about health issues.

As with many other aspects of the nonprofit role in the health sector, however, in recent years nonprofit health insurance has encountered increasing competition from for-profit providers. Private insurance companies have thus undercut Blue Cross and Blue Shield "community rating" plans by offering insurance plans targeted on less risky, and therefore less costly, subsets of a community's population. This has naturally caused Blue Cross and Blue Shield to have to raise its rates to cover the remaining, higher risk populations, prompting even further for-profit

"...nonprofit organizations have pioneered the development of health care finance, beginning with pre-paid insurance in the 1930s and continuing with the invention of the HMO in our own time."

FIGURE 6.11
Nonprofit Role in Health Insurance

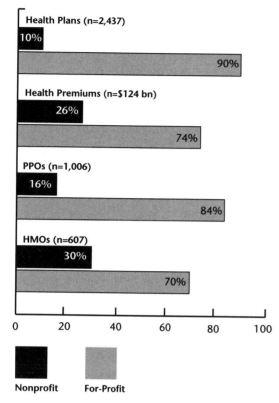

Source: See Endnotes 15 and 16.

competition. As a consequence, the nonprofit share of the health insurance market has steadily narrowed while the proportions of individuals left without insurance coverage has increased. In particular, as shown in Figure 6.11, nonprofit organizations now represent approximately 10 percent of all health insurance plans. Because the nonprofit plans tend to be relatively large, however, they still account for 26 percent of the health premiums.[15] Increasingly, however, the traditional Blue Cross/Blue Shield plans have taken on the character of their for-profit competitors — so much so that Congress canceled their tax exemptions in 1986, prompting many of the Blues to begin pursuing full-fledged transformation into for-profit firms.

As Figure 6.11 also shows, nonprofit organizations retain a significant role in the health maintenance and "preferred provider organization" (PPO) forms of health insurance. According to the latest available evidence, roughly 16 percent of the approximately 1,000 PPOs in the country are nonprofits, as are 30 percent of the approximately 600 HMOs.[16] It remains to be seen whether nonprofits will be able to hold their own in this rapidly changing industry, which requires immense capital outlays for information technology.

Conclusion

The health care sector is thus the largest component of the American social welfare system outside of old-age pensions. It is, moreover, a complex sector, containing many different types of institutions and multiple sources of funds. The primary access to this complex system for most people is through private practitioners operating as for-profit businesses. But much of the institutional care is provided through nonprofit organizations. Although for-profit firms have recently made significant inroads here as well, nonprofits still account for over half of the hospital care, 45 percent of the outpatient clinic care, and nearly 30 percent of the nursing home care. They thus form a vital part of the nation's health care delivery system and have demonstrated durability in the face of rather dramatic recent changes.

The public sector also plays a major role in the nation's health care system, but less as a deliverer of services than as a financer of them. Indeed, government involvement in the delivery of health services has declined sharply in recent years. By contrast, about half of overall health expenditures are financed with public funds. And in the fields of hospital, clinic, and nursing home care, where nonprofit organizations are most involved, the public sector accounts for an even larger share (more than 60 percent of the expenditures).

In short, the health field provides an excellent example of the "mixed economy" that lies at the heart of the American social welfare system, with nonprofit, for-profit, and governmental institutions all playing vital roles, often in close collaboration with one another. At the same time, as pressures for cost reductions have intensified, the position of the nonprofit providers in this mixed economy has come under particular stress, and that of the for-profit providers has grown. What this will mean for the quality, cost, and accessibility of services over the long run, however, remains very much open to debate.

ENDNOTES

1. 1996 data from "National Health Expenditures, 1996," Health Care Financing Administration, Office of the Actuary, Advance Tables, March 1998. 1965 data from "National Health Expenditures, 1987," *Health Care Financing Review*, Vol. 10, No.2 (Winter 1988), p. 112. Inflation factors based on implicit price deflators for services component of personal consumption expenditures as reported in *Economic Report of the President* (February 1998).

2. "National Health Expenditures, 1995," *Health Care Financing Review*, Vol. 18, No.1 (Fall 1996), p. 191.

3. See Chapter Three above. Estimates of private giving to health here include direct contributions plus contributions through religious congregations.

4. The one exception to this general statement may be health construction. As of 1996, for example, 67 percent of the $14.5 billion in health construction was financed by private sources other than private insurance or out-of-pocket patient fees. Some of this, presumably, represented earnings on ancillary activities and endowments. But a considerable portion likely represented charitable contributions. In the case of health research, such other private payments constituted 8 percent of the total income, with government providing the rest (92 percent). Health Care Financing Administration, Office of the Actuary, 1996 Health Care Expenditures.

5. Derived from special tabulations provided by the American Hospital Association, 1998. Data are for 1996. Unless otherwise noted, all data in this section are from this source and from earlier editions of AHA's *Hospital Statistics*.

6. Of the 37,000 clinics, about 28,000 were home health providers and specialized clinics (e.g., blood banks, kidney dialysis centers), and 8,600 were clinics (as opposed to individual offices) of doctors and dentists. This latter category was included in the 1987 Census tabulations for the first time. Such clinics are defined as "general medical clinics staffed by licensed practitioners having M.D. degree" and "not owned and operated by physicians associated for the purpose of carrying on their profession." We assume that at least some of these clinics were

included in earlier censuses of service industries as "outpatient care facilities" or "other health and allied services, not elsewhere classified." See: U.S. Bureau of the Census, *1987 Census of Service Industries,* Appendix A, p. A-16. (Washington: U.S. Government Printing Office, 1989). Data here from U.S. Census Bureau, *1992 Census of Service Industries* (1997).

An alternative estimate of the number of home health agencies in the United States as of 1994 is provided in *The National Home and Hospice Care Survey* (National Center for Health Statistics, February 1997). According to this source, there were 7,900 private home health agencies in existence as of 1994, well below the 10,260 such agencies identified by the U.S. Census Bureau in its 1992 Census of Service Industries. Because the Census also surveyed other types of health clinics and outpatient facilities, we decided to use the Census Bureau estimate here.

7. Based on data provided by the Health Care Financing Administration, Office of the Actuary (1998), Table 11.

8. U.S. Department of Commerce, *Current Business Reports: Service Annual Survey 1996* (1998).

9. Medicare support for nursing home care occurs where Medicare patients are released from hospitals but are still in need of sub-acute care. Many nursing homes have converted excess space into sub-acute care units to accommodate such patients, earning Medicare reimbursement in the process. *Health Care Financing Review* (Fall 1996), p. 189.

10. The estimate of the number of nursing homes here is based on data from the *1992 Census of Service Industries* (1997) and the National Nursing Home Survey conducted by the U.S. Department of Health and Human Services in 1955. These two sources provide very different estimates of the number of private nursing homes in the United States. According to the Census, 20,879 such homes were operating in the United States as of 1992. By contrast, the National Nursing Home Survey identified a total of only 15,300 private homes as of 1995 plus 1,300 public homes, for a total of 16,600. Differences of definition and sampling procedure may explain these marked differences in estimates. Thus, the Census covers "all establishments primarily engaged in providing inpatient nursing and rehabilitative services to patients who require continuous health care, but not hospital services" and that employ at least one person. The National Nursing Home Survey covers all "nursing and related care homes in the coterminous U.S. that had three or more beds, were staffed for use by residents, and routinely provided nursing and personal care services." The proliferation of varieties of long-term care facilities has also complicated the task of coming up with a clear and definitive count of "nursing homes."

Because the Census coverage of the private homes appears more complete, we used the Census estimates for the private homes but added the National Nursing Home Survey estimate for public institutions. This may introduce some imprecision in the estimates since the

National Nursing Home Survey provides data as of 1995 and the Census as of 1992. However, the overall picture that emerges should not be affected significantly. See: Genevieve W. Strahan, "An Overview of Nursing Homes and their Current Residents: Data from the 1995 National Nursing Home Survey," *Advance Data*, No. 280 (January 23, 1997).

11. The employment figure is based on a combination of *1992 Census of Service Industries* (U.S. Census Bureau, 1997) and 1995 National Nursing Home Survey data (Strahan, 1997). The revenue figure applies to 1996 and is based on data generated by the *Service Annual Survey: 1996* (U.S. Census Bureau, 1998).

12. Establishment and employment data here are derived from the *1992 Census of Service Industries* (U.S. Census Bureau, 1997) and earlier editions of the same survey. The revenue data draw on the *Service Annual Survey: 1996* (U.S. Census Bureau, 1998), which gathers data on revenues but not establishments or employment.

13. Strahan (1997), p. 7.

14. For a useful discussion of the origins of Blue Cross and Blue Shield, see: Rosemary Stevens, *In Sickness and in Wealth: American Hospitals in the Twentieth Century* (New York: Basic Books, 1997), pp. 171–199.

15. Based on data provided by the National Association of Insurance Commissioners' database.

16. Data on managed care plans were secured from: AMCRA Foundation (1995), "Managed Care Overview, 1994–5," Washington, D.C.: AMCRA, 1995.

CHAPTER SEVEN

Education

If health is the largest component of the American nonprofit sector, education is the second largest. One out of every five dollars of nonprofit expenditures is spent by nonprofit education institutions, as Figure 3.6 showed. What is more, nonprofit institutions play important roles in all four major segments of the educational system: 1) higher education, 2) elementary and secondary education, 3) vocational education, and 4) library services.

But what exactly is this role, and how does the nonprofit sector compare to government and the for-profit sector in this field?

To answer these questions, this chapter looks first at the basic scale and composition of educational expenditures in America, and then examines the nonprofit role in each of the major spheres of educational activity.

"One out of every five dollars of nonprofit expenditures is spent by nonprofit education institutions."

Education Spending

Overview

Scale and Uses. Americans spent $518 billion on education in the 1995/96 academic year, about half as much as on health, but still a significant 7 percent of the gross domestic product.[1]

As Figure 7.1 shows, the bulk of this spending (58 percent) went for elementary and secondary education. Higher education absorbed another 39 percent. The balance (about 3 percent) went for vocational education and library services.

FIGURE 7.1
Where Education Spending Goes, 1995

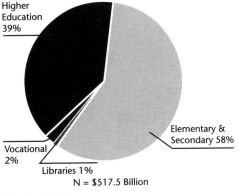

Higher Education 39%

Elementary & Secondary 58%

Vocational 2%

Libraries 1%

N = $517.5 Billion

Source: See Endnote 1.

"Perhaps because of its dependence on government, education spending has not experienced anywhere near as rapid a rate of growth in recent years as has health spending."

Sources of spending. Unlike the situation in the health sphere, where private fees are the dominant source of revenue, in the education sphere most of the spending originates with government. As of 1995, close to 70 percent of total education spending in the United States came from government, almost 90 percent of it from the state and local level (see Figure 7.2). By comparison, private fees and payments accounted for 28 percent of the total and private philanthropy for about 3 percent.[2]

As Figure 7.2 makes clear, however, this situation is largely a reflection of the major role that government plays in the financing of elementary and secondary education in the United States. Thus, 90 percent of all elementary and secondary education funds come from government. By contrast, government provides only 39 percent of the funding for higher education, while 55 percent comes from tuition and fees.[3]

Growth. Perhaps because of its dependence on government, education spending has not experienced anywhere near as rapid a rate of growth in recent years as has health spending. Thus, while the U.S. gross domestic product grew by 74 percent in real terms between 1975 and 1995, education spending grew by a much slower 31 percent. As a share of gross national product, therefore, education spending declined from 7.3 percent in 1975 to 7.1 percent by 1995 (see Figure 7.3).

FIGURE 7.2
Sources of Education Spending, 1995

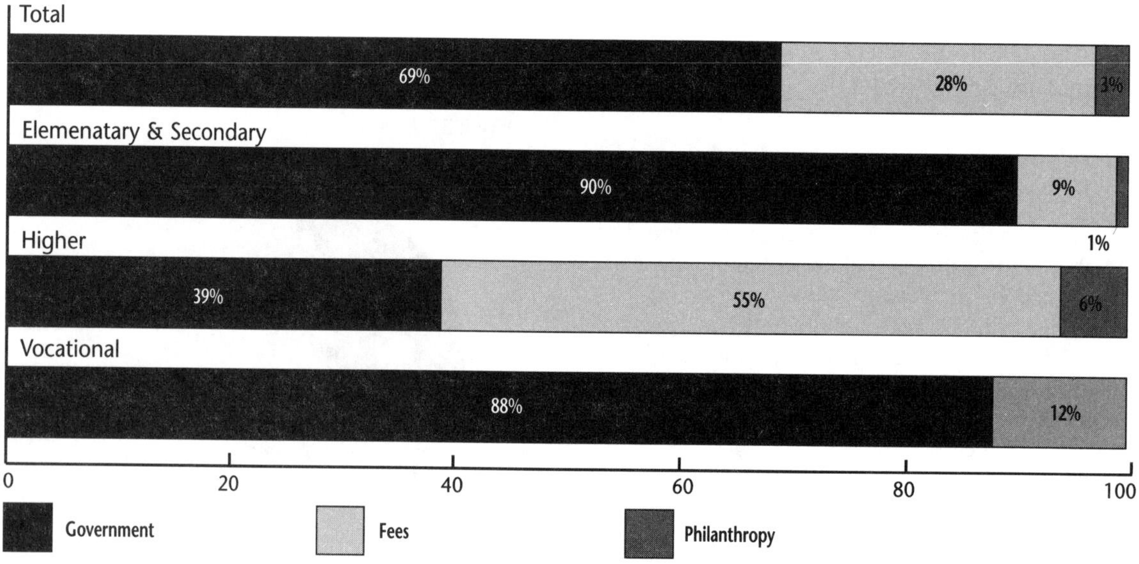

	Government	Fees	Philanthropy
Total	69%	28%	3%
Elemenatary & Secondary	90%	9%	1%
Higher	39%	55%	6%
Vocational	88%	12%	

Source: See Endnotes 2 and 3.

As Figure 7.3 shows, government spending on education grew particularly slowly during this period, lagging well behind the growth of the economy as a whole. Fees and private philanthropic support grew faster, but these represent smaller sources of support. The nation's educational institutions have therefore had to adjust to a declining share of the nation's wealth.

The Role of Philanthropy and the Nonprofit Sector

Although philanthropy plays a relatively minor role in the *financing* of education, as in the case of health the nonprofit sector nevertheless plays a significant role in the *delivery* of education. Overall, as Figure 7.4 shows, nonprofit organizations absorb close to one in every five dollars of education spending. In some fields, such as higher education, moreover, the nonprofit share is considerably larger than this. To understand the role that nonprofit organizations play in the nation's educational system, therefore, it is necessary to examine each of the four major subfields of education in turn.

Higher Education

The most important of these subfields so far as nonprofit organizations are concerned is higher education. As Figure 7.1 shows, almost 40 percent of all education spending goes into higher education, a total of just over $200 billion in 1995.[4]

The Nonprofit Role

Institutions. Nonprofit organizations are a major presence in the higher education field in America. Almost half of all higher education institutions are private nonprofit organizations (see Figure 7.5). Nonprofit prominence is even more striking when we restrict our attention to four-year colleges. More than two-thirds of all four-year colleges and universities in the United States are nonprofit organizations. Unlike many other countries, whose premier universities are frequently government institutions, many of the most distinguished colleges and universities in the United States are private, nonprofit institutions. This includes Harvard, Yale, Princeton, Duke, Stanford, Johns Hopkins, Dartmouth, Brown, Vanderbilt, Rice, Swarthmore, Williams, Vassar, and many others (see Table 7.1).

FIGURE 7.3

Growth in Education Institution Spending, 1975/76-1994/95, by Source (Adjusted for Inflation)*

% Change

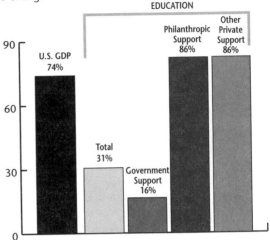

Source: See Endnote 2.

*Based on services component of personal consumption expenditures.

FIGURE 7.4

Shares of Education Spending Flowing to Government, For-Profit, and Nonprofit Institutions, 1995

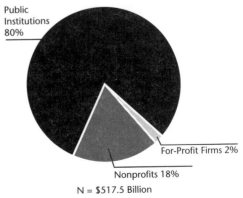

Source: See Endnote 2.

FIGURE 7.5
**The Nonprofit Role in
Higher Education, 1995**

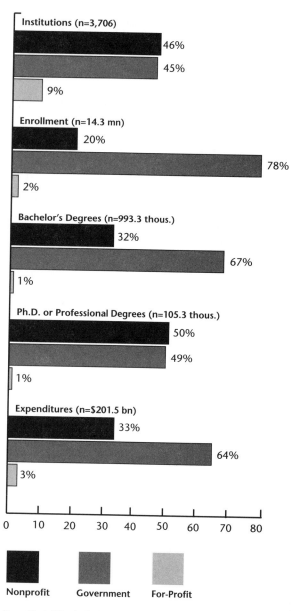

Institutions (n=3,706)
46%
45%
9%

Enrollment (n=14.3 mn)
20%
78%
2%

Bachelor's Degrees (n=993.3 thous.)
32%
67%
1%

Ph.D. or Professional Degrees (n=105.3 thous.)
50%
49%
1%

Expenditures (n=$201.5 bn)
33%
64%
3%

0 10 20 30 40 50 60 70 80

Nonprofit   Government   For-Profit

Source: *Digest of Education Statistics*, 1997, Tables 5, 170.

Enrollment. While nonprofit higher education institutions are quite numerous, they also tend to be smaller than their public counterparts, particularly since the public institutions include a disproportionate share of two-year institutions. With 46 percent of all higher education institutions, nonprofit schools thus account for only 20 percent of all higher education enrollments, as Figure 7.5 also shows.

Degrees. The nonprofit institutions play a much larger role in the granting of higher education degrees, however. This is understandable given the fact that many of the public institutions are two-year colleges that do not issue baccalaureate degrees. For another, the nonprofit institutions traditionally have had especially strong graduate and professional programs. As a result, the private nonprofit institutions account for about a third of all baccalaureate degrees issued in the United States, and just over half of all Ph.D. and professional degrees (e.g., medical degrees, law degrees) (see Figure 7.5).

Expenditures. Reflecting this, nonprofit higher education institutions absorb about one-third of all higher education expenditures (see Figure 7.5) and employ a little under one-third of all higher education staff. All in all, therefore, they play a much more substantial role than the enrollment figures alone would suggest.

Sources of Funds
As noted above, the pattern of funding of higher education in the United States differs considerably from that for other levels of education. In particular, fees and charges play a significantly more important role in the funding of higher education than they do for elementary and secondary education, where government is the dominant source of support.

What Figure 7.6 makes clear is that this distinctive higher education funding pattern is largely a product of the nonprofit institutions. Fully 70 percent of the income of these institutions comes from fees and other sales. Government is a distant second as a source of support, with 17 percent of the revenue. Private gifts, grants, contracts, and endowment earnings together account for the remaining 13 percent of support. Even for the private institutions, therefore, private philanthropy is only the third most important source of support.

The public institutions of higher education, by contrast, rely more heavily on government support, though even here government's contribution is somewhat smaller than might be assumed. Half of the revenue of the public institutions comes from government. But fee and sale income is also significant, accounting for about 44 percent of the total. Finally, private gifts, grants, contracts, and endowment income provide the remaining 5 percent.

Recent Trends

The current structure of American higher education is a product of changes that have occurred largely since the Second World War. Prior to this, the nonprofit sector had an even larger role in the higher education sphere than it does now. As late as 1950, for example, almost two-thirds of all higher education institutions were private nonprofits, and these institutions held half of all the higher education students.[5]

Growth of public higher education, 1950s–1960s. Beginning in the 1950s, and accelerating in the 1960s, however, state and local governments made major investments to build comprehensive systems of public higher education, embracing both two- and four-year institutions. As a consequence, enrollment in American higher education increased dramatically — by 40 percent in the 1950s, and by another 120 percent in the 1960s. Public higher education naturally claimed the lion's share of this increase, boosting its enrollments by 60 percent in the 1950s and 170 percent in the 1960s. By 1980, therefore, close to 80 percent of all students enrolled in higher education in the United States were in public institutions, compared to 20 percent in private ones.

TABLE 7.1

Examples of Private Nonprofit Colleges and Universities in the United States

Harvard University
Princeton University
Yale University
Johns Hopkins University
Stanford University
Duke University
Brown University
University of Pennsylvania
Massachusetts Institute of Technology
University of Chicago
Swarthmore College
Vassar College
Smith College
Williams College
Oberlin College

FIGURE 7.6

Revenue of Public and Private Higher Education Institutions, by Source, 1994/95

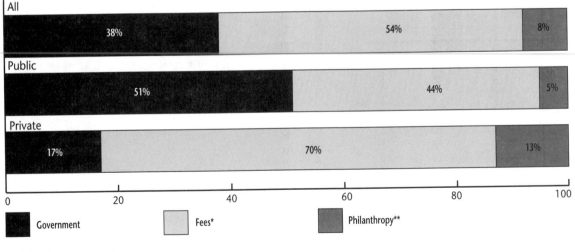

*Includes tuition and other income
**Includes endowment income

Source: *Digest of Educational Statistics*, 1997, Table 328.

FIGURE 7.7
Recent Higher Education Trends, 1975-1995

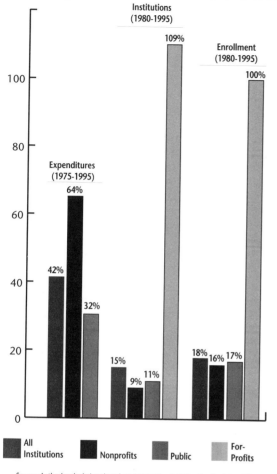

Institutions
(1980-1995)

109%

Enrollment
(1980-1995)

100%

Expenditures
(1975-1995)

64%

42%

32%

15%

9%

11%

18% 16% 17%

All
Institutions

Nonprofits

Public

For-
Profits

Source: Author's calculations based on data in *Digest of Education Statistics*, 1997,
Tables 5, 33, 170.

*"...having weathered a major challenge from
public higher education institutions during
the 1960s and 1970s, private, nonprofit
higher education institutions are
confronting a new challenge from for-profit
institutions in the 1990s."*

Consolidation, 1970s–1980s. Since 1980, however,
changes in higher education have been far less
dramatic. After three decades of rapid expansion, the
growth rate of public higher education has slowed
considerably, restrained particularly by pressures on
government budgets. Between 1975 and 1995, the
expenditures of higher education institutions grew by
42 percent overall. Significantly, private institutions
did better than public ones during these
two decades, boosting their expenditures by nearly 65
percent, compared to 32 percent for the public institutions (see Figure 7.7). Most of this increased revenue
came from increased tuition and fees for services,
however, not charitable giving or government
support. In fact, as a share of income, government
support declined during this period, from more than
20 percent to around 17 percent.

The slowdown in the growth of higher education is
even more evident in figures on the growth in enrollments and in the number of institutions. As Figure
7.7 shows, the number of higher education institutions grew by just 15 percent during the 1980s and
early 1990s, and the number of students enrolled
grew by just 18 percent. Growth was limited among
both the public and nonprofit institutions, moreover.

For-Profit Expansion. The one truly dynamic
element in the higher education picture has been the
emergence of a for-profit presence in the field. Nearly
40 percent of all new higher education institutions
created in the 1980s and early 1990s were for-profit
institutions. In the process, for-profits boosted their
presence in the higher education field from 5 percent
of the institutions to 9 percent. Though still only
representing less than 2 percent of higher education
enrollments, for-profits nevertheless doubled their
enrollments in the process. In other words, having
weathered a major challenge from public higher
education institutions during the 1960s and 1970s,
private, nonprofit higher education institutions are
confronting a new challenge from for-profit institutions in the 1990s.

Elementary and Secondary Education

Overview

If the major locus of nonprofit activity in the education field is at the higher education level, elementary and secondary education is the level at which most of the nation's education expenditures are made. Indeed, as Figure 7.1 noted, elementary and secondary education absorbs nearly 60 percent of all education spending in the United States.

Unlike the higher education level, however, government clearly plays the dominant role at the elementary and secondary level, and has at least since the latter nineteenth century. This is so, moreover, with respect to both the financing and the delivery of such education.[6] Thus, 9 out of every 10 of the dollars spent on elementary and secondary education in the country comes from government. Beyond this, as Figure 7.8 shows, 77 percent of all elementary and secondary school facilities are operated by government agencies, and these institutions account for nearly 90 percent of the enrollments and 92 percent of the expenditures.[7]

Nonprofit Role

Although government — usually local government — clearly plays the dominant role in the elementary and secondary education field in the United States, it hardly occupies this field by itself. To the contrary, a vibrant set of private, nonprofit education institutions also exists. In fact, as of 1995, one out of every four elementary and secondary schools in the country was a nonprofit institution — some 26,000 schools in all. These schools enrolled 5.2 million students, or about 11 percent of all elementary and secondary school students.

Regional Variations. In some sections of the country, moreover, this proportion is considerably higher. In Pennsylvania, for example, the proportion is more than 16 percent; in Delaware it is 17 percent; and in Louisiana and New Jersey it is 15 percent.[8] Generally speaking, the proportion of students in private schools is lowest in the South and the West, and highest in the Northeast and Midwest.

FIGURE 7.8
Nonprofit Share of Elementary and Secondary Education, 1995

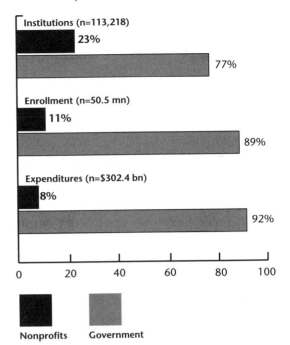

Source: *Digest of Education Statistics*, 1997, Tables 5, 3, 33.

"...one out of every four elementary and secondary schools in the country is a nonprofit institution."

101

FIGURE 7.9

Religious Affiliation of Private Elementary and Secondary Schools, 1996

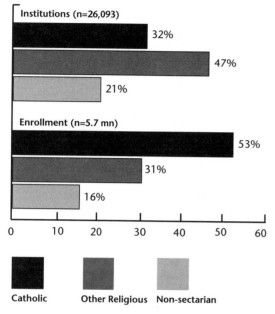

Institutions (n=26,093)
- 32%
- 47%
- 21%

Enrollment (n=5.7 mn)
- 53%
- 31%
- 16%

0   10   20   30   40   50   60

■ Catholic   ■ Other Religious   ▨ Non-sectarian

Source: *Digest of Education Statistics*, 1997, Tables 63, 66.

Religious affiliation. One reason for the variations in the extent of private elementary and secondary education is the close connection between such private education and religion. As Figure 7.9 shows, eighty percent of the private elementary and secondary schools, and 84 percent of the students enrolled in such schools, are in religiously affiliated institutions. Half of these students, and a third of the schools, are Catholic in orientation. The areas of the country with large Catholic populations thus tend to have the largest concentrations of private elementary and secondary schools. Another 30 percent of the students in private schools, and nearly half of all the schools, have some other religious orientation. To a marked extent, therefore, private education at the elementary and secondary level in America is also religious, or religiously affiliated, education.

Recent Trends

Not only have private, nonprofit organizations retained an important foothold in the elementary and secondary education field, but also that foothold has been growing, at least until relatively recently. During the 30 years from the mid-1950s to the mid-1980s, a significant consolidation occurred in public elementary and secondary education. The number of public schools thus declined from almost 120,000 in 1959 to just over 83,000 in 1987.[9] Although enrollments continued to grow, the end of the "baby boom" kept that growth constrained so that there were fewer students in public elementary and secondary education in the late 1980s than there were in the mid-1960s.

Because some of these changes were dictated by demographic realities, they affected private schools as well as public ones. At the same time, however, over the past fifteen years private elementary schools seem to have gained ground on public ones. Thus, as Figure 7.10 shows, the number of private elementary and secondary schools increased by more than 25 percent between 1980 and 1995, compared to a 1 percent growth in the number of public schools. Similarly, the expenditures of these schools grew more rapidly than those of the public institutions. Much of this growth seems to have occurred during the 1980s, when dissatisfaction with public education was particularly intense in the United States. Also at work, very likely, was the growth of fundamentalist religion in some parts of the country and a movement toward private religious education as a protest against Supreme Court decisions outlawing prayer in the public schools. The private nonprofit sector thus served the important function of providing a "safety valve" through which people with different values and opinions could act on them without disrupting the overall social fabric of the nation.

More recently, public schools have staged a recovery while private schools have experienced a bit of a retreat. Thus, between 1987 and 1995, the number of public elementary and secondary schools grew by 5 percent while the number of private schools declined by 3 percent — the product of a continuing consolidation of Catholic education and the slowing of the growth of other religious education. Reflecting this, public school enrollment grew much more rapidly than private school enrollment during this most recent period (12 percent vs. 4 percent). As a consequence, public school enrollment ended up growing slightly faster than private school enrollment over the entire 1980–1995 period, as shown in Figure 7.10.

Vocational Education

Overview

In addition to the formal, academic institutions discussed earlier, nonprofit organizations also play a significant role in the provision of vocational education. Such education is provided through correspondence and trade schools, such as data-processing schools, business and secretarial schools, commercial arts schools, practical nursing schools, and drama and music schools. Data on public-sector activity in this arena is limited, but information on private-sector involvement make it clear that this has become a rapidly growing industry with revenues that had reached nearly $10 billion by 1992.[10]

Nonprofit and For-Profit Roles

For-profit dominance. As Figure 7.11 makes clear, for-profit firms are clearly the dominant element in this industry. As of 1992, such firms accounted for three-fourths of the establishments, three-fourths of the revenues, and three-fourths of the staff.

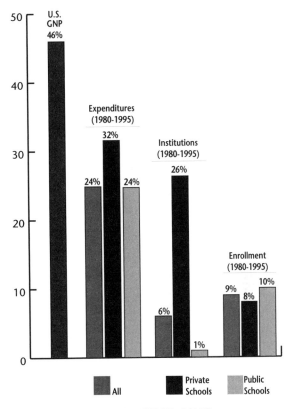

FIGURE 7.10
Recent Trends in Elementary and Secondary Education, 1980–1995

Source: *Digest of Education Statistics*, 1997, Tables 5, 33, 170.

"[during the 1980s in particular], the private nonprofit sector in elementary and secondary education served the important function of providing a 'safety valve' through which people with different values and opinions could act on them without disrupting the overall social fabric of the nation."

FIGURE 7.11
Nonprofit Role in Vocational Education

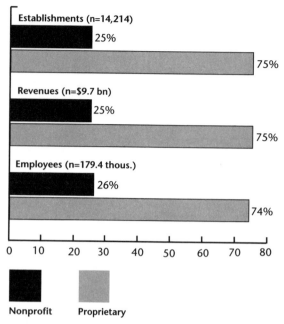

Establishments (n=14,214)
25%
75%

Revenues (n=\$9.7 bn)
25%
75%

Employees (n=179.4 thous.)
26%
74%

0   10   20   30   40   50   60   70   80

■ Nonprofit   ▨ Proprietary

Source: *Census of Service Industries, 1992* (1997), Tables 1a and 1b.

Nonprofit involvement. Despite the commanding for-profit lead, however, nonprofit organizations retain a significant presence in this field. Nonprofits are particularly evident in the "other educational services" portion of this field, where they account for 27 percent of the institutions and 36 percent of the revenues. Included here are music schools, drama schools, student exchange programs, and the like. By contrast, they account for only 19 percent of the strictly vocational schools and 12 percent of the vocational education revenues.

Recent Trends

Overall growth. Nonacademic vocational and specialized training has been one of the most dynamic growth fields within education in recent years. As Figure 7.12 makes clear, between 1982 and 1992, the revenues of private providers of vocational and other specialized education increased by 78 percent after adjusting for inflation. During this same period, overall gross domestic product increased by about 35 percent. Specialized education thus grew twice as fast as the gross domestic product. This is all the more striking in view of the earlier finding that education spending in general has lagged behind the rest of the economy during this period.

For-profit expansion. While nonprofit and for-profit providers both experienced growth during this period, the for-profit firms clearly did better. Thus, between 1982 and 1992, the number of for-profit firms providing such specialized vocational training increased by over 100 percent, the number of workers they employed increased by 95 percent, and the revenues they received jumped 84 percent. The comparable changes for nonprofits, as Figure 7.12 makes clear, were much smaller. With 29 percent of the establishments and 28 percent of the revenue as of 1982 when the period began, in other words, nonprofit providers captured only 19 percent of the growth in establishments and 23 percent of the growth in revenue. Clearly, in this component of the education field, for-profit institutions have established a sizable, and growing, niche, though nonprofit organizations continue to play a meaningful role.

Libraries

One final component of education worth exploring is the provision of library services. To a significant extent, such services have already been covered in our earlier discussion of higher education and elementary education because most higher education and secondary schools have their own libraries.

However, there are also close to 18,000 free-standing libraries.[11] Most of these (90 percent) are public institutions, reflecting the same philosophy that motivated the creation of the system of public elementary and secondary education — the desire to improve the general educational level of the population. Like public education, moreover, these libraries are almost all run by local governments, although a limited amount of federal support is available to them.

Beyond these public libraries and school libraries, however, there are also close to 1,600 private, nonprofit libraries in the United States employing over 16,000 people.[12] These libraries had some $757 million in revenue as of 1995 and represent about 9 percent of all nonschool libraries. If the private college and university libraries were included, moreover, it is probably reasonable to conclude that nonprofit organizations operate at least a third of all adult libraries in the United States.

FIGURE 7.12

Recent Trends in Private Vocational Training, 1982-1992

% Growth

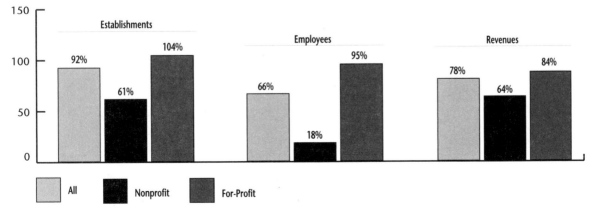

Source: *Census of Service Industries, 1992*, Tables 1a and 1b; 1977, Tables 1 and 2.

Conclusion

Public institutions have long been the predominant providers of education at the elementary and secondary levels in the United States, while private institutions have historically had a major role at the college and university level.

During the past several decades, however, public institutions have expanded rapidly at the higher education level in response to growing public demand for education in the aftermath of World War II. As a result, they now constitute almost half of the institutions and enroll the preponderance of students at the higher education level as well.

"Nonprofit organizations retain an important foothold in the education field,...providing–both at the elementary and secondary level and at the higher education level–an important measure of diversity and choice."

Nevertheless, private nonprofit institutions retain an important foothold in the education field. Not only do they account for nearly half of the higher education institutions, but also they account for at least a third of the enrollments and expenditures and slightly over half of the advanced degrees. What is more, they play a significant, and recently growing, role at the elementary and secondary level as well. Thus, nonprofit organizations are a pivotal part of the American educational system, just as they are of the American health system, with a reputation for quality and independence that helps them provide — both at the elementary and secondary level and at the higher education level — an important measure of diversity and choice.

As in the health field, however, recent years have witnessed a growing for-profit presence in the education area as well. For-profit firms have secured a commanding position in the rapidly growing field of vocational and special education and have been a growing, if still small, presence in higher education. Nonprofit providers in this field are therefore confronting competitive pressures on two fronts at once. How this will affect their operations, and their future, is one of the critical questions that the nonprofit sector faces in the years ahead.

ENDNOTES

1. The principal source of these data on educational spending is the *Digest of Education Statistics, 1997* (Washington, DC: U.S. Department of Education, National Center for Education Statistics, 1997), Tables 33 and 418 (public libraries). However, the *Digest* excludes noncollegiate, postsecondary institutions and contains no data on private libraries. Data on these were obtained from the U.S. Commerce Department's *Annual Survey of Service Industries* for 1995 as reported on the Commerce Department web site. Data reported here represent expenditures of education *institutions* and may therefore include research and other noneducational expenditures.

2. Data on sources of support of elementary, secondary, and higher education from *Digest of Education Statistics, 1997,* Table 33. However, the *Digest* does not distinguish between fees and private philanthropy. Data on philanthropic giving to education was secured from *Giving USA 1997* and Council for Aid to Education, *1996 Voluntary Support of Education* (Prepared by David R. Morgan) (New York: Council for Aid to Education), pp. 3, 8. Government support for vocational education was secured from the *Social Security Bulletin*, various editions. The balance of support for vocational education was assumed to come from fees.

3. See note 2 above for the sources of the income data. The estimate of government's share of higher education income here does not include federally supported student aid that goes to higher education institutions through students' tuition payments. Such income is recorded in the available data sources under fee income.

4. Higher education includes study beyond secondary school at an institution that offers programs terminating in an associate, baccalaureate, or higher degree. Not included is study at a noncollegiate, vocational institution. *Digest of Education Statistics, 1997.*

5. *Digest of Education Statistics,* 1990, Table 3, p. 12; and Table 216, p. 228.

6. A rather different story obtains in the case of day-care and pre-school education. This field is treated in Chapter 8 below as part of social services.

7. *Digest of Education Statistics,* 1997, Tables 5,3,33.

8. *Digest of Education Statistics,* 1997, Tables 63 and 66.

9. *Digest of Education Statistics,* 1990, Tables 84 and 5, pp. 96 and 14.

10. Included in this industry are establishments classified under Standard Industrial Classification (SIC) codes 824 and 829 in the Census of Service Industries — i.e."Vocational schools" and "Schools and educational services not elsewhere classified." The $10 billion estimate is based on U.S. *Census of Service Industries, 1992* (1997). More recent data indicate that the vocational education component alone, which represented 46 percent of the total in 1992, had revenues in 1995 of $6.1 billion. If the rest of this industry grew at roughly the same pace, this would yield an estimate of $13.3 billion for the entire industry as of 1995. See: *Census of Service Industries Annual Survey*, 1995.

11. This figure is derived by adding together the 15,945 public libraries (8,921 central libraries and 7024 branches) identified in the *Digest of Education Statistics, 1997*, Table 418, p. 465, and the 1,804 private libraries identified in the 1992 *U.S. Census of Service Industries*, Tables 1a and 1b. The public figure is for 1994 and excludes bookmobiles.

12. In addition to the private nonprofit libraries, there are 232 private for-profit libraries identified in the U.S. Census of Service Industries for 1992. See: *U.S. Census of Service Industries, 1992*, Table 1a and 1b. SIC code 823 includes "establishments primarily engaged in providing library services, including the circulation of books and other materials for reading, study, and reference."

CHAPTER EIGHT

Social Services

For all their complexity, the fields of health and education are still generally comprehensible to most people. Although there may be uncertainties over the precise definition of an "outpatient clinic," there are few people who do not have some clear idea of what a hospital or a university is.

Not so with the third major field of nonprofit activity: social services. The term itself is ambiguous, and the range of organizations typically grouped under it exceedingly diverse.

Yet, more people probably have contact with nonprofit social service agencies than with any other type, if for no other reason than that they are so numerous. In fact, as Chapter 3 made clear, there are more nonprofit public-benefit social service organizations than any other kind–nearly 66,000 agencies as of 1992 compared to only 3,200 nonprofit hospitals, 6,000 nonprofit nursing homes, and 1,700 nonprofit colleges and universities.[1] In addition, there are many thousand more "mutual benefit organizations" — informal self-help groups, many with few or no paid staff.

What do these organizations do? What is the "social services" field, and what role do nonprofit organizations play in it? How has this role changed in recent years as a result of the significant government spending cutbacks that have occurred? This chapter seeks to answer these questions.

"Although fees and government support play the dominant role in funding social services, nonprofit organizations still play the dominant role in delivering them."

FIGURE 8.1
Spending on Social Services vs. Health and Education

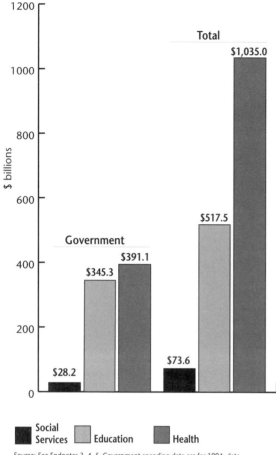

Source: See Endnotes 3, 4, 5. Government spending data are for 1994; data on total social services and education spending are for 1994; health spending data are for 1996.

"Despite its growth during the Great Society era, social service spending still lags far behind that for education and health."

Overview: The Social Service Field

Definition
Although the term "social services" is somewhat amorphous, the basic concept behind it is fairly straightforward. Social services are essentially forms of assistance, other than outright cash aid, that help individuals and families to function in the face of social, economic, or physical problems or needs. Included are day-care services, adoption assistance, family counseling, residential care for the elderly or the physically or mentally handicapped, vocational rehabilitation, disaster assistance, refugee assistance, emergency food assistance, substance abuse treatment, and many more.

Overall Scale
Although the social services field has expanded considerably since the 1960s — the product of some major economic and demographic changes as well as the launching of a number of new government programs — the scale of this field still lags far behind that of either health or education. Thus, of the $1.434 trillion in government social welfare spending as of 1994, only $28.2 billion, or about 2 percent, went for social services.[2] By comparison, education absorbed $345.3 billion in government funding and health $391.1 billion — both well over ten times as much (see Figure 8.1).[3]

Government is only one source of social service spending, of course, but even with nongovernmental funds included, social service spending is a pale reflection of the spending on either health or education. Thus, as of 1994, social services absorbed approximately $73.6 billion in total spending, or a mere 1 percent of gross domestic product.[4] By comparison, as previous chapters have shown, health spending totaled $1.035 billion, or almost 14 percent of the gross domestic product; and education spending totaled $518 billion, or 7 percent of gross domestic product (see Figure 8.1).[5]

Sources of Social Service Spending
As shown in Figure 8.2, the largest single source of social service spending is fees and charges. As of the mid-1990s, this source accounted for 49 percent of total social service spending in the United States. The second largest source of such spending is government, which accounted for 38 percent of the total as of 1994. By contrast, private giving from all sources — individuals, foundations, and corporations — accounted for a considerably smaller 13 percent of social service spending.

The substantial role that fees and service charges play in the financing of social services at the present time reflects the changing character of the social services market in recent years. The aging of the population, the increased labor force participation of women, and the proliferation of drug abuse and related forms of addiction have increased the demand for residential care, counseling, day-care, and related social services on the part of populations that can pay for such services, either directly or through expanded health insurance programs.[6] Also at work have been the general retrenchment in government social welfare expenditures, which put a lid on the expansion on government support, at least in the social services field; and the relatively limited ability of private charity to fill the resulting gap.

Nonprofit, Government, and For-Profit Roles

Despite the dominant role of fees and government support in the *funding* of social services, private, nonprofit organizations still play the dominant role in the actual *delivery* of such services. At the same time, government agencies and for-profit companies also play important parts.

The Nonprofit Role

Overall role. As noted earlier, there were approximately 66,000 nonprofit organizations providing social services in the United States as of the early 1990s.[7] Of these, the most numerous were providers of individual and family services (44 percent) and child day-care (24 percent), as shown in Figure 8.3. The rest provided residential care (23 percent), and job training (9 percent).[8] Individual and family service agencies also rank highest in financial terms with 45 percent of the total revenues; but day-care, with 24 percent of the agencies, accounts for only 10 percent of the revenues.[9] Of the balance, residential care accounts for 29 percent and job training 16 percent.

As Figure 8.4 shows, these nonprofit agencies play a very significant role in the provision of social services in the United States. In particular, they account for:

- 53 percent of the private social service agencies;

- 61 percent of all social service revenues; and

- 55 percent of all social service agency employment — an estimated 1.2 million employees in all.[10]

In addition, nonprofit social service organizations also engage the energies of a sizable army of volunteers. According to recent estimates, these volunteers

FIGURE 8.2

Sources of Social Services Spending, 1994

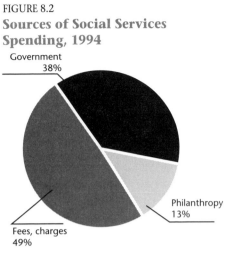

N = $73.6 Billion

Source: See Endnote 4.

FIGURE 8.3

Types of Nonprofit Social Service Agencies, 1992

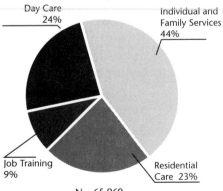

N = 65,969

Source: *Census of Service Industries, 1992* (1997).

contribute time that is equivalent to another 840,000 full-time employees, almost doubling the estimated total of 1.2 million paid employees of these agencies.

Variations by subfield. Although nonprofit organizations play a major role in all facets of the social service field, there are significant variations among the subfields. As shown in Figure 8.5, among private social service agencies, nonprofits comprise:

- 80 percent of the individual and family service agencies;
- 70 percent of the vocational rehabilitation agencies;
- 55 percent of the residential care facilities; and
- 31 percent of the day-care centers.

This picture of substantial nonprofit involvement is even more dramatic in financial terms because nonprofit providers tend to be larger than their for-profit counterparts. Thus, as of 1996 the nonprofit share of private social service agency revenue totals:

- 82 percent in the case of individual and family services;
- 72 percent in the case of job training and vocational rehabilitation;
- 68 percent in the case of residential care; and
- 33 percent in the case of day-care.

FIGURE 8.4
Nonprofit Role in Social Services, 1992/95*

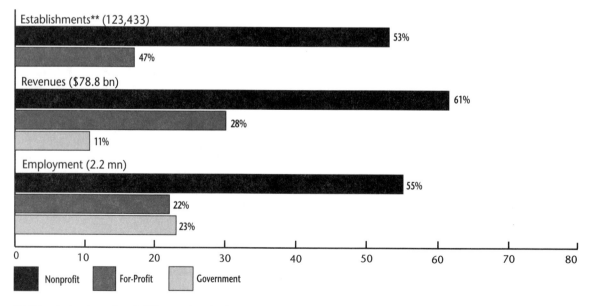

*Establishment and employment figures for 1992; revenue figures for 1995.
**Includes private agencies only.

Souce: See Endnote 10.

In short, the nonprofit sector plays an immense role in the provision of social services.

Financing of Nonprofit Social Service Agencies. Not surprisingly, the pattern of finance for these nonprofit social service agencies closely tracks the pattern of finance for the social service field as a whole, although not completely. The most striking feature is the considerable role of fee income in the revenue base of nonprofit providers. Thus, as Figure 8.6 shows, such fees accounted, as of 1996, for more than 40 percent of all nonprofit social service organization income.[11] Evidently the nonprofit sector's ability to remain a vital force in the social service field in the face of government cutbacks has been due in large measure to its ability to generate essentially commercial forms of support.

Self-Help, Mutual Assistance, and Faith-Based Charity. In addition to the more formal organizations described above, a host of informal organizations are also active in the social service field, although the scope of this activity is more difficult to gauge. One aspect of this is the work of *self-help groups*. The more structured of these, such as Alcoholics Anonymous, are probably captured in the statistics presented above, but others are much more informal and unstructured, consisting of individuals and families

"Evidently, the nonprofit sector's ability to remain a vital force in the social service field has been due in large measure to its ability to generate essentially commercial forms of support."

FIGURE 8.5
Nonprofit vs. For-Profit Providers of Social Services by Subfield

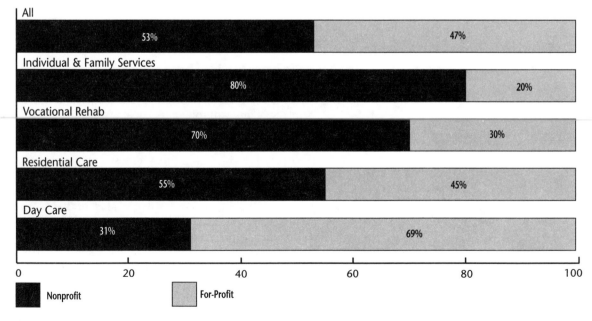

Source: *Census of Service Industries, 1992* (1997).

FIGURE 8.6
Sources of Nonprofit Social Service Agency Income

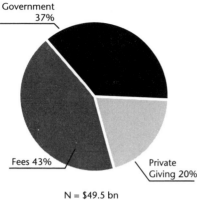

N = $49.5 bn

Source: See Chapter Three, Endnote 31.

"The nonprofit contribution to social services extends well beyond the formal agencies and embraces informal self-help groups and faith-based charities."

who share a common experience, such as loss of a child or the presence of a physical or emotional disability, and who meet together for mutual support. The National Institute of Mental Health identifies three distinct types of such groups: first, groups for people with a physical or mental illness; second, recovery groups for people with problems such as alcoholism, drug addiction, or the like; and, third, groups for certain minorities, such as the handicapped. As many as half a million such groups are estimated to exist in the United States.[12]

In addition to the self-help groups there are numerous other organized, but largely informal, forms of social assistance that also are unlikely to be captured in the official data. According to one recent study, for example, 92 percent of a sample of *religious congregations* reported involvement in one or more human service or welfare activities, at least some of which doubtless takes place through largely informal channels.[13] More generally, grassroots organizations, a number of them religiously affiliated or faith-based, have surfaced in numerous communities across the country to cope with problems of homelessness, hunger, and inadequate job preparation.[14] While many of these are included in the data cited above, others are not. According to one recent survey, for example, 27 percent of a sample of small faith-based human service organizations in Illinois, and 13 percent of other human service agencies, were not included in the Internal Revenue Service listings that form the base for much of our statistical knowledge of the nonprofit sector.[15] In short, the nonprofit contribution to social service provision extends well beyond the contours of the formal agencies described above.

Government Agencies
Although nonprofit organizations are the major providers of social services, government agencies also play a significant role in this field. As we have seen, government is a major financier of social services. But government agencies also help to deliver certain kinds of social services, even though most government-funded services are delivered by others. Thus, some 500,000 government employees are engaged in various "public welfare" activities. Most of these manage the cash assistance programs (e.g., Aid to Families with Dependent Children, and general assistance) at the local level, provide "casework" to client families, and oversee contractual arrangements with private providers to deliver social services to target populations. Public employees also manage the

foster care system that places children without suitable homes in foster care settings. Altogether, as Figure 8.4 showed, about 23 percent of the employees in the social service/public welfare field work for government agencies — a significant proportion, but well below what the level of public spending in this field might suggest.

For-Profit Providers

Finally, for-profit firms have increasingly surfaced as major providers of social services. Such firms accounted for nearly half of the social service agencies and 22 percent of the social service employment as of the early 1990s, as Figure 8.4 shows. Though generally smaller in average size, they accounted for about a third of the revenues as of the mid-1990s.

For-profit providers are concentrated in particular segments of the social service field and in these segments their presence is even larger. Thus, 60 percent of for-profit social service agencies are day-care centers and in this field for-profits constitute close to 70 percent of the providers, as Figure 8.5 shows. Another 30 percent of the for-profit social service agencies are residential care facilities, and in this field for-profits account for 45 percent of the agencies and 32 percent of the revenues.

"...for-profit firms have increasingly surfaced as major providers of social services."

Little reliable information is available about the sources of for-profit social service agency revenue. Almost certainly, fees and service charges comprise a significant portion. This reflects the growth in demand for social services throughout the population, demand that nonprofit organizations have also sought to fill. Thus, the increased workforce participation of women has created a sizable market for day-care services, and effective demand has surfaced as well for other types of counseling and related services. Beyond this, for-profit providers have increasingly entered the competition for government support. The welfare reform legislation of 1996, for example, created new demands for work-readiness and related social service assistance that for-profit firms have increasingly sought to meet.

Recent Trends

The emergence of a sizable for-profit sector in the social services field is but a part of a broader set of changes that has affected this field over the past two decades. Broadly speaking, these changes can be grouped in three major categories: declining government support, overall social services growth, and marketization.

FIGURE 8.7
Key Trends in Social Services, 1977-1996

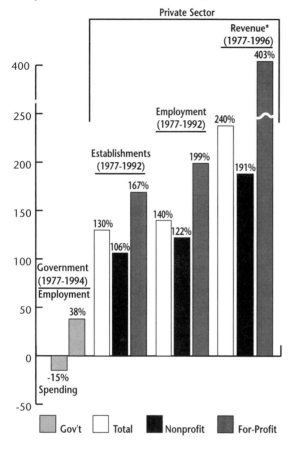

*In constant 1996 dollars based on price deflator for services component of personal consumption expenditures.

Source: See Endnotes 16 and 17.

Declining Government Support

Perhaps the dominant development of the decade of the 1980s in the field of social services was the sharp reversal of the prior growth in government support. From the mid-1960s to the late 1970s, a major expansion of government involvement took place in this field, as efforts were made to combat persistent poverty by providing a variety of supportive services to individuals and families.

As Figure 8.7 makes clear, however, in real, inflation-adjusted terms, that growth essentially stopped in the 1980s and reversed course. Thus, between 1977 and 1994, the real value of government spending on social services declined by 15 percent. Government employment in this field continued to grow, but relatively slowly, and mostly at the state and local level.[16]

Overall Social Services Growth

Despite the reduction in government support, however, considerable growth nevertheless occurred in the social services field during the 1980s and 1990s. Thus, as Figure 8.7 also makes clear:

- The number of private social service agencies recorded by the Census of Service Industries grew by 130 percent between 1977 and 1992;

- The number of employees working for these agencies grew during this same period by 140 percent;

- By 1996, the revenues of these agencies stood close to 240 percent above what they had been in 1977, even after adjusting for inflation.[17]

Marketization

How can we explain this apparent paradox of continued growth despite retrenchment in one of the principal sources of income in this field?

The answer, it seems, is that a significant shift occurred in the character of the social services field, a massive "marketization" of welfare as market relations increasingly penetrated the field.[18] This shift manifested itself in two principal ways:

Increased reliance on fee income. In the first place, a dramatic expansion took place in the scope and scale of fee income in the social services field. Between 1977 and 1994, while goverment social service spending declined by 15 percent and private philanthropy grew by a relatively modest 33 percent (about 1.5 percent per year), fee income jumped by 340 percent. As a consequence, fees went from 14 percent of social service spending in 1977 to

49 percent in 1994, while government support fell from 67 percent of the total to 38 percent.[19]

As noted earlier, this growth in fee income reflects a broadening of the market for social services from its traditional constituency, the poor, to a broader portion of the population. This, in turn, reflects economic and demographic shifts such as the aging of the population and the massive entry of women into the labor force, creating a market for elder care and child care services, among others. Coupled with increased concerns about drug and alcohol addiction within the broad middle of the population, and the increased availability of medical insurance to cover the costs of the counseling and rehabilitation services often required to deal with these problems, the result has been a signficant growth in potential paying customers for social and rehabilitative services.

Much of this growth accrued, naturally enough, to for-profit social service providers. But nonprofit providers benefited as well. Between 1977 and 1996, the income that nonprofit social service agencies received from fees, charges, and related business activities increased by more than 600 percent. Indeed, this source alone accounted for two-thirds of the growth in nonprofit social service agency income during this period, boosting fee income from 13 percent of the total when the period began to 43 percent by the time it ended. By comparison, private giving accounted for only 22 percent of the growth, or half as much. As a consequence, by 1996 fees came to outdistance both government and private giving as a source of nonprofit human service agency income.

"...a significant shift occurred in the character of the social services field during the 1980s and 1990s, a massive 'marketization' of welfare characterized by a dramatic growth of fee income and a substantial expansion of for-profit firms."

Growth of for-profit firms. The growth of fee income in the social service field not only helped offset declines in government support and thus fuel the growth of nonprofit providers; it also helped attract for-profit providers into this field. Already by 1977 for-profit firms were well established in the day-care field, controlling 57 percent of the establishments and 46 percent of the employees. But during the subsequent 15 years, for-profits expanded into other social service fields as well. Thus, as Figure 8.7 shows, between 1977 and 1992, the number of for-profit social service establishments increased by 167 percent, and the number of workers they employed increased by 199 percent — substantially more than the comparable increases for nonprofit providers. By 1996, for-profit social service providers had boosted their revenues by 400 percent over 1977 levels after adjusting for inflation. What is more, for-profit providers seem to have upstaged nonprofit ones in every component of the social service field. This is apparent in Table 8.1, which records the share of private social service agency revenue in each subfield accounted for by for-profit providers as of 1977, and then compares this to the share of revenue *growth* in each subfield between 1977 and 1996 that the for-profit providers captured. As this table shows, *in every subfield* of social services the for-profit providers claimed a larger share of the growth than their share of revenue at the start of the period would have suggested. Thus, with 48 percent of the day-care income in 1977, they captured 74 percent of the growth in such income between 1977 and 1996, or 56 percent more than their proportional share. In other subfields as well, the for-profit share of the growth exceeded the for-profit share of the total at the beginning of the period by proportions that ranged from 30 percent to 176 percent. In the process, for-profit providers moved from accounting for 23 percent of the revenues in this field as of 1977 to accounting for 34 percent as of 1996.

Nor does this process seem likely to abate in the near future. To the contrary, the welfare reform law of 1996, which created a variety of new government social service programs to ease the transition of welfare recipients into work roles, specifically authorized for-profit companies to compete for the resulting contracts, and many are doing so. Shifts in the medical industry also are opening new opportunities for for-profit residential care companies.[20]

In short, as in the other fields examined here, a massive "for-profitization" of social services, one of the more traditional fields of nonprofit activity, appears to be under way. While nonprofit providers are continuing to grow, for-profit competitors are expanding more rapidly in field after field.

> *"...in every subfield of social services, for-profit providers claimed a larger share of the growth between 1977 and 1996 than their share of revenue at the start of the period would have suggested."*

TABLE 8.1
For-Profit Share of Social Service Agency Growth, 1977–1996

	For-Profit Share of:		
	Revenues 1977 A	Revenue Growth 1977–96 B	Ratio B/A
Day Care	48%	74%	156%
Individual & Family Services	8	22	267
Job Training	15	36	233
Residential Care	<u>26</u>	<u>35</u>	130
Total	23%	39%	168%

Source: U.S. Census Bureau, 1977 *Census of Service Industries* and *Census Annual Survey* 1996.

118

Conclusion

The social services field is thus a true mixed economy, with active involvement on the part of nonprofit, government, and for-profit agencies; and extensive support from government revenues, fee income, and private philanthropy. Traditionally, however, private nonprofit agencies have dominated the *delivery* of social services, and, at least since the 1960s, government sources have dominated the *funding* of them. This partnership formed the heart of the nation's human service delivery system for the past three decades, and, at the local level, for numerous decades before that.

During the 1980s, however, a significant disruption occurred in this established pattern, as government support dwindled considerably. Social service agencies seem to have weathered this storm, but they did so largely by moving social services increasingly into the market system. Growth also occurred in private giving in this field, but the really dynamic element appears to have been the growth of commercial forces. In the process, nonprofit organizations have come to rely far more heavily on fees and service charges of various sorts, and they have had to contend with increasingly vigorous for-profit competition in their traditional fields of action. A central question for the future is how this will affect the social role that these organizations are also expected to play.

"During the 1980s a significant disruption occurred in the established pattern of government-nonprofit partnership in the social services field. Nonprofit social service agencies seem to have weathered this storm, but they did so largely by moving increasingly into the market system."

ENDNOTES

1. Included here are establishments classified by the U.S. Census of Service Industries as providing: 1) individual and family social, counseling, welfare, or referral services; 2) training, work experience, or vocational rehabilitation services for the unemployed, the underemployed, the physically challenged, etc.; 3) care of infants or children; or 4) residential care for children, the elderly, or other special categories of persons with some limits on their ability for self-care. Not included are what the Census categorizes as "Social Services N.E.C," which includes community improvement, social change, and neighborhood development organizations. These organizations seem more properly classified as "civic" organizations and are therefore covered in Chapter Ten. U.S. Census Bureau, *1992 Census of Service Industries* (1997).

2. Included here is spending on social services under the basic public assistance program (Title IV of the Social Security Act), vocational rehabilitation, child welfare, child nutrition, and other social welfare services not otherwise classified. Bixby, *Social Security Bulletin*, Vol. 60, No.3, (1997), pp. 42–44.

This estimate may overstate somewhat the actual government expenditures on social services *per se* since it includes child nutrition expenditures (school lunch and school breakfast programs), which might more properly be classified as income transfers rather than social services. These expenditures accounted for a substantial $10.1 billion of the total $28.2 billion in social service expenditures reported here, moreover. On the other hand, however, the estimate here does *not* include the portion of Medicare and Medicaid funding that flows to some social service providers for home health and caretaker services. A reliable estimate of such funding is not available. On balance, therefore, the estimate here probably *understates* the full extent of government support for social service activities. Support for this conclusion can be found in the estimate of the amount of government revenue received by nonprofit social service agencies, as reported by Independent Sector in its *Nonprofit Almanac*. This estimate of government support to nonprofit social services agencies actually exceeds the *total* amount of government social service spending reported here. One explanation for this anomaly may be that the *Almanac* includes government funds that reach nonprofit social service providers through the Medicare and Medicaid programs, which are treated as part of health spending here.

3. Based on data in Bixby, *Social Security Bulletin,* (1997).

4. No data series comparable to that for education and health spending is available on social services spending. The estimate of social service spending reported here was therefore constructed by adding together data on government social service spending from the *Social Security Bulletin* with data on the nongovernmental revenues of nonprofit and for- profit social service agencies drawn, respectively, from Independent Sector and the 1995 *Services Annual Survey* of the Bureau of the Census. Since no estimate of the revenue sources of for-profit social service providers is available, we assumed that 100 percent of these revenues came from fees and charges in 1977 and that these agencies absorbed the balance of government funding in 1994 left after deducting the nonprofit share and a 30 percent government share. In all likelihood, the estimate reported here may *understate* the scale of social service spending for reasons identified in note 2 above.

5. Data on health spending are for 1996 and are derived from U.S. Health Care Financing Administration, Office of the Actuary, "National Health Expenditures, 1996," Advance Tables (March 1998). Data on education spending cover the 1994/95 school year and are from *Digest of Education Statistics,* 1997, Tables 33 and 418. See also Chapter Seven, n. 1.

6. For a discussion of these demographic developments and the implications they have for nonprofit service providers, see: Lester M. Salamon, "The Voluntary Sector and the Future of the Welfare State, *Nonprofit and Voluntary Sector Quarterly,* Vol. 18, No. 1 (Spring 1989), pp. 16–39; and Chapter 12 below.

7. U.S. Census Bureau, *1992 Census of Service Industries* (1997). These are the latest available data. As noted in note 1 above, this figure does not include one category of social service agencies identified in the Census of Service Industries — i.e. "Social Services Not Elsewhere Classified," of which there were 15,757 in 1992. These organization are covered in Chapter Ten, which treats "civic" organizations. Also excluded from this estimate are the numerous agencies that fall outside the Census Bureau's sampling frame or reporting requirements, i.e., agencies that are not registered with the Internal Revenue Service or that do not have at least one paid employee. This likely includes numerous informal self-help groups and small, church-based service providers. The self-help groups may number as many as 500,000, though no solid data exist. With regard to small faith-based groups, recent research has suggested that 13 percent of the agencies in existence, and 27 percent of the religiously affiliated agencies in existence, do not show up on IRS listings. This would suggest at least 6,000–7,000 social service organizations beyond those reported in the available data sources. Kirsten Grønbjerg and Sheila Nelson, "Mapping Small Religious Nonprofit Organizations: An Illinois Profile," *Nonprofit and Voluntary Sector Quarterly*, Vol. 27, No. 1 (March 1998), p. 20.

8. These divisions are naturally somewhat arbitrary because many organizations perform a variety of functions. This is particularly true of the generally large "individual and family services" agencies.

9. Revenue data based on U.S. Census Bureau, *Service Annual Survey: 1995* (1997).

10. Establishment figures here from U.S. Census Bureau, *1992 Census of Service Industries* (1997). In addition to the 123,433 recorded private social service agencies, most states and local jurisdictions also maintain social welfare agencies. The actual number of separate agencies is thus at least as large as the number of local jurisdictions, though this function is sometimes performed at the county level and sometimes at the city level. Estimating the number of government "establishments" in the social service field is thus exceedingly difficult. Accordingly, only the private agencies are reported here.

Revenue figures for for-profit and nonprofit agencies were derived from U.S. Census Bureau, *Service Annual Survey: 1995* (1997). The revenue estimate for government deliverers of social services was computed at 30 percent of total government social service expenditures. This is based on prior research showing that roughly 60 percent of government social service spending took the form of grants and contracts to nonprofit and for-profit social service providers as of the mid-1980s. Given the extensive push for greater contracting-out of human service activities over the past decade, we assume this figure has increased to at least 70 percent.

Data on for-profit and nonprofit employment come from U.S. Census Bureau, *1992 Census of Service Industries* (1997). Data on government employment are from *Statistical Abstract of the U.S.,* 1994, p. 319, and are based on U.S. Bureau of the Census, Public Employment Series GE, No. 1, 1992. Government employment includes all "public welfare" and is therefore probably overstated because it includes employees involved in the administration of the basic public welfare programs in addition to those providing social services.

11. Author's estimates based on Independent Sector preliminary estimates, 1998, and National Center for Charitable Statistics data. See Chapter Three, Endnote 31.

12. U.S. Department of Health and Human Services, Public Health Service, *Surgeon General's Workshop on Self-Help and Public Health* (Washington, DC: U.S. Government Printing Office, 1988), p. 1.

13. Virginia A. Hodgkinson, Murray S. Weitzman, Arthur D. Kirsch, Stephen M. Noga, and Heather Gorski, *From Belief to Commitment: The Community Service Activities and Finances of Religious Congregations in the United States* (Washington: Independent Sector, 1993), pp. 2–3. For further information on religious organizations, see Chapter 11.

14. Robin Garr, *Reinvesting in America: The Grassroots Movements that Are Feeding the Hungry, Housing the Homeless, and Putting Americans Back to Work.* (Reading, MA: Addison-Wesley, 1995).

15. See note 7 above.

16. Government employment data from *Statistical Abstract of the United States,* 1979, p. 313, and 1997, p. 321. Government spending data from *Social Security Bulletin,* Vol. 46, No. 8 (August 1983), p. 10, and Vol. 63, No. 3 (1997), p. 42. Data on government employment are for 1977–1995 and cover all "public welfare." Data on government spending are for 1977–1994.

17. Data on private establishments, employment, and revenues are from U.S. *Census of Service Industries* for 1977 and 1992, and the *Service Annual Survey* for 1996. Estimates of revenue growth may be slightly overstated because 1977 data refer to expenditures only and 1996 data include all revenues.

18. For further detail on this phenomenon, see: Salamon, "The Marketization of Welfare" (1993); Salamon, *Partners in Public Service* (1995), Chapter 14, pp. 220–242.

19. Author's estimates based on sources identified in note 4.

20. See, for example: Jennifer Moore, "A Corporate Challenge for Charities," *Chronicle of Philanthropy,* Vol. X, No. 20 (August 13, 1998), p. 1.

CHAPTER NINE

Arts, Culture, and Recreation

In addition to the role they play in the delivery of health, education, and welfare services, nonprofit organizations also play a major role in the artistic, cultural, and recreational life of the United States. This role can easily be overlooked, however, because arts, culture, and recreation organizations comprise a relatively small part of the entire nonprofit sector (only 8 percent of the organizations and 2 percent of the employment) and because nonprofits tend to be prominent only in a relatively small portion of the arts and recreation field. Yet the importance of the nonprofit sector in this field goes well beyond what numbers alone might suggest. Indeed, most of the serious cultural and artistic activity of the nation is organized by nonprofit organizations, as is a significant share of the nation's recreational activities.

Overview: Culture and Recreation in the United States

Americans devoted just over 8 percent of their total consumption expenditures, approximately $400 billion, to recreation and culture as of 1995, a figure that has been rising steadily over the past several decades and that approximates the amount spent on all levels of education.[1] Included here are purchases of recreational products such as books, videos, recordings, sporting goods, toys, and televisions; as well as expenses related to various recreational, sports, amusement, and cultural activities.

Just over 2 million people are employed in the recreation and arts field. Of these, the vast majority (93 percent) are employed in sports, recreation, and entertainment. Only 7 percent — approximately 138,000 people — are employed in what might reasonably be termed the "arts and culture" portion of

"...most of the serious cultural and artistic activity of the nation is organized by nonprofit organizations."

FIGURE 9.1
Employment in Arts and Recreation Services, 1992

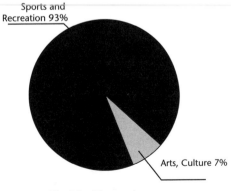

Sports and Recreation 93%

Arts, Culture 7%

N = 2.1 million employees

Source: See Endnote 2.

FIGURE 9.2

Nonprofit, For-Profit, and Government Shares of Arts and Recreation Employment, 1992

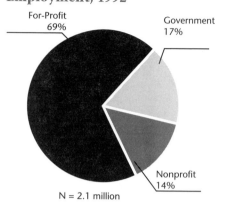

N = 2.1 million

Source: See Endnote 2.

FIGURE 9.3

Nonprofit Arts vs. Recreation Organizations, 1992

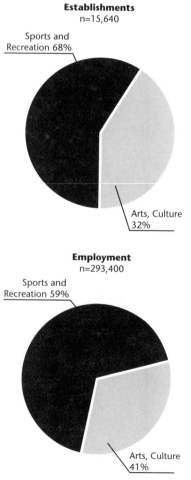

Establishments
n=15,640

Sports and Recreation 68%

Arts, Culture 32%

Employment
n=293,400

Sports and Recreation 59%

Arts, Culture 41%

Source: *U.S. Census of Service Industries, 1992*

the recreation and arts field, including live theater, symphonic and orchestral music, opera, museums, and galleries (see Figure 9.1).[2]

The Nonprofit Role in Recreation and Arts

Nonprofit organizations are involved in both the sports/recreation and the arts and culture segments of this field. Like the other types of providers, most nonprofit activity is in the sports and recreation area. But it is in arts and culture where nonprofits play their most distinctive and significant role.

Nature and Extent of Nonprofit Activity

As Figure 9.2 shows, of the 2.1 million people employed in the recreation and arts field, 14 percent, or approximately 293,000 people, are employed in nonprofit organizations. Of the balance, 17 percent are employed by government agencies, and 69 percent in for-profit organizations providing a wide range of recreational, amusement, and cultural services.[3]

As with the rest of the arts and recreation field, most of the 293,000 people employed in nonprofit organizations in this field are engaged in sports and recreation activities rather than arts and cultural ones. Thus, sports and recreation organizations comprise 68 percent of the close to 16,000 nonprofit arts and recreation establishments and 59 percent of the nonprofit arts and recreation employment, as shown in Figure 9.3. Included here are some 1,200 sporting and recreational camps and over 8,000 sports and recreational clubs, such as country clubs, golf clubs, swimming clubs, and the like.

The remaining 32 percent of the nonprofit organizations in the culture and recreation field, accounting for 41 percent of the employment, are in the arts and culture portion. Included here are hundreds of theaters, symphonies, opera companies, chamber music groups, museums, art galleries, zoos, and botanical gardens that form the backbone of the nation's cultural life.

Nonprofit versus For-Profit and Government Roles
For-profit dominance in sports and recreation.
While most nonprofit cultural and recreational organizations are in the sports and recreation portion of the field, they are far from the dominant force there. Rather, the public and for-profit sectors play a far more significant role than does the nonprofit sector in providing sports and recreational services. Thus, 73 percent of the employment in sports and recreation is in for-profit firms and another 18 percent in government, leaving only 9 percent of the total in nonprofit entities (See Figure 9.4).

These employment numbers can be deceptive, however, because nonprofit organizations mobilize a substantial army of volunteers for sports and recreational activity through Little Leagues, soccer leagues, county fairs, and similar organized community recreation activities. One estimate puts the number of volunteers working for nonprofit cultural organizations at 244,000 full-time equivalent workers as of 1992, roughly equivalent to the 293,000 paid workers.[4] It seems reasonable to assume that a substantial portion of these work in the recreational and sports component of the field. In addition, another 337,000 people are employed in nonprofit social and fraternal membership clubs, which, though not included in the public-benefit portion of the nonprofit sector of principal concern to us here, nevertheless offer significant recreational activities.[5]

Nonprofit dominance in arts and culture. While nonprofit organizations play a significant role in sports and recreation, however, they are even more important in relative terms in the arts and culture portion of the recreation field. Thus, as Figure 9.4 shows:

- Well over half of the *live theaters* in the United States are nonprofits, and they account for 62 percent of the live theatrical employment. To be sure, live theater is not exclusively nonprofit. Many live theatrical companies are for-profit

"...most of the people employed in nonprofit organizations in the culture and recreation field work in the recreation and sports portion of this field rather than the arts and culture portion."

FIGURE 9.4

The Nonprofit Share of Arts and Recreation Establishments and Employment

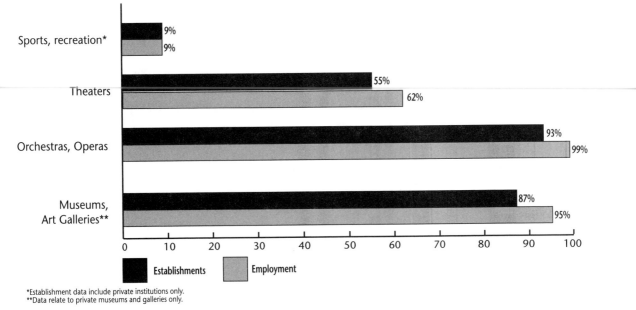

*Establishment data include private institutions only.
**Data relate to private museums and galleries only.

Source: See Endnote 2.

"Not only do nonprofit organizations play a major role in the arts, culture, and recreation field, but private philanthropy also plays a larger part in financing this role than it does in any other."

businesses, particularly in the major cultural centers such as New York. But outside of these centers, most theaters are nonprofit organizations. These nonprofit theaters provide a critical proving ground for new plays and approaches and help to ensure the survival of theater outside the major production centers.

- More than 90 percent of the *orchestras, opera companies, and chamber music groups* in the country are nonprofit organizations, and these organizations account for 99 percent of the employment in this field. For-profit firms are dominant in other aspects of the music and entertainment field (e.g., rock bands, entertainment groups, and the recording industry), but in the field of live classical music, the nonprofit sector holds virtually unrivaled sway. This situation differs markedly from that in Europe and elsewhere in the world, where government-sponsored symphonies and operas are more prevalent.

- Nonprofits are also quite prominent among *museums, art galleries, and zoological gardens.* Eighty-seven percent of the 3,553 private institutions of this sort identified by the Census of Service Industries in the early 1990s are nonprofits, and they account for the lion's share of the employment. Municipal museums and zoos are also quite common, but many of these are formally nonprofit in form as well. Even with the true municipal institutions included, however, it seems likely that nonprofits would remain by far the dominant form for this type of institution.[6]

In short, much of the cultural and artistic life of the country takes place in and through private, nonprofit organizations. The nonprofit sector has provided a convenient mechanism for organizing activity that enriches the cultural and intellectual life of the country but that may not be able meet a market test.

FIGURE 9.5

Sources of Nonprofit Arts and Entertainment Organization Operating Income, 1996

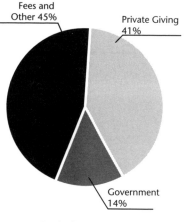

Fees and Other 45%

Private Giving 41%

Government 14%

Total = $10.5 Billion

Source: See Endnote 6.

TABLE 9.1

Revenue Sources of Nonprofit Symphonies, Theaters, and Dance Companies*

Source	Symphonies	Theaters	Dance Companies
Earned Income	59%	62%	61%
Private Giving	34	31	33
Government	7	7	6
Total	100%	100%	100%

*Data are for 1993 for symphonies and dance companies and for 1995 for theaters.
Source: See Endnote 9.

The Role of Private Philanthropy

Not only do nonprofit organizations play a major role in the arts, culture, and recreation field, but private philanthropy also plays a larger part in financing this role than it does in any other. At the same time, even here private philanthropy is not the dominant source of support. Thus, as Figure 9.5 shows, private giving accounts for an estimated 41 percent of the income of nonprofit arts and culture institutions. By comparison, fees, charges, and endowment earnings provide 45 percent of this income and government grants and contracts the remaining 14 percent.[7]

These aggregate data may, however, overstate the role that private giving plays in the financing of arts and cultural activity. One reason for this is that the giving data include the value of donated works of art at the full market value of these gifts, even though this support is not available for use in the operation of the institutions.[8] Supporting this view, recent survey data for symphony orchestras, theaters, and dance companies suggest that earned income is a significantly larger source of revenue than Figure 9.5 suggests, and that private giving and government support are correspondingly smaller, at least for these three types of cultural institutions. Thus, as shown in Table 9.1, for all three of these types of cultural institutions, earned income from ticket sales, endowment earnings, and related business activities comprises approximately 60 percent of revenues. Of the remaining revenue, just over 30 percent comes from private giving and just under 10 percent from government.[9]

Recent Trends

The period from the late 1970s to the early 1990s has been a time of considerable growth in the recreation and arts field in the United States. Overall, the number of establishments in this field grew by 70 percent, the value of the revenues they generated increased by 90 percent, and the number of people they employed increased by nearly 100 percent (see Figure 9.6). What is more, both nonprofit and for-profit organizations participated in this growth, and did so almost equally. Thus, while for-profit revenue increased by 93 percent, nonprofit revenue increased by 76 percent.

While both nonprofit and for-profit organizations experienced considerable growth in the arts and recreation field over the past twenty years, however,

"The past decade and a half has been a time of considerable growth in the recreation and arts field...."

FIGURE 9.6
Recent Trends in Arts and Recreation, 1977-1992

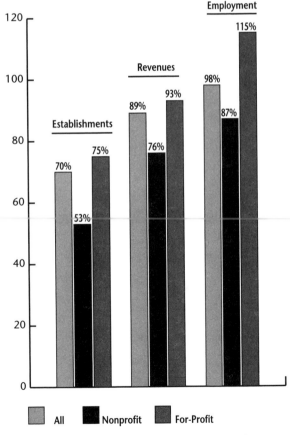

Source: *1977 and 1992 Census of Service Industries Statistical Abstract of the United States, 1979, 1994.*

they prospered in different components of this field. Thus, the for-profit growth was largely confined to the sports and recreation portion of the field while the nonprofit growth was considerably stronger in the arts and culture portion. This point is evident in Figure 9.7, which shows the relative growth of nonprofit and for-profit employment in the fields of recreation and sports, theater, classical music, and museums and galleries.

Recreation and Sports

As Figure 9.7 shows, for-profit firms outperformed nonprofit organizations and government between 1977 and 1992 in the recreation and sports portion of the culture and recreation field, and did so by a substantial margin (119 percent vs. 66 percent growth in employment).[10] This is significant because, as noted earlier, this is clearly the largest component of the recreation and culture field, outdistancing the more narrow "high-culture" subfields of theater, classical music, and museums and galleries by a factor of 13:1. At the same time, as we have seen, for-profits have traditionally dominated this component of the recreation industry, so the recent trends signify no fundamental change in roles and relationships.

Theater, Classical Music, Museums

While for-profits outdistanced nonprofits in the recreation and sports field, however, nonprofits clearly outdistanced for-profits in the high-culture arena. Indeed, their growth here was quite striking not only relative to for-profits, but absolutely as well. Thus, as Figure 9.7 shows:

- Between 1977 and 1992, employment at nonprofit *theaters* jumped over 250 percent, from 6 million to 21 million. This reflected in part a significant expansion in the number of theaters. Between 1977 and 1992, the number of nonprofit live theaters more than doubled, from just under 500 to slightly more than 1,250. At the same time, nonprofit theater revenues also increased substantially, growing by almost 150 percent between 1977 and 1992 after adjusting for inflation. This was three times the growth rate of U.S. gross domestic product, which increased by only 46 percent in real dollar terms during this period. Evidently, a renaissance has been quietly occurring within the nonprofit theater world. In the process, moreover, nonprofit theaters have steadily gained ground on their for-profit counterparts, whose growth lagged far behind that of the nonprofit groups.

"...for-profits outdistanced nonprofits between the late 1970s and the early 1990s in the recreation and sports field, but nonprofits outdistanced for-profits in the 'high-culture' arena."

- A similar story obtains in the case of *nonprofit orchestras, operas, and dance companies.* As Figure 9.7 shows, employment at these institutions grew by more than 125 percent between 1977 and 1992, from just under 16,000 to more than 34,000. Here, again, a considerable broadening of the nonprofit presence in this field took place, as the number of nonprofit orchestras and opera companies swelled from under 300 to just over 700, an increase of nearly 150 percent. At the same time, the number of for-profit institutions in this field declined, both absolutely and relatively, leading to a 50 percent decline in for-profit employment.

- Finally, nonprofit organizations also experienced considerable growth, both absolutely and relatively, in the field of *museums, art galleries, and zoos.* The number of nonprofit institutions in this field grew by a third between 1977 and 1992, from just over 2,200 to nearly 3,100. During the same period, nonprofit employment in the field increased by 103 percent while for-profit employment declined by 13 percent.

More recent data make clear, moreover, that the growth of nonprofit museums, galleries, and zoos has persisted into the 1990s. Thus, the revenue of these institutions grew by 30 percent between 1992 and 1996, or more than 7 percent per year after adjusting for inflation.[11] Indeed a veritable boom in museum construction and attendance has surfaced in the late 1990s.[12]

Sources of Nonprofit Growth

How can we explain this nonprofit growth, particularly in the culture and arts sphere? The answer, it appears, varies depending on the period. In the early part of the period, government support, coupled with foundation initiative, played an important catalytic role. The dramatic expansion of nonprofit theaters reported above, for example, grew out of a program initially developed at the Ford Foundation in the early 1960s and subsequently funded in important part by the National Endowment for the Arts (NEA). The goal of this initiative was nothing less than to create a nationwide network of high-quality professional theaters that could make live theatrical productions accessible to a broad audience of viewers in communities across the country. "The result," as one recent study reports, "was a remarkable era of institution building, which lasted some 30 years. What had originally been a handful of widely scattered

FIGURE 9.7

Recent Trends in Recreation and Arts Employment, by Field and Type of Organization, 1977-1992

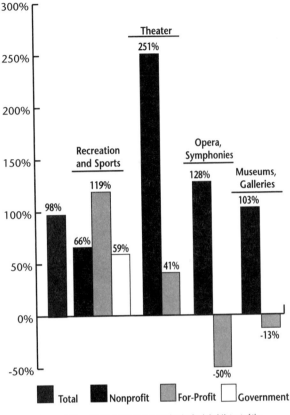

Source: *1977 and 1992 Census of Service Industries Statistical Abstract of the United States, 1979, 1994.*

"The dramatic explosion of nonprofit theaters [between 1977 and 1992] grew out of a program initially developed by the Ford Foundation in the early 1960s and subsequently funded in important part by the National Endowment for the Arts."

TABLE 9.2
**Sources of Growth in Nonprofit
Theater Revenues, 1991–1995**

Source	Share of Change 1991–95
Government	-1%
Private Giving	31
Fees, charges	70
Total	100%

Source: *Theater Facts 1995* (1996), pp. 9–10.

regional theatres became, by the 1994–95 season, a network of hundreds of theatres located throughout the country."[13]

The NEA and its affiliated state agencies also played a pivotal role in the growth of other types of artistic institutions, both through the direct assistance they provided and through the stimulus they created for local government and private charitable support.[14] As one observor has put it: "The NEA changed the arts environment completely. It was the major catalyst in decentralizing the arts."[15]

However, while government seems to have played a critical role in stimulating the growth of nonprofit arts and cultural institutions in the 1960s and 1970s, that role came under fire during the 1980s as a product of conservative fiscal and social policies. Thus, government support for the arts barely kept pace with inflation between 1982 and 1992. Instead, nonprofit arts organizations turned extensively to private charitable support. Such support accounted for 54 percent of the not inconsiderable growth in nonprofit arts organization income between 1982 and 1992, outpacing even earned income, which accounted for 45 percent of the growth.[16]

During the 1990s, a somewhat different dynamic seems to have occurred. With government support still stalled, and the growth of private giving slowing considerably, nonprofit arts and culture institutions seem to have turned more extensively to fees and other earned income. Close to half of all the growth in nonprofit arts organization income came from this source between 1992 and 1996.[17] For some components of the arts and culture subsector, moreover, the share was considerably higher than this. Thus, as Table 9.2 shows, 70 percent of the growth in income of a cross-section of nonprofit theaters between 1991 and 1995 came from earned income. By contrast, government revenue actually declined and private giving contributed 30 percent of the growth.[18]

Behind these numbers lie not only increases in ticket prices for nonprofit cultural events, but also a vast array of other semi-commercial ventures, from bookings of broadway plays to the creation of for-profit companies engaged in real estate development and marketing of museum reproductions.[19] The central issue for the field, as in the other fields of nonprofit action discussed earlier, is what this trend will mean for the distinct mission of the nonprofit institutions.

Conclusions

Nonprofit organizations thus play a critical role in the recreational and cultural life of the United States. Many of the central recreational institutions of local communities — swimming clubs, tennis clubs, Little Leagues, soccer leagues, country clubs — are nonprofit in form. Even more importantly, nonprofit organizations form the backbone of the nation's cultural life, producing most of the live theater, symphonic music, and opera, and providing venues for art and for cultural artifacts.

Much of the expansion of this structure of nonprofit cultural institutions took place over the past 40 years as the product of an important partnership that emerged between government and private philanthropy. Beginning in the 1980s, however, this partnership came under serious strain when government support was significantly reduced. Despite this, nonprofit arts and cultural institutions continued to expand. In part this was due to the generosity of private benefactors. But in somewhat greater part, it was due to the willingness of patrons to pay for the services they received and the ability of arts institutions to find other, semi-commercial, sources of support. It remains to be seen, however, whether the values that gave nonprofit culture its distinctive flavor can be retained in this new funding environment.

ENDNOTES

1. The exact figure is 8.2 percent as of 1995, a 25 percent increase from 1985, when it stood at 6.6 percent of personal income. *Statistical Abstract of the United States, 1997*, p. 252.

2. Data on for-profit and nonprofit employment in arts and recreational services from *1992 Census of Service Industries*, Tables 1a and 1b. Includes data on the following industries: sporting and recreational camps; theatrical producers, bands, orchestras, and entertainers; motion picture production, motion picture theaters, and video tape rental; bowling centers; and sports and recreational services, including amusement services and museums, art galleries, and zoological gardens. Not included are social and fraternal membership organizations such as alumni associations, fraternities, scout organizations, university clubs, veterans' organizations, and youth associations (SIC 869). Such organizations do contribute to the recreational life of the country, but, as membership organizations, they are considered part of the member-serving portion of the nonprofit sector rather than the public-serving portion that is our principal focus here. However, while most organizations covered under

Standard Industrial Classification 869 in the Census are excluded from our discussion, one component is covered in the analysis of advocacy organizations in Chapter Ten. These are the civic associations (i.e., citizens associations, consumer education organizations, and advocacy organizations).

Government employment covers employment in "parks and recreation" from U.S. Bureau of the Census, *Government Finances*, Series GF, No. 5 (1992) as reported in *Statistical Abstract of the United States* (1994), p. 298, Table 464.

The arts and culture portion of this field as defined here includes employment in establishments classified in the Census of Service Industries as: 1) producers of live theatrical productions; 2) symphony orchestras, opera companies, and chamber music organizations; and 3) museums, art galleries, and botanical and zoological gardens. Unfortunately, separate data are not available on public sector employment in these three sub-industries. All public employment in the parks and recreation field is therefore assumed to fall into the sports and recreation portion.

3. Adding the social and fraternal membership organizations (see note 2) would boost the nonprofit employment by an additional 337,300 workers and bring the nonprofit total to 26 percent. This assumes, based on previous work, that 95 percent of the organizations, and a corresponding share of the employment, reported by the Census of Service Industries under "civic, social, and fraternal" organizations represent the social and fraternal organizations and 5 percent the civic organizations.

4. *Nonprofit Almanac*, 1996–1997, p. 150.

5. See note 3. Including these employees would boost the nonprofit share of recreation and sports employment from 9 percent to 22 percent.

6. Unfortunately, solid data on the number of government museums and galleries are not available. One estimate puts the share of art galleries that are public agencies at 12 percent, with an additional 14 percent affiliated with public universities. Among history museums and science museums, the public share is estimated to range from 40 to 60 percent. See: Paul DiMaggio, "Nonprofit Organizations in the Production and Distribution of Culture," in Walter Powell, ed. *The Nonprofit Sector: A Research Handbook* (New Haven: Yale University Press, 1987), p. 198.

7. Based on preliminary estimates provided by Murray Weitzman, Independent Sector, 1998. Of the $17.7 billion of government spending on "parks and recreation," an estimated $1 billion goes for arts and culture. Overall figure from *Statistical Abstract of the United States,1997*, Table 464; estimate of arts and culture share from Nina Kressner Cobb, *Looking Ahead: Private Sector Giving to the Arts and the Humanities* (Washington: President's Committee on the Arts and the Humanities, n.d. [1997]), p. 17.

8. Reflecting this, *Giving USA,* the principal source of data on private giving, estimates private giving to arts, culture, and humanities institutions at $10.92 billion in 1996 *(Giving USA 1997,* p. 201). But this almost exceeds the $14.7 billion in total revenue for all nonprofit arts, recreational, and amusement organizations reported by the Census Bureau for 1995. The Independent Sector estimate of private giving to arts and culture institutions in 1996, at $4.3 billion, is more believable and is the one used here. Even so, it is likely that some donated art is included in the Independent Sector estimate as well.

9. Data on nonprofit symphonies and dance companies apply to 1993 and are from the American Arts Alliance and the American Symphony Orchestra League as reported in Charles S. Clark, "Arts Funding," *CQ Researcher,* Vol. 4, No. 39 (October 21, 1994), p. 916. Data on theaters cover 1995 and are from Steven Samuels and Alisha Tonsic, *Theater Facts 1995* (New York: Theater Communications Group, 1996), pp. 7–8.

10. Nonprofit employment from 1977 and 1992 Census of Service Industries. Government employment from *Statistical Abstract of the United States,* 1979 (Table 473) and 1994 (Table 464). Government employment is allocated entirely to sports and recreation. Estimates of nonprofit theater, symphony, and museum employment for 1977 were developed by applying to 1977 aggregate data on employment among nonprofit "theatrical producers and miscellaneous theatrical services" and "bands, orchestras, and other entertainers" the proportion of these aggregate categories in 1992 that were reported going to live theater, and to symphonies, operas and chamber music organizations, respectively.

11. Based on data from U.S. Census Bureau, *Services Annual Survey 1996.*

12. See, for example, Jacqueline Trescott, "Exhibiting a New Enthusiasm: Across U.S., Museum Construction, Attendance Are on the Rise," *The Washington Post* (June 21, 1998), p. 1.

13. Samuels and Tonsic, *Theater Facts 1995,* p. 2.

14. John Urice, "The Future of the State Arts Agency Movement in the 1990s: Decline and Effect," *The Journal of Arts Management, Law, and Society* (Spring 1992), Vol. 22, No. 1, cited in Nina Kressner Cobb, *Looking Ahead: Private Sector Giving to the Arts and the Humanities* (Washington: President's Committee on the Arts and the Humanities, n.d. [1997]), p. 17.

15. Cobb, *Looking Ahead,* p. 18.

16. As noted earlier, however, these data may overstate the value of private giving by including the value of contributed works of art. Calculating private giving as a share of total operating support can therefore be misleading.

17. Based on data provided by Independent Sector, 1998.

18. Samuels and Tonsic, *Theater Facts 1995,* pp. 9-10.

19. See, for example: Chris Jones, "Monster or Mainstay?" *American Theatre* (March 1996).

CHAPTER TEN

Advocacy, Legal Services, and International Aid

Important as the nonprofit sector is in the provision of various services — from health and education to arts and culture — it also plays other, possibly even more important, roles as well.

This chapter examines two of the most fundamental of these other roles: first, the nonprofit role in *civic advocacy*, the representation of views or interests, particularly public interests, in the shaping of public policy; and second, the nonprofit role in *international assistance*, the effort to relieve suffering and promote economic growth in less developed countries. In both, the nonprofit sector makes unique, and quite substantial, contributions.

Nonprofit Advocacy Activity

Advocacy, the representation of interests and concerns, usually in the political process, is one of the most distinctive functions of the nonprofit sector. Through their involvement in this function, nonprofit organizations consequently embody one of the most cherished values in American life: the right of free expression and its corollary, the right to associate together to give effective voice to common concerns. This right has received particular attention in recent decades as part of a general movement toward empowerment of the poor, of consumers, of women, of racial and ethnic minorities, and of numerous other segments of the population. Indeed, as one long-time student of the nonprofit sector has argued, this advocacy function may be the most important one the sector performs, and certainly the one "for which society is most dependent on it."[1]

"Through their involvement in advocacy, nonprofit organizations embody one of the most cherished values in American life: the right of free expression and its corollary, the right to associate together to give effective voice to common concerns."

TABLE 10.1

Illustrative Washington-Based Nonprofit Business and Professional Associations

American Apparel Manufacturers Association

American Association for Adult and Continuing Education

American Association of Advertising Agencies

American Association of Crop Insurers

American Association of Neurological Surgeons

American Bankers Association

American Concrete Pavement Association

American Electronics Association

American Gear Manufacturers Association

American Guild of Organists

American Hotel and Motel Association

American Low Power Television Association

American Road and Transportation Builders

American Sugarbeet Growers Association

National Asphalt Pavement Association

National Association for Hospital Admitting Managers

National Association of Beverage Importers

National Association of Broadcasters

National Association of Insurance Brokers

National Association of Scissors and Sheers Manufacturers

National Association of Manufacturers

National Association of Margarine Manufacturers

National Food Processor Association

National Wood, Window, and Door Association

Source: *BellAtlantic, District of Columbia White Pages* (1998).

"Despite an onslaught of civil rights, consumer, and environmental advocacy in the 1960s and 1970s, business dominance of the Washington interest-group scene was more pervasive by the early 1980s than it had been two decades earlier."

Private-Interest Advocacy

The nonprofit role in advocacy is most highly developed within the member-serving segment of the nonprofit sector. Most of the nearly 76,000 nonprofit, business and professional associations in the United States, not to mention the 67,000 labor and agricultural organizations, devote at least a part of their efforts toward the representation and promotion of the interests and views of their business or profession in the political process. They do this by contributing to political campaigns, conducting research on issues affecting their members, testifying before Congress and state legislatures, and presenting the views of their constituencies to political leaders, the press, and the general public in dozens of different ways.

As the scope of government involvement in national life has grown, so too has the scope and density of this private-interest representation, particularly in the nation's capital. The Washington, D.C. telephone directory alone contains close to ten pages of listings of "national association" or "American association" of this or that, beginning with the American Apparel Manufacturing Association and ending with the National Wool Growers Association (see Table 10.1). Few facets of national economic or professional life are not represented by at least one, and usually more than one, business or professional association. Despite an explosion of groups representing the interests of broad publics and the disadvantaged during the 1960s and 1970s, the advocacy system still retains a decided business "tilt," even in Washington, where public-interest advocacy is more highly developed than at the state or local level. Indeed, according to one recent study, despite an onslaught of civil rights, consumer, and environmental advocacy in the 1960s and 1970s,[2] business dominance of the Washington interest-group scene was more pervasive by the early 1980s than it had been two decades earlier. Thus, although the overall number of interests represented in Washington increased greatly, the number representing business interests increased even faster so that the business proportion of the total swelled from 57 percent to 72 percent between 1960 and 1980, while that for citizens' groups declined from 9 percent to 5 percent and the proportion for labor decreased from 11 percent to 2 percent (See Figure 10.1).[3] Indeed, so pervasive has the representation of interests become that some observers despair about the impact that this "interest-group liberalism" is having on the national capacity to formulate and implement meaningful policy.[4]

Public-Interest Advocacy

More important for our purposes than this extensive business and professional advocacy is the advocacy activity of public-serving nonprofit organizations. Indeed, a whole class of public-interest advocacy organizations has emerged in recent decades specializing in the identification, analysis, and development of potential solutions to public, or community, problems. Beyond this, however, numerous public-benefit service agencies (e.g., social service providers) include advocacy as a part of their activity, or belong to regional or national associations that advocate on behalf of the clients that the agencies serve. Finally, at the community level there are thousands of civic organizations through which individuals engage in community life.

Types of Advocacy Activity. To understand the nonprofit role in public-interest advocacy, it is necessary to distinguish three types of advocacy-related activity that are treated differently under U.S. law:

- **Issue Advocacy.** The first type is basic "issue advocacy." Issue advocacy consists of research, education, and dissemination activity related to identifying problems or potential solutions to them. Nonprofit public-benefit organizations — i.e., those eligible to receive tax-deductible contributions — are permitted to engage in such issue advocacy basically without limit.

- **Lobbying.** A second type of advocacy activity goes beyond providing general information about an issue or problem in the direction of trying to influence actual decisions on pending legislation. This type of advocacy is called "lobbying." The major difference between advocacy and lobbying is that the latter involves an attempt to influence the outcome of *a specific piece of legislation.*

  Nonprofit public-benefit organizations [i.e., 501(c)(3) organizations] are permitted to engage in such lobbying activity, but they are not allowed to devote a "substantial part" of their activities to it. Since 1976, such organizations have had two options for determining what constitutes a "substantial part" of their activities for this purpose: first, they can rely on a common-sense notion of what is "substantial," taking account of the circumstances of the organization and the nature of the situation; or second, they can "elect" to come under a set of specific mathematical guidelines about the share of their expenditures they can devote to lobbying (i.e., 20 percent of the first $500,000 of expenditures and a declining

FIGURE 10.1
The Washington Interest-Group System, 1980s

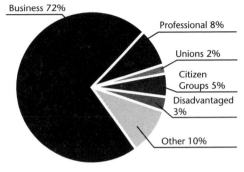

Business 72%
Professional 8%
Unions 2%
Citizen Groups 5%
Disadvantaged 3%
Other 10%

Source: See Endnote 3.

"...a whole class of public-interest advocacy organizations has emerged in recent decades specializing in the identification, analysis, and development of potential solutions to public, or community problems."

"Nonprofit public-benefit organizations are permitted to engage in issue advocacy basically without limit so long as it does not cross the line into active legislative lobbying, on which there are limits."

"The nonprofit sector has been the principal vehicle for most of the major social movements that have animated and energized American life over the past century or more–the women's suffrage movement, the civil rights movement, the environmental movement, the consumer movement, the abortion rights movement, the anti-abortion movement, the gay rights movement, and many more."

percentage of amounts over that up to a total of $1 million).[5] Whichever method is used, charities can exclude from "lobbying costs" any amounts spent on generating or disseminating nonpartisan research, responding to legislative requests for information, protecting the organization itself, communicating with the members of the organization about a piece of legislation (so long as no request is made to the member to communicate with the legislature about the legislation), and routinely communicating with government officials. In short, a wide range of activity is still permitted without running afoul of the limitations on nonprofit lobbying. Finally, charities that wish to engage in lobbying beyond the limits set in the law can choose to surrender their 501(c)(3) status and register as 501(c)(4) organizations, which have no restrictions on their lobbying. However, as 501(c)(4) organizations they lose their eligibility to receive tax-deductible contributions.

- **Political activity.** The third basic type of advocacy activity is "political campaign activity." Political campaign activity is involvement in a political campaign to support or oppose a candidate for public office. Nonprofit charitable organizations [501(c)(3) organizations] are absolutely prohibited from engaging in such campaign activity.[6]

Extent of Nonprofit Advocacy. Given its different forms, it is difficult to be very precise about the exact scope of the public-interest advocacy activity of nonprofit organizations. What we do know, however, is the following:

- **Nonprofit role in recent social movement activity.** The nonprofit sector has been the principal vehicle for most of the major social movements that have animated and energized American life over the past century or more — the women's suffrage movement, the civil rights movement, the environmental movement, the consumer movement, the women's rights movement, the abortion rights movement, the anti-abortion movement, the gay rights movement, and many more. To the extent that such movements have taken organizational expression, it is through nonprofit organizations that they have been able to function. The sector has thus provided a convenient safety valve for public concerns and a mechanism for mobilizing citizen action and attention on matters of public importance.

- **Nonprofit political action [501(c)(4)] organizations.** Reflecting the restrictions on nonprofit lobbying, a significant portion of nonprofit advocacy takes place through specially organized nonprofit advocacy organizations, many of which are organized under Section 501(c)(4) of the Internal Revenue Code. Close to 140,000 such 501(c)(4) organizations were registered with the Internal Revenue Service as of 1995. Interestingly, the number of such organizations has grown only modestly in recent years. Thus, while the total number of nonprofit organizations registered with the internal revenue service increased by 21 percent between 1987 and 1995, the number of 501(c)(4) organizations barely grew by 1 percent.[7] Nevertheless, this range of organizations has brought a degree of parity to the representational universe, providing vehicles through which broad public concerns can be reflected in the political process.

- **Advocacy activity by other nonprofits.** Beyond the dedicated lobbying organizations, a considerable amount of public-benefit advocacy takes place through 501(c)(3) organizations. As noted, such organizations are permitted to engage in issue advocacy essentially without limit, and can engage as well in lobbying so long as it is not a "substantial part" of the organizations' activity. A recent survey of nonprofit human service and arts organizations found that while only 4 percent of the organizations are *principally* involved in advocacy, about one-fourth of them take part in advocacy activities at least to some extent.[8] This includes research, information development, information sharing, identification of public problems, work with the press, and so forth. Because the scale of the nonprofit sector has grown considerably in the past three decades, this translates into a considerable advocacy force. At the same time, it is clear that a substantial number of nonprofit organizations shy away from this crucial function of the nonprofit sector.

- **Specialized national advocacy organizations.** Whether they are organized as 501(c)(3)'s or 501(c)(4)'s, a considerable number of specialized public-interest advocacy organizations have taken their place in Washington, D.C., along with the more numerous private-interest organizations. Some of these represent other nonprofit organizations, such as the American Association of Museums or the National Assembly of National Voluntary Health and Social Welfare Organiza-

"...about one-fourth of the nation's nonprofit human service agencies report taking part in advocacy activities at least to some extent."

TABLE 10.2
Selected Washington-Based Public-Interest Advocacy Organizations

Accuracy in Media
American Conservation Union
Americans for Democratic Action
Common Cause
Federation for American Immigration Reform
National Abortion Rights Action League
National Coalition to Ban Handguns
National Right to Life Committee
American Civil Liberties Union
Consumer Federation of America
Independent Sector
National Association of Railroad Passengers
National Urban Coalition
Migrant Legal Action Program
National Council of Negro Women
Environmental Law Institute
Conservation Foundation
National Wildlife Federation
The Nature Conservancy

Source: *Washington '88: A Comprehensive Directory of the Key Institutions and Leaders of the National Capital Area,* edited by J. Russell, A. O'Shea, Ba. Bachman (Washington: Columbia Books, Inc., 1988).

"Evidently, the growing push for empowerment at the local level is manifesting itself in a considerable growth of nonprofit civic organizations."

tions. Others, however, represent otherwise unrepresented or underrepresented groups or perspectives, such as the American Association of Retired Persons, the American Diabetes Association, the American Digestive Disease Society, or the National Association for Music Therapy (see Table 10.2).

Increasingly, moreover, public-interest organizations have had to focus their activities at the state level as well. Major national organizations thus often work with state-level affiliates, while others are really federations controlled by their local affiliates.

• **Civic associations.** In addition to the national or state-oriented advocacy activity, a great deal of advocacy activity also takes place through nonprofit civic organizations. Many of these organizations are informal neighborhood clubs that serve social as well as civic functions. But many are formally incorporated nonprofit organizations functioning to help develop housing and jobs in local areas. These latter were encouraged by the antipoverty program of the mid-1960s, which fostered the creation of Community Action Agencies involving the participation of the poor; and by the federal Community Development Block Grant Program, which has encouraged, and to some extent funded, the formation of neighborhood organizations to help oversee the process of community development in inner-city neighborhoods.

These organizations often provide a mechanism for neighborhood involvement in local decision-making. The Planning Department of the City of Baltimore, Maryland, for example, maintains a register of over 600 neighborhood or community organizations in the city that are regularly consulted on property development and other issues in their areas.[9] More generally, the Census Bureau identified close to 18,000 organizations as of the early 1990s that are engaged in community improvement, social change, neighborhood development, consumer education, or public advocacy. These organizations employed over 200,000 employees and had revenues as of 1995 of close to $22 billion.[10]

From all indications, this nonprofit civic activity has grown significantly in recent years. Thus, as reflected in Figure 10.2, the number of nonprofit civic organizations grew by close to 70 percent between 1977 and 1992, and the number of people they employed grew by close to 50 percent. As of 1995, the revenue of these organizations stood more than 200 percent above its 1977 level, after adjusting for inflation. By contrast, the overall U.S. gross domestic product grew by a much smaller 58 percent during this same period. Evidently, the growing push for empowerment at the local level is manifesting itself in a considerable growth of nonprofit civic organizations.

- **Advocacy Funding.** Interestingly, the funding of civic organizations does not diverge as sharply from the funding pattern of other nonprofit organizations as might be supposed. In particular, government plays a larger role in this field than might be expected, accounting for half of the funding, as shown in Figure 10.3.[11] Evidently, government has recognized even more fully than private funding sources the importance to a vital democracy of active citizen engagement.

Legal Service Organizations

One of the more interesting features of nonprofit public-interest policy advocacy during the past two decades has been the use of the legal system to promote policy changes. At the heart of this development has been an array of specialized nonprofit, public-interest legal organizations in such fields as environmental protection, civil rights, consumer rights, and the like. Many of these organizations were specially created to pursue public-interest policy change through legal action. Others grew out of the efforts sparked by the federal antipoverty program of the 1960s to make legal services available to the poor.

Thanks to a Supreme Court ruling in 1966, which changed the definition of "standing" in certain legal cases, it became possible for these public-interest legal organizations to bring cases not only on behalf of particular injured individuals, but also on behalf of entire classes of similarly situated persons. This made it possible to claim sufficient damages to warrant the costs of a case, even though the damages sustained by any individual member of the affected group may have been relatively small.

Many of the nonprofit advocacy organizations pursuing legal changes are doubtless classified by the Census Bureau as environmental, or civil rights, or housing organizations. But as of the early 1990s there were also 1,725 nonprofit legal aid organizations in existence with some 21,300 employees, as shown in Table 10.3. By the mid-1990s, these organizations had revenues of some $1.3 billion. This represents an increase of nearly 60 percent in the number of agencies, and over 70 percent in the employment and revenues, compared to 1977.

FIGURE 10.2

Growth of Nonprofit Civic Organizations, 1977-1992/95

% Change

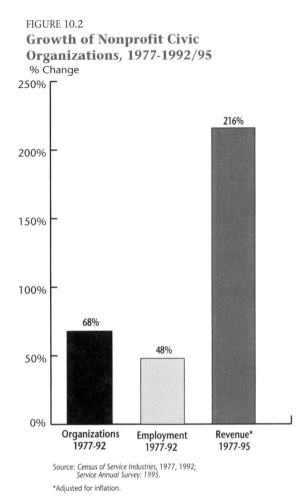

Source: *Census of Service Industries,* 1977, 1992; *Service Annual Survey: 1995.*

*Adjusted for inflation.

FIGURE 10.3

Sources of Revenue of Nonprofit Civic Organizations, 1996

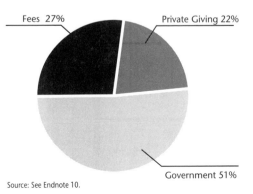

Source: See Endnote 10.

How many of these organizations are principally engaged in policy advocacy and class-action law as opposed to more traditional legal services (e.g., divorces, wills, property settlements) for indigent clients is difficult to say. During the 1970s, major efforts were made by the Nixon administration to restrict the advocacy work of the federally funded legal service organizations and limit them to more traditional legal services. Cutbacks in the funding of these services during the Reagan administration further hampered their efforts. What is more, the nonprofit legal service and legal advocacy organizations are a pale reflection of the 152,000 for-profit legal firms employing close to 1 million employees identified in Census records.[12] Nevertheless, this range of organizations has provided an important public-interest dimension to legal representation in the country and has attracted at least a modicum of private support.

Nonprofit Foreign Assistance

Nonprofit International Activities

Nonprofit organizations also play an important role in international activities. Internal Revenue Service sources identify at least 1,500 organizations actively engaged in such international work. Included here are organizations promoting peace and understanding among nations, channeling private philanthropic resources to favored institutions overseas (so-called "friend of" organizations), contributing to the alleviation of distress or the promotion of development, or improving knowledge of other countries.

International Assistance Organizations

Scale. Perhaps the most visible and important portion of this international nonprofit activity is that involving international relief and development. As of the latter 1990s, there were 424 U.S. private, voluntary organizations (PVOs) involved in international relief and development assistance registered

TABLE 10.3
Nonprofit Legal Service Organizations

| Dimension | Amount | | % Change |
	1977	1992/95*	1977–92/95*
Establishments	1,101	1,725	+57%
Employees	12,440	21,341	+72%
Revenues (Millions, 1995 $)	$720	$1,290	+79%

Source: *Census of Service Industries,* 1977 and 1992; *Service Annual Survey: 1995*
*Revenue data for 1995; all other for 1992.

with the U.S. Agency for International Development.[13] These organizations had revenues that year totaling $8.7 billion, of which an estimated $5.7 billion went into international activities.[14] By comparison, total U.S. government development assistance that year amounted to only $7.6 billion.[15] Nonprofit foreign assistance agencies thus spend almost as much as the U.S. government on international relief and development.

"Nonprofit foreign assistance agencies spend almost as much as the U.S. government on international relief and development."

Revenue Sources. As is the case with domestic nonprofit organizations, however, not all of the revenue that private, nonprofit foreign assistance organizations spend comes from private giving. On the contrary, the same widespread pattern of government–nonprofit cooperation that is evident on the domestic scene also operates in U.S. nonprofit activities abroad. Thus, as Figure 10.4 shows, 28 percent of the income of nonprofit foreign aid organizations came from government as of 1996. By

FIGURE 10.4

Sources of Income of Nonprofit Foreign Aid Organizations: Total and Selected Agencies

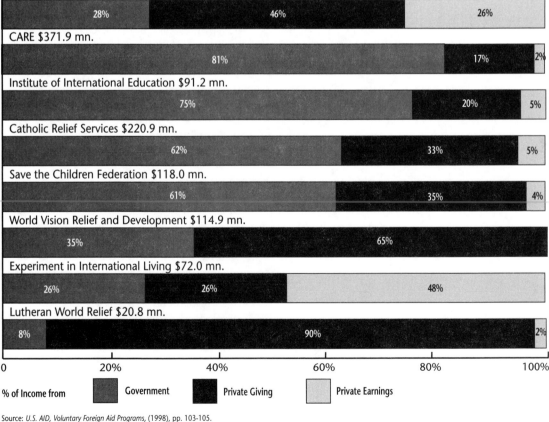

All Agencies $8.7 bn. — 28% | 46% | 26%
CARE $371.9 mn. — 81% | 17% | 2%
Institute of International Education $91.2 mn. — 75% | 20% | 5%
Catholic Relief Services $220.9 mn. — 62% | 33% | 5%
Save the Children Federation $118.0 mn. — 61% | 35% | 4%
World Vision Relief and Development $114.9 mn. — 35% | 65%
Experiment in International Living $72.0 mn. — 26% | 26% | 48%
Lutheran World Relief $20.8 mn. — 8% | 90% | 2%

% of Income from — Government — Private Giving — Private Earnings

Source: *U.S. AID, Voluntary Foreign Aid Programs*, (1998), pp. 103-105.

FIGURE 10.5

Sources of Growth of U.S. Nonprofit Foreign Assistance Agency Activity, 1980-1996

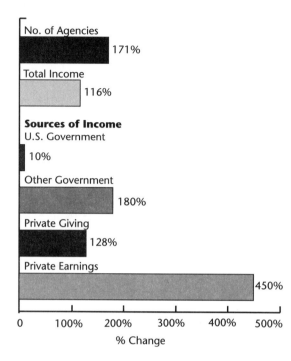

comparison, private giving provided 46 percent of the income of these agencies and private earnings 26 percent.[16]

Government support is even more important than these averages suggest among the largest private voluntary relief and development agencies. Thus, as Figure 10.4 also shows, Catholic Relief Services got 62 percent of its $221 million budget from government in 1996, CARE received 81 percent of its $372 million, and Save the Children Federation received 61 percent of its $118 million.

Recent Trends. This pattern of government support, though substantial, is nevertheless much more restricted than was the case in the recent past. Indeed, like many other parts of the nonprofit sector, the nonprofit foreign assistance community has been affected by a number of dramatic changes in recent years. Foremost among these changes have been the following:[17]

- *A substantial growth in the numbers of agencies in the field.* As shown in Figure 10.5, the number of PVOs registered with the U.S. Agency for International Development more than doubled between 1980 and 1998, increasing from 156 to 424. This reflects the growing globalization of the economy and the increased preoccupation with international disasters.

- *A significant broadening of the function of these agencies from relief to development.*[18] One reflection of this is the fact that the share of government support to these agencies that took the form of Public Law 480 surplus food distribution and other in-kind assistance declined from 59 percent in 1980 to only 15 percent in 1998. By contrast, the share that took the form of direct grants and contracts increased from 41 percent to 85 percent;

- *A significant decline in the government share of support.* Despite a long-standing partnership between government and private voluntary organizations in the provision of overseas relief, U.S. PVOs have had to contend in recent years with a significant reduction in the growth of U.S. development assistance. Although the number of agencies registered with the U.S. Agency for International Development more than doubled between 1980 and 1998, the real value of government support to these agencies increased by only 10 percent. As a share of total support, therefore, U.S. government support fell from 41 percent in 1980 to 21 percent in 1996.

- *Modest growth in private charitable support.* Fortunately, private charitable support increased markedly during this period, as Figure 10.5 shows. Much of this growth took the form of donated supplies and services, however, rather than actual contributions. Thus, of the $4.7 billion growth in income registered by PVOs affiliated with USAID between 1980 and 1996, only $1.1 billion came from private contributions.

- *Robust growth in private earnings and support from other governments and international organizations.* Far more important in permitting U.S. PVO's to respond to growing international assistance crises was the income they managed to secure from various commercial activities and from other governments and international organizations. The commercial income of these agencies grew by 450 percent between 1980 and 1996, contributing $1.8 billion to the overall income growth and boosting the share of total income coming from such commercial sources from 10 percent in 1980 to 26 percent in 1996. Similarly, US PVOs managed to reach out to international organizations to boost their income further. As a consequence, overall PVO income grew by 116 percent despite the fall-off of government support.

"U.S. private voluntary organizations have had to contend in recent years with a significant reduction in the growth of U.S. development assistance....While growth in private giving has helped them cope, far more important has been the increased income they managed to secure from other governments, international organizations, and commercial activities."

Conclusion

Beyond their significant domestic service roles, American nonprofit organizations thus play other vital functions in American national life. For one thing, they provide critical vehicles for advocacy and civic action, ensuring a free and open "civil society" in which different groupings of individuals can make their views known in the policy process at both the national and local levels. Nonprofit organizations are in this sense "empowering" institutions, providing a mechanism for joint action on behalf of even the least well-represented groups or views.

In addition, however, nonprofit organizations are also active in the international sphere, extending the reach of traditional, government-to-government relief and development aid, and mobilizing considerable quantities of private resources as well.

To be sure, in neither respect does the nonprofit sector respond adequately to all the needs that exist. What is more, important changes have challenged these roles of the nonprofit sector in recent years. Yet the sector nevertheless provides a mechanism for channeling what energies and resources can be mobilized for these purposes to useful ends.

"Beyond their significant service roles, American nonprofit organizations also provide critical vehicles for advocacy and civic action, ensuring a free and open 'civil society' in which different groupings of individuals can make their views known...."

ENDNOTES

1. Brian O'Connell, *People Power: Service, Advocacy, Empowerment* (New York: The Foundation Center, 1994), p. 49.

2. See, for example: Jeffrey Berry, *Lobbying for the People: The Political Behavior of Public Interest Groups.* (Princeton: Princeton University Press, 1977); and Jeffrey M. Berry, "Citizen Groups and the Changing Nature of Interest Groups in America," *Annals of the American Academy of Political Science,* No. 528 (July 1993), pp. 30–41.

3. Kay Lehman Schlozman and John T. Tierney, *Organized Interests and American Democracy* (New York: Harper and Row, Publishers, 1986), pp.77–78.

4. Theodore Lowi, *The End of Liberalism* (New York: W. W. Norton, 1979).

5. In addition to the basic limitation on lobbying expenditures as a share of total organizational expenditures, organizations that elect to follow the more specific rules are also prohibited from devoting more than 25 percent of their allowable lobbying expenditures to grassroots lobbying, i.e., influencing the general public on legislative matters. The penalty for exceeding these limitations on lobbying is an excise tax of 25 percent of the excess lobbying expenditures. For further detail, see: Hopkins, *The Law of Tax-Exempt Organizations* (1992), pp. 300–326.

6. A slight variation on political campaign activity is permissible, however. This is activity designed to influence the *nomination* or *appointment* of any individual to public office and not just the election. All tax-exempt organizations, including charitable ones, are permitted to engage in such "political activity." However, they must pay taxes on any income so used at the highest corporate tax rate. Hopkins, *The Law of Tax-Exempt Organizations* (1992), pp. 327–351.

7. Internal Revenue Service, *Annual Report,* various years, as reported in Independent Sector, *Nonprofit Almanac,* 1996, p. 38.

8. Lester M. Salamon, James C. Musselwhite, Jr., and Carol J. DeVita, "Partners in Public Service: Government and the Nonprofit Sector in the American Welfare State," Working Papers, Independent Sector Research Forum (1986); and unpublished tabulations of the Salamon/Urban Institute Nonprofit Sector Survey.

9. Baltimore City Department of Planning, *Baltimore City's Community Association Directory* (1991).

10. The Standard Industrial Classification used in the Census data makes it difficult to locate "civic" or "advocacy" organizations very precisely. Such organizations are included in two groupings of organizations in the Census data system: (1) SIC 839, "Social Services Not Elsewhere Classified," which includes community improvement, social change, and neighborhood development organizations, but also includes organizations such as the United Way that solicit funds for distribution to other nonprofit social welfare agencies as well as social service planning agencies; and (2) SIC 864, "Civic, Social, and Fraternal Associations," which includes citizens' associations,

consumer education and public advocacy organizations, but also includes fraternities, sororities, singing societies, university clubs, and other essentially social organizations. For purposes of our discussion here, we include all of the SIC 839 organizations and 5 percent of the SIC 864 organizations. Data on number of organizations and employment are drawn from the *1992 Census of Service Industries.* Data on revenues are from the *Service Annual Survey: 1995.* For derivation of the 5 percent figure, see Chapter 9, Endnote 3.

11. Author's estimates based on data drawn from Independent Sector, 1998, preliminary estimates.

12. *1992 Census of Service Industries,* Table 1A.

13. U.S. Agency for International Development, *Voluntary Foreign Aid Programs 1998,* (Washington: U.S. Agency for International Development, 1998), pp. 104–5.

14. See U.S. AID, *Voluntary Foreign Aid Programs 1998*, p. 105.

15. U.S. Office of Management and Budget, *Budget of the United States Government, Fiscal Year 1998* (Washington: U.S. Government Printing Office, 1997), p. 252.

16. Computed from data in U.S. AID, *Voluntary Foreign Aid Programs 1998*, pp. 104-5.

17. Based on data from U.S. Agency for International Development, *Voluntary Foreign Aid Programs,* 1981 and 1998 editions.

18. Advisory Committee on Voluntary Foreign Aid, *An Assessment of the State of the USAID/PVO Partnership,* (Washington, D.C.: Advisory Committee on Voluntary Foreign Aid, June 1997), p.3.

CHAPTER ELEVEN

Religion

Not only do nonprofit organizations provide a major mechanism for the pursuit of civic and secular concerns; they are also the principal vehicle for the pursuit of spiritual ones. The practice of religion is one of the purposes explicitly identified in the Internal Revenue Code as entitling organizations to exemption from income taxation, and virtually all churches and related religious institutions in the country are nonprofit in form. Indeed, religious institutions are near the epicenter of American philanthropy: they absorb well over half of all private charitable contributions, and account for a disproportionate share of the private voluntary effort. In turn, they provide useful support, financial and otherwise, to other components of the nonprofit world. Although they differ in purpose from the other nonprofit organizations we have examined thus far, no account of the U.S. nonprofit sector would therefore be complete without some attention to the religious institutions the sector also contains.

Previous chapters have already treated some aspects of religion's place in the American nonprofit scene. Many of the hospitals, educational institutions, and social service agencies examined earlier have some affiliation with religious institutions, though most of them nevertheless operate as separate institutions. In this chapter, by contrast, we focus on the religious community proper, i.e., on the places of religious worship such as churches, mosques, synagogues, temples, and related institutions through which the practice of religion is carried out.

To do so, we begin by examining the special position that religious organizations occupy in American law and the difficult definitional issues this poses. We then look at the scale of the religious-

"Religious institutions are near the epicenter of American philanthropy."

organization universe and the financial base on which it rests. Against this backdrop we turn to the non-religious functions that many of these institutions also perform. A final section then examines some of the key trends that are affecting America's religious institutions at the present time.

The Special Position of Religion

Religious institutions enjoy a privileged position in American law, even compared to other types of nonprofit organizations. This position derives from the First Amendment to the U.S. Constitution, which forbids Congress from passing any law that might have the effect of "establishing" or advancing one or more religions or impeding their "free exercise." One consequence of this provision is that religious organizations are exempt from the general requirement on other charitable organizations to secure official recognition of their tax-exempt status from the Internal Revenue Service. Rather, religious organizations are automatically presumed to be exempt from taxation and eligible to receive tax-deductible gifts, whether or not they officially secure recognition of this exemption. As a consequence, only a fraction of the churches and other religious organizations believed to exist in the nation are formally recorded on Internal Revenue Service records. In addition, religious organizations are exempt from the requirement to file an annual information return (Form 990) detailing their receipts and expenditures, as is required of other nonprofits.

Because of the First Amendment's proscriptions, moreover, neither Congress nor the courts have been eager to spell out what constitutes a "religion" for these purposes, with the result that considerable ambiguity exists. In one celebrated case, a court did deny a claim for tax exemption made by a self-proclaimed religious order, the Neo-American Church, which identified as its chief religious precept the obligation of adherents to imbibe psychedelic substances such as LSD and marijuana that were said to constitute "the true Host of the Church."[1] More generally, the courts have sidestepped the question of what constitutes a "religion" and have only denied exempt status where it becomes clear that the chief purpose of an organization, whether religious or other, is tax evasion and the financial enrichment of the founder.

Not only is there no clear definition of what constitutes a religion for purposes of tax-exempt status, but also there is no clear definition of what constitutes a "church" or other place of religious worship. This has become increasingly problematic,

"Religious institutions enjoy a privileged position in American law, even compared to other types of nonprofit organizations."

however, because of the rise of so-called "personal churches" in which the personal finances of the religious leader and those of the "church" or religious organization become thoroughly intermixed. To avoid fraud, therefore, courts have come to require certain minimum attributes to qualify an entity as a "church" or other religious congregation, such as the existence of a congregation or body of believers who assemble regularly to worship, a set of beliefs, and the actual conduct of some form of organized religious worship.[2]

The Scale of America's Religious Subsector

Number of Churches. Even when defined in this way, it is clear that religious institutions are a substantial presence on the American nonprofit scene. As shown in Table 11.1, at the present time at least 350,000 churches or other religious congregations exist in the United States.[3] This represents over 20 percent of all identifiable nonprofit organizations in the country, and 30 percent of the public-serving, or charitable, type of organizations.

As reflected in Table 11.2, the vast majority of these churches, representing 91 percent of the total, are Protestant in denomination. Roman Catholic churches are the second largest in number, with close to 7 percent. The remaining religions combined account for fewer than 3 percent of all congregations.

This picture does not begin to convey the vast assortment of different sects and denominations that characterize the American religious scene, however. Indeed, the latest edition of the *Yearbook of American and Canadian Churches* lists nearly 170 different religious denominations in the United States, ranging from the Advent Christian Church, with 318 churches and 26,552 members, to the Wisconsin Evangelical Lutheran Synod, with 1,235 churches and 413,000 members. Even this compilation misses

TABLE 11.1
The American Religious Sector Circa 1996*

Indicator	Amount
Denominations	~ 200
Places of worship (thousands)	351.9
Members (millions)	170.0
Revenues ($billion)	77.1
Employment (millions)	1.0
Volunteers (millions, FTE)	2.4

Sources: See Endnotes 3, 4, 5, 7, 8
*Employment data are for 1994; volunteer data are for 1992.

"Religious congregations represent over 20 percent of all identifiable nonprofit organizations in the United States, and these organizations receive 60 percent of all the country's charitable contributions and account for over 40 percent of the volunteer time."

Table 11.2
U.S. Churches and Church Membership, 1996*

Denomination	Churches		Members (millions)	
	Number	%	Number	%
Protestant	319,109	90.7%	93.3	54.9%
Roman Catholic	22,728	6.5	61.2	36.0
Jewish	2,755	0.8	5.9	3.5
Orthodox/Other Catholic	1,506	0.4	4.7	2.8
Buddhist, Eastern	1,772	0.5	4.1	2.4
Islamic	1,500	0.4	0.5	0.3
Other	2,510	0.7	0.1	0.1
Total	351,880	100%	170.0	100%

*Dates vary somewhat by denomination.
Source: See Endnotes 3 and 4.

FIGURE 11.1

FIGURE 11.1
Sources of Revenue of Religious Organizations, 1996

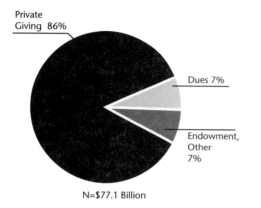

Private
Giving 86%

Dues 7%

Endowment,
Other
7%

N=$77.1 Billion

Source: See Endnote 6.

many of the smaller denominations. Indeed, other recent editions of this *Yearbook* have recorded well over 200 denominations.

Number of Members. Over 170 million Americans are members of these churches.[4] This means that close to two-thirds of the population is officially considered to belong to a religious congregation of some sort.

Of these, as Table 11.2 shows, the majority are Protestants, as is the case with the majority of churches. However, the Protestant dominance is not nearly so large in terms of members as it is in terms of numbers of institutions since many of the Protestant churches tend to be small. Thus 55 percent of the religious congregation members belong to Protestant congregations, 36 percent to Roman Catholic congregations, and about 10 percent to the remaining religions, including Judaism, Orthodox or other Catholic denominations, eastern churches, Islam, and others.

The degree of religious diversity may not be as great as these figures suggest, however. Rather, of the 200 religious denominations known to exist in the United States, the top three — the Roman Catholic Church, the Southern Baptist Convention, and the United Methodist Church — account for over half of all congregation members. While there is considerable religious diversity, therefore, a relative handful of denominations dominate the religious landscape.

Revenues. Although the importance of religious organizations is best measured in other terms, these organizations also turn out to be important in purely economic terms. As reported in Table 11.1, religious organizations had revenues in excess of $77 billion in 1996.[5] This is four times the scale of the nonprofit arts and culture sector and almost double the revenues of nonprofit social service agencies.

As noted in Figure 11.1, the vast majority (86 percent) of this revenue comes from private giving.[6] Indeed, as Figure 11.2 shows, religious institutions absorb over 60 percent of all individual charitable contributions in the United States. The balance of the support comes from dues and fees, endowment earnings, and miscellaneous sources.

Employment. Religious organizations are also major employers. Over 1 million people worked for religious congregations in the United States as of 1994, almost as many as work for nonprofit social service agencies.[7] In addition, these organizations attracted volunteer effort that was the equivalent of 2.4 million additional full-time workers.[8] As reflected in Figure 11.2, religious congregations thus absorb

43 percent of the volunteer activity in the country, substantially more than any other component of the nonprofit sector.

Religion's Contribution to Other Fields

Most of the revenues flowing to religious congregations goes to support religious worship and religious education. However, religious institutions also channel substantial financial resources and volunteer effort to other uses. According to the *Yearbook of American and Canadian Churches*, American churches devote 12 percent of their revenues to "benevolences;" but "benevolences" here refers not just to various non-religious services such as soup kitchens and homeless shelters, but also the support of religious institutions outside of the local congregation, such as seminaries, religious schools, and the parent denominational bodies.[9] Some portion of this sum is therefore still used for fundamentally religious worship purposes. Based on surveys conducted in the early 1990s, it seems reasonable to conclude that approximately 9 percent of the revenues of religious congregations goes to support non-religious charitable activities and needy individuals.[10]

Financial resources are not the only ones that religious congregations contribute to societal problem-solving, however. Also important is the time that clergy, other paid staff, and volunteers mobilized by religious congregations devote to a variety of service activities. As it turns out, the range of such activities is quite substantial. Thus a recent survey reported that:

- 92 percent of surveyed congregations are involved in human service activities;
- 90 percent are involved in health services;
- 74 percent are involved in international activities;
- 62 percent are involved in civic or public advocacy activities;
- 53 percent are engaged in education; and
- 50 percent are involved in arts and culture activities.[11]

Judging from the nature of the activities, it seems likely that the beneficiaries of much of this congregation involvement are largely congregation members. Thus, for example, the human service programs include congregational youth groups, marriage counseling, family counseling, and programs for single adults. Similarly, the most common health program is visitation or support for hospital patients or hospice residents; and a substantial share of the arts and culture activity consists of choral singing that is likely related to congregational choirs even if it excludes the actual participation in religious services.

FIGURE 11.2

Religion's Share of All Individual Giving and Volunteering

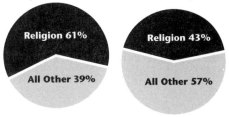

Individual Giving, 1996   Volunteer Time, 1992

Religion 61%   Religion 43%

All Other 39%   All Other 57%

Source: See Endnotes 6 and 8.

"Congregations function as important mobilizers and orchestrators of volunteer effort and financial support for a broad range of other nonprofit organizations."

FIGURE 11.3

Trends in Religious Organization Revenue and Employment, 1977-1994/96

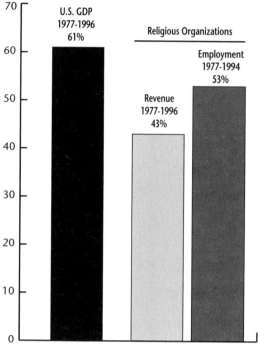

Source: See Endnotes 13 and 14.

"Over the past 20 years, the growth of religious congregations has lagged behind the growth of other types of nonprofit organizations, and of the economy as a whole."

What is more, only a small share of the activity in the key fields of human services, civic action, and international aid are run by the congregations themselves. To be sure, a significant number of so-called "faith-based charities" — nonprofit institutions closely affiliated with religious congregations — have emerged in recent years.[12] But most congregational social welfare activity is operated in conjunction with other nonprofit agencies. As such, it is probably captured in the data reported earlier on these other types of agencies.

Nevertheless, it seems clear that congregations perform functions for their members that might otherwise have to be performed by other agencies. What is more, congregations function as important mobilizers and orchestrators of volunteer effort and financial support for a broad range of other nonprofit organizations. It is notable, therefore, that half of all congregations reported involvement in meal services and food kitchens, that over 60 percent reported involvement in overseas relief, that 34 percent reported involvement in civil rights and social justice campaigns, that 25–30 percent reported participation in programs for abused women, and that 20 percent reported working on affordable housing — all of these being important charitable activities.[13]

Recent Trends

The American religious community has undergone immense changes in recent years as the nature and composition of the U.S. population and the character of U.S. life have changed.

Slow Growth of Organizational Revenues and Employment

In the first place, over the past 20 years the growth of religious congregations has lagged behind the growth of other types of nonprofit organizations, and of the economy as a whole. Thus, as Figure 11.3 shows, the inflation-adjusted value of congregation revenues grew by only 43 percent between 1977 and 1996, well behind the 61 percent growth rate registered by the U.S. economy as a whole and only half as large as the 96 percent growth rate of the nonprofit sector as a whole.[14]

Similarly, employment in U.S. congregations grew by only 53 percent between 1977 and 1994.[15] By comparison, employment in nonprofit social service agencies grew by well over 100 percent during this same period.

Limited Growth in Private Giving

Underlying this relatively limited growth in the size and scale of religious congregations has been the relatively limited growth of private charitable giving in the United States. Since religious congregations are particularly dependent on private giving, this has translated into a serious constraint on the growth of the religious institutions. According to one recent study of a sample of Protestant denominations for which historical data were available, per member giving to churches grew by only 18 percent between 1968 and 1991, after adjusting for inflation.[16] All of the limited increase that occurred, moreover, was absorbed by congregational finances. By contrast, after adjusting for inflation, per member giving to "benevolences" actually declined.

Even more troubling, while the absolute value of contributions to churches increased slightly, church giving as a share of personal income declined. In 1968, per member giving *as a share of personal income* was 3.09 percent. By 1991 it had fallen to 2.54 percent, a drop of nearly 20 percent. What is more, the decline was particularly marked for benevolences as opposed to congregational finances (-32 percent vs. -14 percent). Evidently, Americans are increasingly finding uses for their available income other than contributing to their religious congregations.

"A significant secularization has affected major areas of American life, leading to a weakening of the historic bonds to established religious institutions even while new religious affiliations are emerging.

Shifting Balance between Mainline and Less Traditional Congregations

Not only are contributions per member declining as a share of personal income, the number of members has been declining, or growing more slowly than the growth of population, for many denominations, including some of the largest in the country. According to one recent study of church membership, the number of adherents to 80 religious denominations for which data could be assembled over time increased by approximately 12 percent between 1980 and 1990, compared to a population growth rate of almost 10 percent. Church membership thus just barely kept pace with the growth of population.[17]

However, these aggregate data obscure some major shifts in denominational fortunes. In particular, 31 of the 80 denominations reported actual declines in membership over this period and another 16 reported growth rates below the growth rate of the population. Well over half of the denominations thus lost ground relative to the size of the population during this period.

What is more, the pattern of gains and losses was not distributed randomly across the denominations. Rather, the mainline churches generally lost members while the less established churches, many of them with a strong evangelical flavor, experienced often substantial growth. Thus, of 14 denominations in this study of membership change that are affiliated with the National Council of the Churches of Christ, a mainline body, eleven, or almost 80 percent, reported actual membership declines between 1980 and 1990, and one other reported growth that lagged behind the growth rate of the general population. Included here, moreover, were such major denominations as the Episcopal Church (-13.4 percent), the Presbyterian Church (-11.5 percent), the United Church of Christ (-4.9 percent), the United Methodist Church (-4.0 percent), and the American Baptist Churches (-2.5 percent). While the rate of decline for these mainline denominations seems to have moderated in more recent years, and while some established denominations, such as the Roman Catholic Church, are experiencing growth, the fact remains that membership among the mainline denominations seems to be in "steady decline," with significant implications for the nonprofit institutions these adherents are expected to support.[18]

Conclusion

In short, the nonprofit sector includes not only institutions that deliver services and advocate on behalf of public issues. It also houses the institutions that look after the spiritual health of the nation. These institutions have long played a vital role in sustaining a tradition of voluntary giving and voluntary action, and they retain that role today.

At the same time, like so many other components of the American nonprofit scene, the religious institutions face important challenges. A significant secularization has affected major areas of American life, leading to a weakening of the historic bonds to established religious institutions. This is manifested in declining memberships and declining shares of personal income devoted to religious giving. At the same time, new religious bodies are emerging, many of them more traditional in their approaches and more evangelical in their style. Which of these two streams of development will gain the upper hand, and how the two will be reconciled, is difficult to predict at this time. But it seems clear that some significant institutional adjustment still lies ahead.

ENDNOTES

1. Hopkins, *Law of Tax-Exempt Organizations* (1992), pp. 223–224.

2. For a discussion of the dilemma of defining "churches" for tax-exemption purposes, see: Hopkins, *Law of Tax-Exempt Organizations* (1992), pp. 218–228.

3. The number of Christian and non-denominational churches was derived from the *Yearbook of American and Canadian Churches 1998*, 66th Issue, edited by Eileen Lindner. (Nashville: Abingdon Press, 1998). These data generally cover 1996, though some denominations reported 1995, 1994, or 1997 data. Data on Jewish synagogues was derived from the Council of Jewish Federations, 1998. Data on mosques was derived from the American Muslim Council. Information on Buddhism and other Eastern religions was based on estimates provided in the 1991 edition of the *Yearbook of American and Canadian Churches,* (New York: National Council of the Churches of Christ, 1991) p. 270.

4. See note 3 for sources of membership data. In addition to the sources cited there, membership data on Jewish congregations comes from the 1991 *Yearbook of American and Canadian Churches,* p. 270; and on Muslim congregations from a 1990 survey of religious affiliation summarized in the *1997 Yearbook of American and Canadian Churches,* p. 1. Great care must be taken in interpreting these figures because the data are based on self-reporting by religious bodies and the different bodies use different definitions of membership. Thus, for example, Roman Catholics count all baptized individuals, including infants, whereas some Protestant bodies include only those persons who have been formally received into the church, which generally occurs later in life, thereby excluding many millions of young children. Data on the number of Jewish congregants include all individuals in households in which one or more Jews reside and therefore include non-Jews living in such households as a result of intermarriage. Similarly, except in the case of Muslims, the numbers reported here do not represent the number of people who *identify* themselves as adherents to particular religions, which may be larger or smaller than the numbers reported by the religious bodies as constituting their "membership."

5. Independent Sector, 1998.

6. Independent Sector estimates, 1998.

7. U.S. Census Bureau data as reported in *Nonprofit Almanac, 1996*, p. 145.

8. *Nonprofit Almanac, 1996*, Table 3.11, p. 150.

9. *Yearbook of American and Canadian Churches 1998*, p. 325. More specifically, benevolences includes any activities beyond the local congregation, including denominational support, global missions, seminary support, and contributions to agencies in the local community. John and Sylvia Ronsvalle, "The State of Church Giving through 1991," *Yearbook of American and Canadian Churches 1994*, p. 13.

10. This assumes that at least half of the 10 percent of all congregational expenditures identified in a 1992 Independent Sector survey of U.S. congregations as going to "denominational organizations and charities" went to the denominational organizations and half to the charities, and that the remaining 4 percent of all congregational expenditures identified in this survey as going to "other organizations and individuals" went to support the needy. By comparison, the *Nonprofit Almanac* reports that approximately 11 percent of religious organization revenue goes to support other types of organizations, though it is not clear whether this includes religiously affiliated schools and seminaries. Independent Sector, 1998 estimates; Virginia A. Hodgkinson and Murray S. Weitzman, *From Belief to Commitment: The Community Service Activities and Finances of Religious Congregations in the United States* (Washington: Independent Sector, 1992), p. 1.

11. Hodgkinson and Weitzman, *From Belief to Commitment* (1992), pp. 23–24.

12. One recent analysis puts the number of faith-based charities registered with the Internal Revenue Service at approximately 10,000. A further study suggests that there may be 25 percent more such institutions that are not registered with the IRS and therefore not included in most of the available data systems. See: Tom Pollack, "A Profile of Religious Organizations in the IRS Business Master File and Return Transaction Files," A Paper Prepared for Presentation at the ARNOVA Conference, 1997.

13. Hodgkinson and Weitzman, *From Belief to Commitment* (1992), pp. 23–24.

14. 1977 data from *Nonprofit Almanac, 1996;* 1996 data from Independent Sector, 1998, Preliminary estimates.

15. Bureau of Labor Statistics and Bureau of Census data as reported in *Nonprofit Almanac, 1996,* Table 3.6, p. 145.

16. John and Sylvia Ronsvalle, "The State of Church Giving Through 1991," *Yearbook of American and Canadian Churches 1994* (Nashville: Abingdon Press, 1994), p. 12.

17. *Yearbook of American and Canadian Churches 1993.* (Nashville: Abingdon Press, 1993), pp. 14–15.

18. "The Church in the 90s: Trends and Developments," *Yearbook of American and Canadian Churches 1997.* (Nashville: Abingdon, 1997), p. 9.

PART THREE

Looking to the Future

CHAPTER TWELVE

Trends and Challenges

As the previous chapters have made clear, the nonprofit sector remains a vital force in American society, enlivening American democracy and enriching national life in countless ways. This set of organizations helps to meet human needs, give expression to diverse values, foster social bonds, voice citizen concerns, hold government accountable, and generally mobilize private initiative in the pursuit of public purposes.

At the same time, as previous chapters have also made clear, America's nonprofit sector functions in a context of dynamic change. Many of the changes affecting this sector are strengthening it in important ways, but others pose significant risks.

The purpose of this chapter is to examine these changes and to identify the opportunities and threats they seem to hold for the nation's nonprofit sector in the years ahead.[1] Such an analysis is not only important for the future of the American nonprofit sector, moreover. It also has implications for the significant efforts that are now under way to build viable private nonprofit, or "civil society," sectors elsewhere in the world — in the developed countries of Western Europe and Asia, in Central and Eastern Europe, and in the developing world.[2]

"America's nonprofit sector functions in a context of dynamic change."

Supportive Trends

As a first step in this direction, it may be useful to focus on a number of trends that seem to hold important promise for the nonprofit sector's future development. Six of these in particular seem especially noteworthy.

"The aging of the population and the dramatic increase in female labor force participation both suggest growing needs for nonprofit services."

1. Social and Demographic Developments[3]

In the first place, nonprofit organizations are being affected by a number of demographic trends that are boosting the demand for the kinds of services that these organizations provide, and these trends seem likely to persist. Among the more salient of these trends are the following:

- **Aging of the Population.** As shown in Table 12.1, between 1960 and 1996, the number of people aged sixty-five and older in the United States doubled while the overall population barely increased by 50 percent.[4] This trend is now projected to continue over the next two decades at least, so that by 2025 the number of people aged sixty-five and over is expected to be nearly four times greater than it was in 1960. Among the elderly, moreover, the proportion that is over seventy-five is projected to grow especially rapidly so that it will reach 50 percent by the year 2025.

  This demographic shift is significant because it translates into increased demand for nursing home care and related forms of assisted living, as well as for health care more generally. As we have seen, these are fields in which nonprofit organizations are deeply involved. What is more, this development also suggests continued political support for government programs that assist the elderly, such as Medicare and Medicaid, and hence for a stream of revenue to support this nonprofit activity.

- **Transformation of the Role of Women.** A second notable social trend with important implications for nonprofit organizations has been the striking transformation in the role of women that has been under way for the past several decades. While this transformation has many dimensions, one of the most important is the surge in female labor force participation. Between 1960 and 1996, the labor force participation rate of women increased from 30.5 percent to 59.3 percent.[5] Even more dramatic, the labor force participation rate for married women with children under the age of six rose from 18.6 percent in 1960 to 62.7 percent in 1996, and even for single women with children under six it reached 55.1 percent.[6] Aside from its social and

TABLE 12.1

Growth of Elderly Population in U.S., 1960–2025 (millions)

	1960	1996	2025 Est.	% Change 1960–1996	% Change 1996–2025
Population over 65	16.7	33.9	62.0	103%	271%
Total Population	180.7	265.6	335.1	47%	85%

Source: *U.S. Statistical Abstract,* 1997 and 1982/83

162

economic implications, this dramatic shift has triggered a substantial increase in the need for child day-care, another field in which nonprofit organizations play an important role.

- **Shifts in Family Structure.** Significant changes have also occurred in the American family structure and these, too, have important implications for nonprofit agencies. In 1960, there was one divorce for every four marriages. By 1980, this figure had jumped to one divorce for every two marriages, and it has remained there through the mid-1990s.[7] During this same period, the number of children involved in divorces increased from 463,000 in 1960 to more than 1 million throughout the 1980s and 1990s. Since divorce typically involves a certain amount of emotional trauma, and often brings with it significant loss of economic status, this shift also translates into increased need for human services of the sort that many nonprofit agencies offer. Also contributing to this increased demand is the tremendous surge that has occurred in out-of-wedlock births. Between 1960 and 1980, the proportion of all births that were to unwed mothers increased from 5 percent to 18 percent, and by 1994 it had reached 33 percent. This represents a fivefold increase in the number of out-of-wedlock births, from 224,000 in 1960 to 1.3 million by 1994.[8]

- **Substance Abuse.** Changes have also occurred in the prevalence of substance abuse in American society. One reflection of this is the striking increase that has occurred in the number of people receiving substance abuse treatment services over the past two decades. Thus, as recently as 1977, the number of people using such services stood at approximately 235,000. By 1995 it was over 1 million.[9]

- **Increased Leisure Time and Expenditures.** Finally, Americans are engaging more extensively in leisure activities and devoting increasing shares of their income to it. As shown in Figure 12.1, recreation expenditures grew two-thirds faster than the overall gross domestic product between 1970 and 1995. While recreation encompasses far more than nonprofit culture and arts activities, the fact is that nonprofits have claimed more than their proportional share of the growth that has occurred. Indeed, as Figure 12.1 shows, the expenditures on live theater, opera, symphonies, and other nonprofit culture activity grew at a rate that was twice that for recreation as a whole.[10] There thus seems reasonable grounds for concluding that the

FIGURE 12.1

Growth of U.S. Recreation Expenditures, 1970-1995

Inflation Adjusted

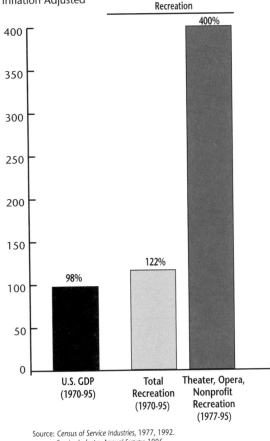

Source: *Census of Service Industries,* 1977, 1992.
Service Industry Annual Survey: 1995.
Statistical Abstract of the United States, 1982-83 and 1997.

general growth in leisure time and recreational expenditures will translate into increased demand for nonprofit services in the culture and arts area.

In short, far from declining, the demand for services of the sort that nonprofit organizations are able to provide seems on the rise, driven by a variety of major social and demographic forces that seem unlikely to subside in the foreseeable future.

2. Increased Visibility

A second major development of considerable importance to the future of the nonprofit sector is the increased visibility this sector has attained in recent years. In part, this visibility has been a byproduct of conservative fiscal policies. A central argument advanced by Ronald Reagan and his conservative allies to justify cuts in government spending in the early 1980s was that private, nonprofit organizations and private, voluntary activity could substitute for government spending across a broad front.[11] Whatever the merits of this view, it focused renewed attention on the nation's nonprofit institutions and the role they play in national life. Well before the Reagan administration came to power, however, steps were being taken by leading figures in the world of philanthropy and nonprofit action to bolster the image of the nonprofit sector. One concrete manifestation of this was the formation in 1980 of an umbrella group called Independent Sector designed to serve as a common "meeting ground" for all elements within the nonprofit and philanthropic community and a mechanism for increasing awareness of this sector within the academic world, among opinion leaders, and within the general public. Partly as a result of its efforts, scholarly attention to this sector has exploded, a new Nonprofit Sector Research Fund has been created, and a specialized press has come into existence focusing squarely on this sector.

3. Professionalization

Along with increased visibility and growing demand for their services, nonprofit organizations have become increasingly professionalized. No longer the preserve only of hearty volunteers, nonprofit organizations had become major employers by the late 1970s, and their attraction of paid staff has continued into the mid-1990s. Indeed, between the late 1970s and the mid-1990s, the paid staff of nonprofit organizations has grown at an annual rate that is more than 60 percent higher than that of all nonagricultural employment.[12] By 1994, therefore, public-benefit nonprofit organizations employed 9.7 million paid workers, or nearly 7 percent of the U. S. total. In the

"...scholarly attention to this sector has exploded, a new Nonprofit Sector Research Fund has been created, and a specialized nonprofit press has come into existence."

process, many of these organizations have become quite complex institutions. Unable to sustain themselves from traditional charitable sources, these organizations have had to develop sophisticated funding strategies involving government grants and contracts, fees for service, and a variety of earned-income schemes. Even traditional charitable fundraising has grown enormously more complex, utilizing elaborate telemarketing, direct mail, and donor "planned giving" arrangements.

Not surprisingly, to cope with this increased complexity, nonprofit management has had to become increasingly professional. As one recent account has noted: "Although some nonprofit industries, such as education and health care, had been professionally managed for decades, by the end of the Reagan era, professionalization had penetrated every area in which nonprofits operated, including religion."[13]

To meet the resulting demand for more professionalized staff, new nonprofit management training programs have been organized at universities throughout the country. As of 1997, 76 such programs had been created, up from only 17 as recently as 1990.[14] Of these, 43 percent operate as parts of public administration or policy studies programs, 14 percent are concentrations within essentially business management schools, and the rest are either free-standing or parts of other departments.

While this professionalization has its costs, as will be detailed below, it also brings with it the potential for improving the quality of nonprofit operations and attracting higher quality personnel. This, in turn, can contribute to the sector's reputation for effectiveness and competence.

4. Reinvigoration of the Grass-Roots Base

While the nonprofit sector has grown increasingly professional, there is also evidence of continued vitality in the grass-roots base of the sector throughout the country. Challenging academic concerns about a loss of vital "social capital,"[15] journalist Robin Garr, for example, has detected a widespread process of community reinvention underway in America. Responding to the twin challenges of federal budget cuts and economic recession in the early 1980s, a wide assortment of emergency feeding programs, temporary housing facilities, AIDS clinics, and self-help groups of various sorts popped up in communities across the land. As problems persisted, moreover, "emergency facilities evolved into congregate shelters, soup kitchens, and food banks, and ultimately into multiple-purpose

"Responding to the twin challenges of federal budget cuts and economic recession in the early 1980s, a wide assortment of emergency feeding programs, temporary housing facilities, AIDS clinics, and self-help groups of various sorts popped up in communities across the land."

organizations that didn't just feed the hungry and homeless people, but sought to identify their problems and do whatever was needed to move them back into the mainstream."[16]

Not only the needs of the poor, but recently other needs as well have been the focus of grass-roots civic action. Data assembled by Professor Sydney Verba of Harvard, for example, reveals that almost 80 percent of Americans reported an affiliation with at least one association as of the early 1990s.[17] This included 44 percent who were affiliated with a charitable or social service organization, 25 percent with an education organization, 23 percent with a business or professional association, and 21 percent with a hobby, sports, or leisure association. While labor union participation may have declined, new social movements have emerged to take labor's place as vehicles for recruiting new participants into civic life. The environmental movement, for example, has experienced a massive upsurge in recent years, doubling or tripling its members since 1980. Nor is this merely the "paper" membership sometimes assumed. Rather, a vibrant grass-roots culture has emerged involving hundreds of thousands of people. "On almost a daily basis," reports one account, "a plethora of meetings, social gatherings, hikes, bike trips, clean-up projects, rallies, nature workshops, and the like are held in communities across the nation by local chapters of national environmental organizations, as well as ad-hoc community groups."[18] From this and related data, a leading pollster concludes, to quote the title of his review article, "The Data Just Don't Show Erosion of America's Social Capital."[19] Evidently, the wellsprings of voluntary action continue to bubble in contemporary American society.

"...almost 80 percent of Americans reported an affiliation with at least one association as of the early 1990s."

5. Intergenerational Transfer of Wealth

A fifth potentially promising development for the nonprofit sector is the *intergenerational transfer of wealth* between the Depression-era generation and the postwar baby boomers that is anticipated over the next forty years. According to an influential 1993 study by economists Robert Avery and Michael Rendell of Cornell University, an extraordinary $10 trillion will be transferred in this process. This wealth accumulated in the hands of the Depression-era generation as a consequence of their relatively high propensity to save; their fortuitous investment during the 1950s and 1960s in relatively low-cost houses that then escalated in value during the real estate boom of the 1970s; and the stock market surge of the 1980s and 1990s, which substantially boosted the value of

"...a striking intergenerational transfer of wealth is anticipated over the next forty years, creating substantial opportunities for charitable bequests."

their investments. Also contributing have been powerful economic trends and policies that have substantially increased income levels at the upper end of the income scale, accentuating income inequalities but leaving substantial sums of money in the hands of smaller numbers of people. Between 1979 and 1992, for example, the share of the nation's wealth controlled by the top 1 percent of households climbed from 20 percent to over 40 percent. Indeed, one third of the projected intergenerational transfer is expected to go to 1 percent of the baby-boomer generation, for an average inheritance of $1.6 million per person among this select few.[20]

To be sure, the lengthening life expectancy noted above may dissipate much of this wealth in heavy health care and nursing home expenses. What is more, the stock market volatility of 1998 provides a powerful reminder of the ephemeral quality of much of this presumed new wealth. Nevertheless, with so much money "in play," substantial opportunities likely exist for the expansion of charitable bequests. The experience of the 1980s is certainly encouraging in this respect. During that decade alone, about a third of all foundations now in existence were formed, including 3,000 with assets of at least $1 million.[21]

6. A New Approach to Corporate Philanthropy

Finally, new strategies of corporate social involvement have surfaced that hold promise of further encouragement to nonprofit action. While corporate giving has proved far more disappointing than many hoped in the early 1980s, numerous corporations have begun integrating social responsibility activities into their overall corporate business strategies. This has been done in part to win consumer confidence and in part to foster greater employee loyalty and morale, and thus to promote the "total quality" commitment that firms have increasingly pursued.

The great virtue of this new strategic approach to corporate social responsibility is that it makes corporate managers available to nonprofit organizations not simply as donors, but as allies and collaborators in a wide range of socially important missions, from improving the well-being of children to protecting natural resources. While there are dangers of exploitation of the good names of nonprofit organizations to promote the narrow commercial objectives of companies, there are also intriguing possibilities for extremely productive partnerships that could pay off handsomely for nonprofit organizations and those they serve.[22]

"Thanks to a new strategic approach to social involvement on the part of many corporations, corporate managers are becoming available to nonprofit organizations not simply as donors, but as allies and collaborators...."

Major Challenges

While the American nonprofit sector stands to benefit from a number of supportive trends, however, it also faces enormous challenges. In part, these challenges grow out of limitations in the positive trends. Despite the significant evidence of continued revitalization of the organizational base of the sector, for example, the new grass-roots organizations have increasingly come up against the hard realities of institutional survival on the basis of private charitable support alone and have therefore found it necessary to turn to governmental resources like the older organizations before them. Similarly, while the prospect of significant intergenerational wealth transfer and a changing corporate posture toward the voluntary sector offer much-needed relief, the extent of this relief is open to serious question. After all, charitable giving is not the only potential use of the new wealth, and investment managers have been hard at work devising more profitable alternatives. What is more, the projected inheritances may never materialize, or never materialize to the extent anticipated, if life expectancy continues to expand and medical or nursing care costs absorb more than the anticipated share of the accumulation. Certainly the recent record of bequest giving offers little encouragement. Far from increasing, the relative level of such giving has been on the decline. Similarly, the reorientation of corporate philanthropy has recently run headlong into the imperatives of corporate downsizing. In re-engineering the corporation, many corporate managements are re-engineering the corporate philanthropy function out of existence.

Under these circumstances, the pressures on the nation's nonprofit sector are likely to persist. More specifically, the nonprofit sector faces four rather serious challenges at the present time.

1. The Fiscal Challenge

The first of these challenges is essentially fiscal in character. As previous chapters have made clear, much of the growth of the nonprofit sector in the United States took place during the 1960s and 1970s and was fueled in large part by government support. In a sense, government became the principal philanthropist of the nonprofit sector, significantly boosting nonprofit revenues in a wide variety of fields and freeing the sector of its total dependence on the far-less-reliable base of private charitable support.

With the election of the Reagan administration in 1980 and the launching of a major program of fiscal retrenchment, however, this widespread pattern of

> *"While the American nonprofit sector stands to benefit from a number of supportive trends, it also faces enormous challenges."*

government–nonprofit partnership was subjected to considerable strain. Convinced that government had displaced nonprofit organizations, the Reagan administration set out to get government out of the sector's way, and Congress initially went along with many of the early cuts. Overlooked in the process, however, was the extent to which the programs being cut delivered support to the nonprofit organizations that were supposed to pick up the slack. As a consequence, not only were significant reductions in federal spending enacted in many of the key fields where nonprofit organizations are active, at least outside of health care; but also these reductions translated into revenue losses for nonprofit organizations in these fields.

Although spending levels recovered somewhat in the late 1980s and early 1990s, the election of a highly conservative Congress in 1994 revived the retrenchment process. As of 1998, therefore, the real value of federal spending on programs of special interest to nonprofit organizations, outside of the health field, still stood some 25 percent *below* what it had been in Fiscal Year 1980, almost two decades before. This, in turn, has translated into revenue losses for a broad cross-section of nonprofit organizations in such fields as employment and training, community development, international assistance, social services, and education. Thus the value of federal support to nonprofit community development and international aid organizations as of 1998 was 46 percent and 41 percent, respectively, below its 1980 level; while for nonprofit organizations in the fields of social services, education, and employment and training federal support ended up as of FY 1998 still 11 percent below its level in 1980.[23] Indeed, the revenue that nonprofit organizations lost from the federal government over the period 1980 to 1994 alone was equivalent to the *total amount of foundation grants they received between 1970 and 1990!* The upshot has been a considerable fiscal squeeze on the nation's nonprofit organizations.

Nor does this process seem likely to abate in the foreseeable future, despite the elimination of the national budget deficit in the latter 1990s. To the contrary, the budget proposals advanced by the Clinton administration in February 1998 would exact further reductions in federal support to nonprofit organizations, at least outside of the health field. Under these proposals, federal support to nonprofit organizations outside of health would decline an additional 2 percent between FY 1998 and FY 2003. This translates into an additional cumulative loss of $13 billion in revenue compared to what would be

"...because of federal budgetary stringency, nonprofit organizations have confronted a significant fiscal squeeze over the past decade and a half, and this squeeze is likely to continue."

available if FY 1980 spending levels were to be maintained over this period. Worse yet, the Congress appears headed for even steeper reductions.

Compounding the fiscal situation facing nonprofit organizations is the fact that charitable giving has not grown fast enough to offset the cuts and allow the sector to respond to the needs that exist. Recent data indicate that the share of household income being devoted to charitable giving has actually been declining — from an average of 1.86 percent during the 1970s to 1.78 percent during the 1980s and 1.72 percent during the early 1990s. Reflecting this, giving grew by *less than 1 percent in real terms during the early 1990s*. Similarly, the average contribution per return among upper income taxpayers has declined steadily from the early 1980s to the early 1990s — from over $200,000 in 1980 to just over $60,000 in 1993.[24] Reflecting these trends, far from filling in for government cutbacks, private giving actually lost ground as a source of nonprofit income during the decade that began with the Reagan budget cuts, falling from 15 percent of total nonprofit revenue in 1982 to 10 percent in 1996.[25] Although there is some evidence that private individual giving may have grown more substantially in the mid-1990s, the stock market volatility of 1998 suggests that this gain may not be permanent.

2. Intensified Economic Competition

In the face of this budgetary pressure, nonprofit organizations have either had to reduce their services or find alternative sources of support.[26] From the evidence at hand, it seems clear that the sector has mostly pursued the latter of these courses. Reflecting this, nonprofit revenue actually grew faster between 1977 and 1996 than the U.S. economy as a whole (96 percent vs. 62 percent), as Figure 5.6 showed. What is more, this growth was not limited to the hospital and health sector, which has traditionally grown faster than the general economy. Rather, the income of social service and arts and culture organizations grew even faster, and only education organization income lagged behind.

One explanation for this growth was that the budget cuts of the early 1980s barely touched the entitlement programs in the health field, such as Medicare and Medicaid, which continued to pump public resources into the health and nursing home portion of the nonprofit sector. In addition, state and local governments boosted their own levels of support in a number of fields. As a consequence, despite declines in government support in some areas, government assistance still contributed 40 percent of the increased revenues that nonprofit organizations captured during the 1980s and early 1990s.

Even more important as a source of nonprofit growth, however, was *fee and service-charge revenue.* As we have seen, this source alone accounted for 55 percent of the growth of the nonprofit sector during the 1977–1996 period. By contrast, private giving accounted for only 4 percent, well below the share with which it started. What is more, this pattern was not restricted simply to health and higher education, where fees have historically played a significant role. Rather, social service agencies more than tripled their share of income coming from fees and charges. In short, faced with the possibility of significant government cutbacks and unable to generate sufficient income from private giving, American nonprofit organizations moved much more massively into the commercial market.

However, while this "marketization"[27] has enabled nonprofit organizations to survive the Reagan-era budget cuts and prosper, it has also exposed them to a second serious challenge, the challenge of economic competition. In a sense, the nonprofit sector has been the victim of its own success. Having created, or newly entered, markets that could yield substantial commercial returns, it is now encountering intense competition from for-profit providers attracted to these same markets and better able to generate the capital investments that technological changes in these fields make increasingly necessary. In the process, operating margins are being squeezed so severely that it is undermining the ability of the nonprofit providers to subsidize the "mission-related" activities, such as charity care or research, that pushed them into these markets in the first place. This has, in turn, narrowed the differences between nonprofit and for-profit providers, raising fundamental questions about the justification for the tax advantages that nonprofit organizations enjoy and inducing nonprofits to convert to for-profit status in order to attract the capital required to survive.

In this way, through a series of incremental steps, the basic viability of the nonprofit form appears to be under challenge in a number of fields. While it may be premature to conclude, paraphrasing T.S. Eliot's "The Hollow Men," that this is the way the nonprofit sector will end, "not with a bang but a whimper," the fact remains that numerous nonprofit organizations are facing serious challenges of precisely this sort. As previous chapters have shown, moreover, these pressures are widespread. In particular:

- **In health care**, while the overall number of hospitals was declining between 1980 and 1989 as a result of overall competitive pressures, the number of for-profit hospitals increased by 30 percent and the number of beds they control grew by 41 percent. Moreover, this trend continued into the 1990s. Thus, between 1989 and 1996, the number of for-profit hospitals and for-profit hospital beds increased by 8 percent and 11 percent, respectively, while the number of nonprofit hospitals and beds declined by 8 percent and 12 percent, respectively. What is more, nonprofit Blue Cross and Blue Shield insurance organizations are undergoing similar transformations in major markets from California to New York.[28]

"...the real story of the past two decades is the steady penetration of for-profit firms into domains that were once the nearly exclusive preserve of nonprofit providers...."

What lies behind these changes are a series of profound shifts in the basic structure of the health care market, as both private employers and the government health insurance programs have moved away from cost-based reimbursement for medical services toward pre-paid insurance plans that put a premium on lowering hospital costs. These shifts have also necessitated complex consortia arrangements in order to attract sufficient numbers of patients, which in turn have required heavy capital investments in information systems and marketing activities. Because of their inability to offer investors a return on their equity, nonprofit hospitals have found it difficult to raise the needed capital and thus to compete effectively in this arena.

- In **human services** as well, considerable growth has occurred in nonprofit income from fees and charges, attracting for-profit providers into the field. As we have seen, moreover, the for-profit providers seem to be gaining the edge in a number of areas. Thus, they accounted for 70 percent of the growth in day-care employment and three-quarters of the growth in home health employment between 1977 and 1992 even though they started the period with far smaller shares in both. The appearance of HMO-type arrangements in the social services field makes it clear, moreover, that these trends are likely to continue.

- Even in **education**, for-profit firms appear to be challenging the nonprofit sector's role.

In short, despite recent complaints from small businessmen about "unfair competition" from nonprofits, the real story of the past two decades is the steady penetration of for-profit firms into domains that were once the nearly exclusive preserve of nonprofit providers, threatening the nonprofit sector's continued existence, and certainly its prominence, in the process.

3. The Effectiveness Challenge

In addition to the fiscal and economic challenges confronting the nonprofit sector at the present time is a third challenge, a veritable crisis of effectiveness.

Because they do not meet a "market test," nonprofits are always vulnerable to charges of inefficiency and ineffectiveness. However, the scope and severity of these charges have grown massively in recent years. In fact, the competence of the nonprofit sector has been challenged on at least four different grounds.

"...nonprofit organizations generally lack meaningful bases for demonstrating the value of what they do."

Programmatic Opposition. In the first place, nonprofit organizations, particularly in the human service field, have been implicated in the general assault on public social programs that has animated national political debate for more than a decade now. Despite considerable contrary evidence,[29] the persistence of poverty, the alarming growth of urban crime, the epidemic of teen-age pregnancy, and the continuation of welfare dependency have been taken as evidence that these programs do not work. The resulting open season on government social programs has caught significant components of the nonprofit sector in the cross-fire, particularly since the sector has been involved in administering many of the discredited programs.

Worse than that, the very motives of the nonprofit agencies have been called into question. Involvement in government programs "changes charities' incentives," charges one recent critique, "giving them reasons to keep caseloads up instead of getting them down by successfully turning around peoples' lives."[30] Nonprofits thus stand accused not only of being ineffective, but also of preferring not to solve the problems they are purportedly addressing.

Reconceptualization of Social Assistance. Underlying this critique of public social programs is a profound rethinking of the causes of poverty and of the interventions likely to reduce it. The central change here involves a loss of faith in the traditional premise of professional social work, with its emphasis on casework and individualized services as the cure for poverty and distress. During the 1960s, this precept was translated into public policy through the 1962 amendments to the Social Security Act and, later, through portions of the Economic Opportunity Act of 1964, both of which made federal resources available to purchase social services for poor people in the hope that this would allow them to escape the "culture of poverty" in which they were enmeshed.

This "services strategy" has now been challenged by critics on both the right and the left. Those on the right have argued that the growth of supportive services and income assistance for the poor ultimately proved counter-productive because they created disincentives to work and undermined fundamental values of self-reliance. Those on the left, by contrast, point to the structural shifts in the economy that have eliminated much of the market for blue-collar labor, and not a lack of services, as the real causes of poverty, unemployment, and the social maladies that flow from them. Both sides seem to agree, however, that the traditional skills of the nonprofit human service sector have become increasingly irrelevant to the problems facing the poor. More important than social services in the new paradigm is job-readiness, and ultimately a job. Under these circumstances, the employer rather than the social worker becomes the pivot of social policy. While private nonprofit organizations may still play a role in the alleviation of poverty, the real action has shifted to the business community and the educational system. This is clearly reflected in the welfare reform law of 1996, which ended the entitlement to assistance and placed much heavier emphasis on employment as a condition of assistance. All of this threatens to push the nonprofit sector more to the periphery of social problem-solving, at least so far as the poor are concerned.

The Accountability Movement. Complicating matters further is the fact that nonprofit organizations generally lack meaningful bases for demonstrating the value of what they do. Indeed, nonprofit organizations have often resisted demands for greater accountability on grounds that responding to such demands might interfere with the independence that gives the sector its special character. Instead, nonprofits have tended to point to their not-for-profit status as *ipso facto* evidence of their trustworthiness and effectiveness.

Increasingly, however, these implicit claims by nonprofit providers have been subjected to serious challenge as a result not only of a number of recent scandals, but also of growing questions about the basic efficiency and effectiveness of nonprofit

"Recent thinking is making the employer rather than the social worker the pivot of social policy."

agencies. "Unlike publicly traded companies," management expert Regina Herzlinger has thus noted, "the performance of nonprofits and governments is shrouded behind a veil of secrecy that is lifted only when blatant disasters occur."[31] This is problematic, she argues, because nonprofit organizations generally lack the three basic accountability mechanisms of business: the self-interest of owners, competition, and the ultimate bottom-line measure of profitability. This has prompted calls on the part of even advocates of the sector for more formalized mechanisms for holding nonprofit organizations accountable for the pursuit of their charitable missions.[32]

The Professionalization Critique. One response to this criticism has been to professionalize the operation of nonprofit organizations. But this has opened these organizations to another line of criticism that takes them to task for becoming a principal locus for the "overprofessionalization" of societal problem-solving. This line of argument has a long lineage in American politics, but it has taken on new energy in recent years as critics on both the left and the right have pummeled nonprofit providers for their tendency toward professionalization and have called for a return to the simple virtues of self-help, faith-based charity, or other community-based approaches. According to this line of thinking, the professionalization of social concerns, by redefining basic human needs as "problems" that only professionals can resolve, has alienated people from the helping relationships they could establish with their neighbors and kin. "Through the propagation of belief in authoritative expertise," Northwestern University Professor John McKnight thus notes, "professionals cut through the social fabric of community and sow clienthood where citizenship once grew."[33]

4. The Legitimacy Challenge

All of this, finally, has led to a fourth challenge for the nonprofit sector, a much more serious and profound crisis of legitimacy that is questioning the whole concept of the nonprofit sector. Ironically, the nonprofit sector's success in adjusting to the realities of postwar, and then post-Reagan, American society may be costing it the support of significant elements of the American public as a massive mismatch has opened between the sector's actual operations and popular conceptions of what it is supposed to be like, conceptions that the sector itself has helped to promote.

"... nonprofit organizations are increasingly taken to task for becoming a principal locus for the overprofessionalization of societal problem-solving."

"Ironically, the nonprofit sector's success in adjusting to the realities of postwar, and then post-Reagan, American society may be costing it the support of significant elements of the American public...."

"...a massive mismatch has opened between the nonprofit sector's actual operations and popular conceptions of what it is supposed to be like....."

In its public persona, the nonprofit sector still holds to a quaint nineteenth-century image of charity and altruism, of small voluntary groups ministering to the needy and downtrodden. In reality, however, the actual operations of the nonprofit sector have become far more complex. Thus, for example, instead of private philanthropy, fees and service charges are now the sector's principal source of support. Similarly, the sector's complex relationships with government have also not been fully integrated into prevailing conceptions of the sector and consequently remain somehow suspect. Even the nonprofit sector's involvement in advocacy has been called into question. Having joined with government to respond to public needs, nonprofit organizations are now in the uncomfortable position of appearing to advocate not on behalf of the clients and communities they serve, but in their own self interest, for the budgets and programs that support their own operations, a point that conservative critics of government spending have made a particular point of attack.

Taking advantage of the resulting questioning, local governments have been increasingly emboldened to challenge the tax exemptions of nonprofit organizations. Such challenges have surfaced vigorously in Pennsylvania, New York, New Hampshire, Oregon, Maine, Wisconsin, and Colorado.

More recently, Congressional critics brought the same questioning to one of the other fundamental functions of the voluntary sector — its advocacy and representational function. Under the so-called Istook Amendment, named after its Congressional sponsor, nonprofit organizations receiving federal grants could not use more than 5 percent of their total revenues, including their private revenues, for a broad range of advocacy activities. This would significantly broaden existing restrictions on nonprofit lobbying and advocacy. Though ultimately defeated, this amendment evidences the considerable questioning of nonprofit activity that has surfaced recently.

Indeed, recent surveys suggest a distressing loss of public confidence in nonprofit institutions. A Gallup survey in 1994, for example, showed that only about one-third of the American population felt "a great deal" or "quite a lot" of confidence in nonprofit organizations outside of religion or education. This is well above the 15 percent who expressed this level of confidence in the federal government and the 23 percent who had "a great deal" or "quite a lot" of confidence in state governments. But it was still far behind the 47 percent confidence levels the federal government enjoyed in 1975, and the 52 percent and 48 percent levels that small businesses and the military enjoyed as of 1994.[34]

Needed: A Renewal Strategy

Whether the supportive trends or the significant challenges facing the nonprofit sector at the present time will prevail is difficult to determine with any precision. To a significant extent, the answer to this question will depend on forces outside the sector's control — the shifting realities of political life, the resulting patterns of government policy, and broader economic trends. Nevertheless, how well the sector will be able to take advantage of the opportunities and fend off the perils will depend also on how well prepared it is, and how well prepared it makes those on whom it relies.

From the evidence at hand, it appears that this preparation is far from adequate. To correct this, a serious strategy of *renewal* seems to be needed. Such a renewal strategy could usefully involve five basic tasks.

"To cope with the challenges it faces, the American nonprofit sector needs a comprehensive renewal strategy."

Values and Visioning

In the first place, renewal requires a re-examination of basic values. As John Gardner has put it in his book, *Self-Renewal*, "Anyone concerned about the continuous renewal of society must be concerned for the renewal of that society's values and beliefs."[35] For a variety of reasons, the evolution of the nonprofit sector in the United States has leaped beyond existing concepts about how this set of institutions is supposed to operate:

- Traditional concepts of charity and altruism, of care for the less fortunate, now sit uneasily with the reality of large-scale charitable enterprises headed by well-paid professionals and providing assistance to far more than those in greatest financial need.

- The religious taproots of the charitable sector, with their emphasis on sacrifice and duty, must now make room for new impulses stressing empowerment, self-realization, self-help, and even self-interest.

- A sector whose mythology celebrates independence must now come to terms with the need for close working relationships with business and government to solve pressing public problems.

- Traditional notions of arms-length philanthropy, alms-giving, and service as the principal vehicles of nonprofit action must be reconciled with new demands for citizen involvement, for active engagement in societal problem-solving, and even for direct means for deciding which public goods are worthy of support.

Rather than seeing these challenges facing the nonprofit sector as an excuse for retreat into some mythical golden age of nonprofit independence, or a time for continued drift toward greater commercialization, a renewal strategy would view them as an occasion, and an opportunity, for *renewal*, for rethinking the nonprofit sector's role and operations, for re-examining the prevailing mythology in the light of contemporary realities, and for achieving a new consensus, a new settlement, regarding the functions of nonprofit organizations, the relationships they have with citizens, with government, and with business, and the way they will operate in the years ahead. This may require the formation of Civil Society Commissions embracing government, nonprofit, and business leaders in local areas throughout the country and more explicit attention to underlying values in the training of nonprofit managers and in the development of organizational plans.

"In addition to renewing the sector's basic values, more effective efforts need to be made to monitor the fiscal and operational health of the nonprofit sector on a timely basis...."

Monitoring

In addition to renewing the sector's basic values, more effective efforts need to be made to monitor the fiscal and operational health of the nonprofit sector on a timely basis, to chart the sector's position *vis-a-vis* government and the business sector, and to identify challenges before they become irreversible. Although the information now available on the nonprofit sector in the United States is vastly improved over what it was a decade and a half ago, up-to-date information on how policy changes are affecting this set of institutions, and how nonprofit organizations are faring in their competition with for-profit businesses, is generally lacking. The Census of Service Industries, which regularly charts such matters, does so only every five years, and several years typically elapse between the taking of the Census and the reporting of the results. Internal Revenue Service data are potentially available, but are imperfect at best. For-profit firms would not stand for the lack of basic information that still afflicts much of the nonprofit sector and steps are needed to create a more effective monitoring system than now exists.

Reconnecting the Sector to its Citizen Base

In addition to renewing values and monitoring trends, more concrete actions may also be needed to revitalize America's nonprofit sector and connect it more securely to its citizen base. Illustrative of the kinds of actions that might usefully be considered are the following:

- Replacement of the current system of charitable tax deductions with a more direct "charity tax credit" that would reward contributions equally rather than offering more sizable incentives to high-income taxpayers, as is now the case;[36]

- Deregulation of nonprofit advocacy and policy involvement to stimulate greater nonprofit involvement in civic life;

- Greater use of matching grants by government — to tie public funding more directly to citizen desires and provide incentives for nonprofit organizations to preserve their volunteer and charitable bases of support.

Educating

Fourthly, to close the gap that has opened between popular beliefs and actual nonprofit operations, a sizable media campaign is needed. The point of this campaign should not be to celebrate nonprofit successes or reinforce the standard mythology about the importance of voluntarism and the accomplishments of private charity. What is needed instead is an explicit acknowledgment of the modern reality of collaborative problem-solving, of *nonprofit organizations working collaboratively with government and the business sector to respond to societal needs*. This is a complex message to be sure, but it is the one that accurately reflects the realities that currently exist, and that are likely to persist into the foreseeable future.

"What is needed is an explicit acknowledgment of the modern reality of collaborative problem-solving, of nonprofit organizations working collaboratively with government and the business sector to respond to societal needs."

Improving Accountability

Finally, in the wake of a number of celebrated scandals and much questioning of the legitimacy of nonprofit tax exemptions, efforts are needed to restore public trust in both the effectiveness and the honorableness of this sector. This will require strengthening the accountability mechanisms within the nonprofit sector and greater attention to measuring nonprofit results.

Conclusion and Implications

The building of sustainable nonprofit, or civil society, sectors has been a focus of immense concern in many parts of the world in recent years, from the newly emerging democracies of Central and Eastern Europe to the post-colonial regions of Africa, Asia, and Latin America. Taken for granted in these deliberations, however, has been the assumption that such a sector is already securely in place in much of the developed world, and certainly in the United States.

What the discussion here has made clear, however, is that the survival and prosperity of nonprofit institutions is not only at issue in the emerging democracies of the East and South, it is also very much in question in mature market economies such as the United States. Indeed, the very maturation and growth of nonprofit institutions may paradoxically pose challenges to their continued viability and support. Certainly in the United States, where a somewhat naive myth of voluntarism has long enveloped the nonprofit sector, recent years have witnessed a steady broadening of the gap between what nonprofit organizations have had to do to prosper and grow and what popular mythologies have expected them to do to retain public support. The upshot has been a crisis of legitimacy for America's nonprofit sector that has manifested itself in declining public confidence, growing demands for greater accountability, challenges to tax-exempt status, questioning of the sector's advocacy role, and a growing unease about a whole range of pay and perquisite issues.

What this suggests is that the nonprofit sector is an inherently fragile organism, even in societies like the United States where commitment to this type of organization is an integral part of national heritage. More than that, the role and character of these organizations can no more be frozen in time than those of other types of institutions: they must evolve in response to new circumstances and adapt to new opportunities and needs.

Those committed to the sustenance of a sphere of independent action outside the market and the state, whether in the United States or elsewhere, can therefore not afford to take the survival of this set of institutions for granted. To the contrary, they must continuously re-examine this sector in the light of broader societal trends and re-position it as needed to keep it vital as conditions change.

ENDNOTES

1. The discussion here draws heavily on Lester M. Salamon, *Holding the Center: America's Nonprofit Sector at a Crossroads* (New York: The Nathan Cummings Foundation, 1997).

2. Lester M. Salamon, "The Rise of the Nonprofit Sector," *Foreign Affairs*, 73, 4 (July/August 1994), pp. 109–122.

3. For more detail on many of the trends reported here, see Lester M. Salamon, "The Voluntary Sector and the Future of the Welfare State," *Nonprofit and Voluntary Sector Quarterly*, 1989 (1), pp. 11–24.

4. U.S. Bureau of the Census, *Statistical Abstract of the United States, 1997*, Tables 24 and 47; *1982/83*, Tables 27 and 30.

5. U.S. Bureau of the Census, *Statistical Abstract of the United States, 1997*, Table 620.

6. U.S. Bureau of the Census, *Statistical Abstract of the United States, 1997*, Table 631, p. 404.

7. U.S. Bureau of the Census, *Statistical Abstract of the United States, 1997*, Table 145, p. 105.

8. 1994 data from U.S. Bureau of the Census, *Statistical Abstract of the United States, 1997*, Table 97, p. 79.

9. 1995 data from U.S. Bureau of the Census, *Statistical Abstract of the United States, 1997*, Table 219, p. 144; 1977 data from U.S. Bureau of the Census, *Statistical Abstract of the United States, 1982/3*, Table 197, p. 124.

10. Based on data in *1977 Census of Service Industries* and *Service Annual Survey: 1995*.

11. For a discussion of the Reagan approach, see: Lester M. Salamon, "Nonprofit Organizations: The Lost Opportunity," in John L. Palmer and Isabel V. Sawhill, eds., *The Reagan Record* (Washington, D.C.: The Urban Institute, 1984), pp. 261–286.

12. The paid employment of public-benefit nonprofit organizations grew at an annual average rate of 3.3 percent between 1977 and 1994, compared to 1.9 percent for all nonagricultural employment. Bureau of Labor Statistics data as reported in *Nonprofit Almanac, 1996*, p. 129.

13. Peter Dobkin Hall, "Historical Perspectives on Nonprofit Organizations," in Robert D. Herman, ed., *The Jossey-Bass Handbook of Nonprofit Leadership and Management* (San Francisco: Jossey-Bass Publishers, 1994), p. 28.

14. Included here are only programs that offer three or more courses. Naomi Wish and Roseanne Mirabella, "Nonprofit Management Education: Current Offerings and Practices in University-Based Programs," *Nonprofit Management and Leadership*, Vol. 9, No. 1 (Fall 1998).

15. Concern about the deterioration of "social capital" in the United States has been expressed most vividly by Harvard political scientist Robert Putnam. See: Robert Putnam, "Bowling Alone: America's Declining Social Capital," *The Journal of Democracy* (Winter 1995).

16. Robin Garr, *Reinvesting in America: The Grassroots Movements that Are Feeding the Hungry, Housing the Homeless, and Putting Americans Back to Work* (Reading, MA: Addison-Wesley Publishing Company, 1995).

17. Sydney Verba et al. *Voice and Equality*, (Cambridge, MA: Harvard University Press, 1995), p. 63.

18. George Pettinico, "Civic Participation Alive and Well in Today's Environmental Groups," *The Public Perspective,* (June/July 1996).

19. Everett C. Ladd. "The Data Just Don't Show Erosion of America's Social Capital," *The Public Perspective* (June/July 1996), p. 1.

20. *Top Heavy* (New York: Twentieth Century Fund, 1995), Table A-1. For a summary of the recent thinking on this intergenerational wealth transfer, see: Harvey D. Shapiro, "The Coming Inheritance Bonanza," *Institutional Investor,* Vol XXXVIII, No. 6 (June 1994), pp. 143–148.

21. Loren Renz, *Foundation Giving, 1995.* (New York: The Foundation Center. 1995), p. 3.

22. Craig Smith, "The New Corporate Philanthropy," *Harvard Business Review* (May/June 1994), p. 107; Jane Nelson, *Business as Partners in Development: Creating Wealth for Countries, Companies, and Communities.* (London: Prince of Wales Business Leaders Forum, 1996).

23. Lester M. Salamon and Alan J. Abramson, *The Federal Budget and the Nonprofit Sector: President Clinton's FY 1999 Budget Proposals.* Report to Independent Sector, 1998

24. Internal Revenue Service data as reported in *Nonprofit Almanac, 1996–1997: Dimensions of the Independent Sector* (1996), pp. 88, 91.

25. See Chapter Three, Endnote 31.

26. A third option — increasing efficiency — is also theoretically available. However, this option has only limited applicability to many of the fields of nonprofit action given their labor-intensive, personal-care character.

27. Lester M. Salamon, "The Marketization of Welfare: Changing Nonprofit and For-Profit Roles in the American Welfare State," *Social Service Review,* Vol 67, No. 1 (March 1993), pp. 16–39.

28. American Hospital Association, *Hospital Statistics 1996.* (Chicago: American Hospital Association, 1998); Mort Freudenheim, "Health Plans in New Jersey Face Rivalries," *New York Times* (May 30, 1996); M. Freudenheim, "For Blue Cross at Crossroads, A Fight to Save Role for System," *New York Times* (June 15, 1996); M. Freudenheim, "Empire Blue Cross Seeks Permission to Earn Profits," *New York Times* (September 26, 1996).

29. See, for example: Lisbeth Schorr, *Within Our Reach: Breaking the Cycle of Disadvantage.* (New York: Anchor Books, 1988).

30. K. Dennis, "Charities on the Dole," *Policy Review: The Journal of American Citizenship,* (1996), p. 76.

31. Regina Herzlinger, "Can Public Trust in Nonprofits and Governments Be Restored? " *Harvard Business Review* (March/April, 1996), p.96.

32. Joel Fleischman, "To Merit and Preserve the Public's Trust in Not-For-Profit Organizations: The Urgent Need for New Strategies for Regulatory Reform," in Charles Clotfelter and Thomas Ehrlich, eds, *The Future of Philanthropy in a Changing America* (Bloomington: Indiana University Press, forthcoming).

33. John McKnight, *The Careless Society: Community and its Counterfeits*. (New York: Basic Books, 1995).

34. Independent Sector, *Giving and Volunteering in the United States: Findings of a National Survey* (analyzed by Virginia A. Hodgkinson and Murray S. Weitzman), 1996 Edition. (Washington: Independent Sector, 1996), p. 3–73.

35. John Gardner, *Self-Renewal: The Individual and the Innovative Society*. Revised edition. (New York: W. W. Norton, 1981), p. 115.

36. Under the current tax-deduction system, taxpayers deduct their charitable contributions from their taxable income and then pay taxes on the balance. The higher the tax bracket the taxpayer is in, therefore, the greater the deduction that a given contribution is worth. Under a "tax credit" system, by contrast, all or a portion of the value of a gift is deducted directly from the taxpayer's bill. Hence taxpayers get the same tax benefits from a given gift regardless of which tax bracket they are in.

CHAPTER THIRTEEN

Conclusions

Perhaps the central conclusion that flows from the foregoing chapters is that private, nonprofit organizations continue to play a significant role in American society despite the expanded role of government over the past half-century or more. This runs counter to much conventional wisdom, which has viewed this expansion of government action as fundamentally hostile to the preservation of a vibrant private, nonprofit sector. In fact, however, as we have seen, the growth of government activity in the American context has done at least as much to strengthen the nonprofit sector as to threaten it, and probably far more so. Because of American hostility to centralized government bureaucracies and the presence of significant nonprofit providers in many of the fields that government has entered, we have tended to rely heavily on nonprofit providers to deliver even publicly funded services — in health, in education, in social services, and even in arts and culture. As a consequence, the growth of government has helped to expand the nonprofit role, not limit or eliminate it, and as a consequence nonprofit organizations retain a significant foothold in virtually every sphere of human service.

This situation poses a serious challenge to the traditional terms and concepts commonly used to depict our social welfare system. Although government provides most of the funds in many of the key social welfare fields, private institutions deliver most of the services. Does this make the system public or private? Unfortunately, we do not even have the words to portray the situation. In some fields, such as hospital care, nonprofit organizations clearly play the largest role. In others, such as nursing home care, for-profit institutions are the major

> *"...the growth of government activity in the American context has done at least as much to strengthen the nonprofit sector as to threaten it, and probably far more so."*

"...nonprofit organizations are far more than deliverers of services: they also promote cultural values, facilitate citizen engagement in the policy process, build community, embody important national norms, and help us satisfy our spiritual needs."

"Penetrating the myths and improving understanding of this important set of institutions has become a matter of special urgency."

providers. Does this make the system mostly philanthropic or mostly commercial? Like the elephant examined by three blind men in the ancient tale, the American social welfare system appears to be a different beast depending on who touches it and where. It is, in fact, not a single system at all — whether governmental, nonprofit, or for-profit — but all three together. If "public–private partnership" is not a perfect way to characterize the reality that exists, it certainly comes closer than any of the other alternative concepts. But even this concept has limitations, because nonprofit organizations are often also in the position of criticizing and prodding government rather than simply cooperating with it to carry out public objectives. Indeed, as we have seen, these organizations are far more than deliverers of services: they also promote cultural values, facilitate citizen engagement in the policy process, build community, embody important national norms, and help us satisfy our spiritual needs.

While the "mixed" character of the American social welfare system makes it more difficult to comprehend and explain, it may also make it stronger and more capable of change. In a sense, Americans have surrendered the comprehensiveness and coherence of the social welfare systems of many European countries for the pluralism and adaptability of a much looser and more diverse system of mixed public and private care. In doing so, however, we have also taken on an added challenge of analysis and education to make our complex system comprehensible to our own citizenry and government officials as well as to those abroad interested in comprehending its lessons.

Unfortunately, ideological stereotypes and political rhetoric have kept us from meeting this challenge very effectively. As a consequence, the nonprofit sector remains shrouded in myths and barely perceptible to large portions of the American public. This is problematic not only because of the vital place these organizations continue to occupy in our national life, but also because of the serious risks they confront at the present time, risks arising from shifts in government policy, increased competition from for-profit providers, and a growing questioning of the contribution these organizations make. Penetrating the myths and improving understanding of this important set of institutions has thus become a matter of special urgency. If this primer has helped to contribute to such understanding, it will have served its purpose well.

References

AAFRC Trust for Philanthropy, Ann E. Kaplan, ed., *Giving USA:* 1997 (New York: AAFRC Trust for Philanthropy, 1997 [and earlier years]).

Advisory Committee on Voluntary Foreign Aid, *An Assessment of the State of the USAID/PVO Partnership* (Washington, DC: Advisory Committee on Voluntary Foreign Aid, June 1997).

AMCRA Foundation, "Managed Care Overview, 1994–5," (Washington, DC: AMCRA, 1995).

American Heart Association, World Wide Web Site, January 20, 1998.

American Hospital Association, *Hospital Statistics,* various years and special analyses (Chicago: American Hospital Association, various years).

Avery, R. and M. Rendell, "Inheritance and Wealth," Paper Prepared for Delivery at the American Statistical Association, 1993.

Bailey, A., "Health Care's Merger Mania," *Chronicle of Philanthropy,* (November 16, 1995).

Baltimore City Department of Planning, *Baltimore City's Community Association Directory* (1991).

Ben-Ner, Avner and Theresa van Hoomissen, "Nonprofit Organizations in the Mixed Economy: A Demand and Supply Analysis," in Avner Ben-Ner and Benedeto Gui, eds., *The Nonprofit Sector in the Mixed Economy* (Ann Arbor: The University of Michigan Press, 1993).

Berry, Jeffrey M., "Citizen Groups and the Changing Nature of Interest Groups in America," *Annals of the American Academy of Political Science,* No. 528 (July 1993), pp. 30–41.

Berry, Jeffrey M., *Lobbying for the People: The Political Behavior of Public Interest Groups* (Princeton: Princeton University Press, 1977).

Bixby, Ann Kallman, "Overview of Public Social Welfare Expenditures, Fiscal Year 1989," *Social Security Bulletin,* Vol. 54, No. 10 (November 1991).

Bixby, Ann Kallman, "Public Social Welfare Expenditures, Fiscal Years 1965–87," *Social Security Bulletin,* Vol. 53, No. 2 (February 1991), pp. 1–25.

Bixby, Ann Kallman, "Public Social Welfare Expenditures, Fiscal Year 1994, *Social Security Bulletin,* Vol. 60, No. 3 (1997), p. 40.

Bixby, Ann Kallman, "Social Welfare Expenditures, 1963–83," *Social Security Bulletin,* Vol. 49, No. 2 (February 1986), pp. 12–21.

Brenton, Maria, *The Voluntary Sector in British Social Services* (London: Longman, 1985).

Brilliant, Eleanor, *The United Way: Dilemmas of Organized Charity* (New York: Columbia University Press, 1991).

Brown, M., "Commentary: The Commercialization of America's Voluntary Health Care System," *Health Care Management Review,* 21:3 (1996), pp. 13–18.

Charities Aid Foundation, *Charity Trends,* 13th ed. (London: Charities Aid Foundation, 1990).

Clark, Charles S., "Arts Funding," *CQ Researcher,* Vol. 4, No. 39 (October 21, 1994).

Cobb, Nina Kressner, *Looking Ahead: Private Sector Giving to the Arts and the Humanities* (Washington, DC: President's Committee on the Arts and the Humanities, n.d. [1977]).

Coleman, James S., *Foundations of Social Theory* (Cambridge, MA: Harvard University Press, 1990).

Commission on Philanthropy and Public Needs, *Giving in America: Toward a Stronger Voluntary Sector* (Washington, DC: Commission on Private Philanthropy and Public Needs, 1975).

Council for Aid to Education, *1996 Voluntary Support of Education* (prepared by David Morgan) (New York: Council for Aid to Education).

Council for Aid to Education, *Voluntary Support of Education,* 1986–87 (New York: Council for Aid to Education, 1988).

Dennis, Kimberly, "Charities on the Dole," *Policy Review: The Journal of American Citizenship* (March/April 1996), p. 5.

de Tocqueville, Alexis, *Democracy in America.* The Henry Reeve Text, Vol. II (New York: Vintage Books, 1945 [1835]).

DiMaggio, Paul, "Nonprofit Organizations in the Production and Distribution of Culture," in Walter

Powell, ed., *The Nonprofit Sector: A Research Handbook* (New Haven: Yale University Press,1987), pp. 195–220.

Fetter, F., *"The Subsidizing of Private Charities,"* American Journal of Sociology (1901–2), pp. 359–85.

Fisher, J., *The Road from Rio: Sustainable Development and the Nongovernmental Movement in the Third World* (Connecticut: Praeger, 1993).

Fleischman, Joel, "To Merit and Preserve the Public's Trust in Non-For-Profit Organizations: The Urgent Need for New Strategies for Regulatory Reform," in Charles Clotfelter and Thomas Erlich, eds., *The Future of Philanthropy in a Changing America* (Bloomington: Indiana University Press, forthcoming).

Foundation Center, *Foundation Giving* [1998 and earlier editions], compiled by Loren Renz, Crystal Mandler, and Rikard Treiber (New York: The Foundation Center).

Foundation Center, *Foundations Today,* 7th ed. Compiled by Loren Renz (New York: The Foundation Center, 1990).

Freudenheim, Mort, "Empire Blue Cross Seeks Permission to Earn Profits," *New York Times* (September 26, 1996).

Freudenheim, Mort, "For Blue Cross at Crossroads, A Fight to Save Role for System," *New York Times* (June 15, 1996).

Freudenheim, Mort, "Health Plans in New Jersey Face Rivalries," *New York Times* (May 30, 1996).

Gardner, John, *Self-Renewal: The Individual and the Innovative Society,* Revised Edition (New York: W.W. Norton, 1981).

Garr, Robin, *Reinvesting in America: The Grassroots Movements that Are Feeding the Hungry, Housing the Homeless and Putting Americans Back to Work* (Reading, MA: Addison- Wesley, 1995).

Gidron, Benjamin, Ralph Kramer, and Lester M. Salamon, eds., *Government and the Nonprofit Sector: Emerging Relationships in Welfare States* (San Francisco: Jossey-Bass, 1992).

Grønbjerg, Kirsten and Sheila Nelson, "Mapping Small Religious Nonprofit Organizations: An Illinois Profile," *Nonprofit and Voluntary Sector Quarterly,* Vol. 27, No. 1 (March 1998), pp. 13–31.

Hall, Peter Dobkin, "A Historical Overview of the Private Nonprofit Sector," in Walter Powell, ed., *The Nonprofit Sector: A Research Handbook* (New Haven: Yale University Press, 1987), pp. 3–26.

Hall, Peter Dobkin, "Historical Perspectives on Nonprofit Organizations," in Robert D. Herman, ed., *The Jossey-Bass Handbook of Nonprofit Leadership and Management* (San Francisco: Jossey-Bass, 1994), pp. 3–43.

Hansmann, Henry, "The Role of Nonprofit Enterprise," *Yale Law Journal,* Vol. 89 (1990), pp.835–901.

Hansmann, Henry, "Why Are Nonprofit Organizations Exempted from Corporate Income Taxation," in Michelle J. White, ed., *Nonprofit Firms in a Three-Sector Economy, COUPE Papers* (Washington, DC: The Urban Institute Press, 1981).

Hart and Teeter, "A National Public Opinion Survey Conducted for the Council for Excellence in Government" (Washington, DC: Council for Excellence in Government, 1995).

Hasan, M., "Let's End the Nonprofit Charade," *New England Journal of Medicine,* 334:16 (1995), pp. 1055–8.

Herzlinger, Regina, "Can Public Trust in Nonprofits and Governments Be Restored?" *Harvard Business Review* (March/April, 1996), pp. 97–107.

Hodgkinson, Virginia A., Murray S. Weitzman, Christopher Toppe, and Stephen M. Noga, *Nonprofit Almanac 1992–1993: Dimensions of the Independent Sector* (San Francisco: Jossey-Bass, 1992).

Hodgkinson, Virginia A. and Murray S. Weitzman with John A. Abrahams, Eric A. Crutchfield, and David R. Stevenson, *Nonprofit Almanac 1996–1997: Dimensions of the Independent Sector* (San Francisco: Jossey Bass, 1996).

Hopkins, Bruce R., *The Law of Tax-Exempt Organizations,* 6th ed. (New York: John Wiley and Sons, 1992).

Independent Sector, *America's Nonprofit Sector in Brief* (Washington, DC: Independent Sector, Spring 1998).

Independent Sector, *From Belief to Commitment: The Community Service Activities and Finances of Religious Congregations in the United States.* Findings From National Survey. 1993 Edition. Analyzed by Hodgkinson, Virginia A. and Murray S. Weitzman with Arthur D. Kirsch, Stephen M. Noga, and Heather A. Gorski (Washington: Independent Sector, 1993), pp. 2–3.

Independent Sector, *Giving and Volunteering in the United States.* Analyzed by Virginia A. Hodgkinson and Murray Weitzman (Washington, DC: Independent Sector, 1996).

James, Estelle, "The Nonprofit Sector in Comparative Perspective," in Walter Powell, ed., *The Nonprofit*

Sector: A Research Handbook (New Haven: Yale University Press, 1987), pp. 397–415.

Jones, Chris, "Monster or Mainstay?" *American Theatre* (March 1996).

Kendall, Jeremy and Martin Knapp, "The United Kingdom," in Lester M. Salamon and Helmut K. Anheier, eds., *Defining the Nonprofit Sector: A Cross-National Analysis* (Manchester, U.K.: Manchester University Press, 1996), p. 249–279.

Kramer, Ralph, *Voluntary Agencies in the Welfare State* (Berkeley: University of California Press, 1981).

Krashinsky, Michael, "Stakeholder Theories of the Nonprofit Sector: One Cut at the Economic Literature," *Voluntas*, Vol. 8, No. 2 (1997), pp. 149–161.

Ladd, Everett C., "The Data Just Don't Show Erosion of America's Social Capital," *The Public Perspective* (June/July 1996), pp. 1–8.

Logan, D., D. Roy, and L. Regelbrugge, *Global Corporate Citizenship–Rationale and Strategies* (Washington, DC: The Hitachi Foundation, 1997).

Lowi, Theodore, *The End of Liberalism* (New York: W.W. Norton, 1979).

Lubove, Roy, *The Struggle for Social Security, 1900–1935* (Cambridge: Harvard University Press, 1968).

McKnight, John, *The Careless Society: Community and its Counterfeits* (New York: Basic Books, 1995).

Meyer, H., T. Hudson, J.E. Cain, S.L. Carr, and D. Zacharias, "Selling...or Selling Out." *Hospitals and Health Networks*, (June 5, 1996), pp. 21–46.

Moore, Jennifer, "A Corporate Challenge for Charities," *Chronicle of Philanthropy*, Vol. X, No. 20 (August 13, 1998), p.1.

National Center for Health Statistics, *National Home and Hospice Care Survey* (February 1997).

National Commission on Philanthropy and Civic Renewal, *Giving Better/Giving Smarter: Renewing Philanthropy in America*, Report of the National Commission on Philanthropy and Civic Renewal (Washington, DC: National Commission on Philanthropy and Civic Renewal, 1997).

Nelson, Jane, *Business as Partners in Development: Creating Wealth for Countries, Companies , and Communities* (London: Prince of Wales Business Leaders Forum, 1996).

Nielsen, Waldemar, *The Endangered Sector* (New York: Columbia University Press, 1979).

O'Connell, Brian, *People Power: Service, Advocacy, Empowerment* (New York: The Foundation Center, 1994).

O'Neill, Michael, *The Third America: The Emergence of the Nonprofit Sector in the United States* (San Francisco: Jossey-Bass, 1989).

Organization for Economic Cooperation and Development (OECD), *National Accounts,* Vol. II (Paris: OECD, 1997).

Organization for Economic Cooperation and Development (OECD), *National Accounts, Detailed Tables, 1976–1988* (Paris: OECD, 1991).

Pettinico, George, "Civic Participation Alive and Well in Today's Environmental Groups," *The Public Perspective* (June/July 1996).

Pollack, Tom, "A Profile of Religious Organizations in the IRS Business Master File and Return Transaction Files," A Paper Prepared for Presentation at the ARNOVA Conference, 1997.

Potter, M. and Longest, B. "The Divergence of Federal and State Policies on the Charitable Tax Exemption of Nonprofit Hospitals," *Journal of Health Politics, Policy, and Law,* 19:2 (Summer 1994), pp. 393–419.

Powell, Walter, ed. *The Nonprofit Sector: A Research Handbook* (New Haven: Yale University Press, 1987).

Price Waterhouse LLP and Caplin & Drysdale, Chartered, *Impact of Tax Restructuring on Tax-Exempt Organizations* (Washington, DC: Council on Foundations and Independent Sector, 1997).

Putnam, Robert, "Bowling Alone: America's Declining Social Capital," *The Journal of Democracy,* Vol. 6, No. 1 (January 1995), pp. 65–78.

Putnam, Robert, *Making Democracy Work: Civic Traditions in Modern Italy* (Princeton: Princeton University Press, 1993).

Ranci, Constanzo, "Government Policy and Future Issue," in P. Barbetta, ed., *The Nonprofit Sector in Italy,* Johns Hopkins Nonprofit Sector Series, ed. by L.M. Salamon and H.K. Anheier (U.K.: Manchester University Press, 1997), pp. 226–280.

Ronsvale, John and Sylvia, "The State of Church Giving Through 1991," *Yearbook of American and Canadian Churches 1994* (Nashville: Abingdon Press, 1994), pp. 12–15.

Russell, J., A. O'Shea, and B. Bachman, eds. *Washington 88: A Comprehensive Directory of the Key Institutions and Leaders of the National Capital Area* (Washington, DC: Columbia Books, Inc., 1988).

Salamon, Lester M., ed., *Beyond Privatization: The Tools of Government Action* (Washington, DC: The Urban Institute Press, 1989).

Salamon, Lester M., *Holding the Center: America's Nonprofit Sector at a Crossroads* (New York: Nathan Cummings Foundation, 1997).

Salamon, Lester M., "The Marketization of Welfare: Changing Nonprofit and For-Profit Roles in the American Welfare State," *Social Service Review,* Vol. 67, No. 1 (March 1993), pp. 17–39.

Salamon, Lester M., "Nonprofit Organizations: The Lost Opportunity," in John L. Palmer and Isabel Sawhill, eds., *The Reagan Record* (Cambridge: Ballinger Publishing Co., 1984), pp. 261–286.

Salamon, Lester M., "Of Market Failure, Voluntary Failure, and Third-Party Government: Toward a Theory of Government-Nonprofit Relations in the Modern Welfare State," *Journal of Voluntary Action Research,* Vol. 16, Nos. 1–2, (1987), pp. 29–49, reprinted in Lester M. Salamon, *Partners in Public Service: Government-Nonprofit Relations in the Modern Welfare State* (Baltimore, Johns Hopkins University Press, 1995), pp. 33–49.

Salamon, Lester M., *Partners in Public Service: Government-Nonprofit Relations in the Modern Welfare State* (Baltimore: Johns Hopkins University Press, 1995).

Salamon, Lester M., "Partners in Public Service: The Scope and Theory of Government-Nonprofit Relations," in W. Powell, ed., *The Nonprofit Sector: A Research Handbook* (New York: Yale University Press, 1987), pp. 99–117.

Salamon, Lester M., "Rethinking Public Management: Third-Party Government and the Changing Forms of Government Action," *Public Policy 29* (1981), pp. 255–275.

Salamon, Lester M., "The Rise of the Nonprofit Sector," *Foreign Affairs,* Vol. 73, No. 4 (July/August 1994), pp. 109–122.

Salamon, Lester M., "The Voluntary Sector and the Future of the Welfare State," *Nonprofit and Voluntary Sector Quarterly,* Vol. 18, No. 1 (Spring 1989), pp. 16–39.

Salamon, Lester M., *Welfare: The Elusive Consensus—Where We Are, How We Got Here, and What's Ahead* (New York: Praeger Publishers, 1977).

Salamon, Lester M., and Alan J. Abramson, *The Federal Budget and the Nonprofit Sector* (Washington, DC: The Urban Institute, 1982), pp. 219–243.

Salamon, Lester M., and Alan J. Abramson, *The Federal Budget and the Nonprofit Sector* (Washington, DC: The Urban Institute Press, 1986).

Salamon, Lester M., and Alan J. Abramson, *The Federal Budget and the Nonprofit Sector: President Clinton's FY 1999 Budget Proposals.* Report to Independent Sector (Baltimore: Johns Hopkins Institute for Policy Studies, 1998).

Salamon, Lester M., and Alan J. Abramson, "The Nonprofit Sector." in John L. Palmer and Isabel Sawhill, eds., *The Reagan Experiment* (Washington, DC: The Urban Institute Press, 1982), pp. 219–243.

Salamon, Lester M., David M. Altschuler, and Jaana Myllyluoma, *More Than Just Charity: The Baltimore Area Nonprofit Sector in a Time of Change* (Baltimore: The Johns Hopkins Institute for Policy Studies, 1990).

Salamon, Lester M. and Helmut K. Anheier, *Defining the Nonprofit Sector: A Comparative Analysis* (Manchester, U.K.: Manchester University Press, 1997).

Salamon, Lester M. and Helmut K. Anheier, "In Search of the Nonprofit Sector: The Problem of Definition," *Voluntas,* Vol. 3., No. 2 (1992), pp. 125–151.

Salamon, Lester M. and Helmut K. Anheier, *The Emerging Nonprofit Sector* (U.K.: Manchester University Press, 1996).

Salamon, Lester M. and Helmut K. Anheier, *The Emerging Sector Revisited: A Summary* (Baltimore: Johns Hopkins Institute for Policy Studies, 1998).

Salamon, Lester M., James C. Musselwhite, Jr., and Carol J. DeVita, "Partners in Public Service: Government and the Nonprofit Sector in the American Welfare State." Working Papers, Independent Sector Research Forum (March 1986).

Samuels, Steven and Alisha Tonsic, *Theater Facts 1995* (New York: Theater Communications Group, 1996).

Schlozman, Kay Lehman, and John T. Tierney, *Organized Interests and American Democracy* (New York: Harper and Row, 1986).

Schorr, Lisbeth, *Within Our Reach: Breaking the Cycle of Disadvantage* (New York: Anchor Books, 1988).

Shapiro, Harvey D., "The Coming Inheritance Bonanza," *Institutional Investor,* Vol. XXXVIII, No. 6 (June 1994), pp. 143–148.

Sirrocco, Al, "Nursing and Related Care Homes as Reported from the 1986 Inventory of Long-Term Care Places," *Advance Data,* No. 147 (January 22, 1988).

Smith, Craig, "The New Corporate Philanthropy," *Harvard Business Review* (May/June 1994), pp. 105–116.

Smith, David Horton, "The Rest of the Nonprofit Sector: Grassroots Associations as the Dark Matter

Ignored in Prevailing 'Flat Earth' Maps of the Sector," *Nonprofit and Voluntary Sector Quarterly,* Vol. 26, No. 2 (June 1997), pp. 114–131.

Smith, Steven and Michael Lipsky, *Nonprofits For Hire: The Welfare State in the Age of Contracting* (Cambridge: Harvard University Press, 1993).

Stevens, Rosemary, *In Sickness and in Wealth: American Hospitals in the Twentieth Century* (New York: Basic Books, 1997).

Strahan, Genevieve W., "An Overview of Nursing Homes and their Current Residents: Data from the 1995 National Nursing Home Survey," *Advance Data,* No. 280 (January 28, 1997).

Top Heavy (New York: Twentieth Century Fund, 1995).

Trescott, Jacqueline, "Exhibiting a New Enthusiasm: Across U.S., Museum Construction, Attendance are on the Rise," *The Washington Post* (June 21, 1998).

Ullman, C. F., "Partners in Reform: Nonprofit Organizations and the Welfare State in France." In W. Powell and E. C. Clemens, eds., *Private Action and the Public Good* (New Haven: Yale University Press, 1998), pp. 163–176.

Urice, John, "The Future of the State Arts Agency Movement in the 1990s: Decline and Effect," *The Journal of Arts Management, Law, and Society* (Spring 1992), Vol. 22, No. 1.

U.S. Agency for International Development, *Voluntary Foreign Aid Programs,* various years (Washington, DC: U.S. Agency for International Development).

U.S. Bureau of the Census, *Census of Service Industries,* various years (Washington, DC: U.S. Government Printing Office).

U.S. Bureau of the Census, *Current Business Reports BS/96, Service Annual Survey: 1996* (Washington, DC: U.S. Government Printing Office, 1998).

U.S. Bureau of the Census, *Statistical Abstract of the United States, 1997,* 117th Edition (Washington, DC: National Technical Information Service, 1997).

U.S. Bureau of the Census, *Statistical Abstract of the United States,* various years (Washington, DC: U.S. Government Printing Office).

U. S. Council of Economic Advisers, *Economic Report of the President,* various years (Washington, DC: U.S. Government Printing Office).

U.S. Department of Education, National Center for Education Statistics, *Digest of Education Statistics,* various years (Washington, DC: U.S. Government Printing Office).

U.S. Department of Health and Human Services, *Public Health Service, Surgeon General's Workshop on Self-Help and Public Health* (Washington, DC: U.S. Government Printing Office, 1988).

U.S. Department of Labor, Bureau of Labor Statistics, *Employment and Earnings, 1996* (Washington, DC: 1998).

U.S. Health Care Financing Administration, Office of the Actuary, "National Health Expenditures, 1996," Advance Tables (March 1998).

U.S. Internal Revenue Service, *Annual Report of the Director* (1997 and prior years).

U.S. Internal Revenue Service, *1995 Data Book* (Washington, DC: U.S. Treasury Department, 1995).

U.S. Internal Revenue Service, *Statistics of Income Bulletin*, Publication 1136 (February 1997).

U.S. Office of Management and Budget, *Budget of the United States Government, Fiscal Year 1998* (Washington, DC: U.S. Government Printing Office, 1997).

Verba, Sydney, et al. *Voice and Equality: Civic Voluntarism in American Politics* (Cambridge, MA: Harvard University Press, 1995).

Warner, A., *American Charities: A Study in Philanthropy and Economics* (New York: Thomas Y. Crowell, 1894).

Weisbrod, Burton, *The Voluntary Nonprofit Sector* (Lexington, MA: Lexington Books, 1978).

Whitehead, John S., *The Separation of College and State: Columbia, Dartmouth, Harvard and Yale, 1776–1876* (New Haven: Yale University Press, 1973).

Wish, Naomi and Roseanne Mirabella, "Nonprofit Management Education: Current Offerings and Practices in University-Based Programs," *Nonprofit Management and Leadership,* Vol. 9, No. 1 (Fall 1998).

Wolch, Jennifer, *The Shadow State* (New York: The Foundation Center, 1990).

Yearbook of American and Canadian Churches, 1990 edition (New York: National Council of the Churches of Christ, 1990).

Yearbook of American and Canadian Churches, 1996 edition, edited by Kenneth B. Bedell (New York: National Council of Churches, 1996).

Yearbook of American and Canadian Churches, 1998 edition, edited by Eileen Lindner (Nashville: Abingdon Press, 1998).

Index